THE COMPLETE IDIOT'S GUIDE® TO

Microsoft®
PowerPoint® 2000

by Nat Gertler

A Division of Macmillan Computer Publishing
201 W. 103rd Street, Indianapolis, IN 46290

**The Complete Idiot's Guide to Microsoft®
PowerPoint® 2000**

Copyright © 1999 by *Que*

International Standard Book Number: 0-7897-1866-9

Library of Congress Catalog Card Number: 99-60554

Printed in the United States of America

First Printing: *May 1999*

01   00   99   4   3   2

Trademarks

Executive Editor
Angela Wethington

Acquisitions Editor
Stephanie J. McComb

Development Editor
Nick Goetz

Managing Editor
Thomas F. Hayes

Project Editor
Tom Stevens

Copy Editor
Keith Cline

Technical Editor
Allen Boyce

Illustrator
Judd Winick

Indexer
Larry Sweazy

Proofreader
Elise Walter

Layout Technicians
Cyndi Davis-Hubler
Christy M. Lemasters

Contents at a Glance

department, your division, or even just you.

Part 3: Fancy, Flashy, Fabulous Features   **137**

Part 4: Sharing the Presentation with Others   **189**

who saw it.

Contents

24 Making Your Presentation a Doozy! (Not a Don'tzy!) 249

25 Express to Impress: Delivering Good Oral Presentations 263

Daddycation

This book is for my father Gene and his wife Poco, who have recently moved to Arizona. (If you've noticed New Jersey suddenly being a quieter place, this is why.)

Ack! Nowledgements!

I'd like to thank the gang at Que for dragging me into yet another of these books. Particular thanks go to Jamie Milazzo who got me to write it (with a tip of the hat to Martha O'Sullivan, wherever she may be, for getting me involved in the previous version), and to Stephanie McComb, for seeing me through it. Points to Nick Goetz and Allen Boyce, Jr. for their editorial work on this book. I'd also like to thank my comic book collaborators for all their understanding during the hectic days spent get-

ting this book done. Special thanks goes to my lady-friend Lara Hughes, who once made me cookies and therefore will always have my affection.

Tell Us What You Think!

As the reader of this book, *you* are our most important critic and commentator. We value your opinion and want to know what we're doing right, what we could do better, what areas you'd like to see us publish in, and any other words of wisdom you're willing to pass our way.

As Executive Editor for the General Desktop Applications team at Macmillan Computer Publishing, I welcome your comments. You can fax, email, or write me directly to let me know what you did or didn't like about this book—as well as what we can do to make our books stronger.

Please note that I cannot help you with technical problems related to the topic of this book, and that due to the high volume of mail I receive, I might not be able to reply to every message.

When you write, please be sure to include this book's title and author as well as your name and phone or fax number. I will carefully review your comments and share them with the author and editors who worked on the book.

Fax: 317-581-4666

Email: office-que@mcp.com

Mail: Executive Editor
           General Desktop Applications
           Macmillan Computer Publishing
           201 West 103rd Street
           Indianapolis, IN 46290 USA

Introduction

Welcome to The Complete Idiot's Guide to Microsoft PowerPoint 2000, your user-friendly, low-calorie guide to using PowerPoint. PowerPoint is a tool that lets you put together slide shows, interactive displays on your computer, and other sorts of presentations. This book will get you using it quickly, easily, and effectively. After you get the hang of PowerPoint, you will find it easy to put together a clear and exciting presentation. Your co-workers will ask you to make presentations for them! Soon, you'll become Executive Vice President in Charge of Presentations. Charged with success, you'll try to take over the company, and lose the power struggle. Jobless and broke, you've got nothing but the clothes on your back and your knowledge of PowerPoint, but that's all you need. You come up with a great idea for a new company, create a convincing presentation to show to the Wall Street bigwigs, and next thing you know you're back on top, more successful than ever! And it will all be thanks to The Complete Idiot's Guide to PowerPoint.

You're welcome.

This Book Is Full of Good Stuff

This book has a lot of good stuff. Early in the book are the basics of using PowerPoint, so you can start putting presentations together quickly. Later in the book you get to see more of PowerPoint's special features so that you can make fancier presentations and ones that look exactly like you want them to. Throughout the book you'll find advice on making creative decisions to let your presentation have impact. There's so much good stuff in here that it's amazing we didn't throw in a pound of chocolate!

Browsing Through the Book

If you're as lazy as I am (and that's saying something!) you probably don't want to spend a lot of time reading about things you're never going to use—and odds are that with all the features of PowerPoint, you'll never use them all. This book is broken up into chapters. There are a few chapters you have to read to get the hang of PowerPoint, but most chapters you can skip reading until you decide you need to know about that specific topic. Each chapter starts with a list of the things you'd learn by reading that chapter, so you can decide whether to skip it. Think of it as a buffet of knowledge, and you can always come back for seconds!

Part 1: A Running Start

The chapters are grouped into parts. The first part is designed to get you going with PowerPoint. There's a chapter that lets you know what PowerPoint is, what it does, and what it's good for. Immediately following we get you up and running, putting together a simple presentation, including information about how to save presentations on your hard disk and get them back later, and how to display them on your computer screen. Then there's a chapter on how to get help when you have a PowerPoint question, which will come in handy no matter what you're doing. All in all, Part 1 is a must-read, and should be the first thing you read.

Part 2: Building Your Presentation

You can put a lot of things into a presentation, such as text, charts and graphs, lists, logos, pictures, and chocolate (which is good for bribing customers during sales presentations). I can't help you with chocolate, but the rest of these elements are each covered in chapters of Part 2. The first chapter, which tells you how to arrange the basic units of a presentation, is a must-read, and odds are you'll be using text and have to read that one as well. For the rest, just take a look at the first paragraph, see what the section is about, and skip over it if you don't need it. You can always come back to them later, if necessary.

Part 3: Fancy, Flashy, Fabulous Features

Part 3 is full of chapters on things such as flying text, interactivity, moving pictures, sound, and other whiz-bang effects that'll make your presentation as fancy as a Stephen Spielberg movie (or at least a Buzby Berkeley musical). Depending on what sort of presentation you're giving, however, you may not be able to use these things. After all, there's no way to put a movie onto an overhead projector sheet, and if you figure out a way to get sound onto a piece of paper, you'll be earning so many millions that you'll be able to hire someone to make presentations for you. (I am certainly willing to accept such a job at a huge salary!) If you're going to be showing your presentations on a computer display, on a Web page, or on video tape, you should look at this part and see what each chapter has to offer. If you're just doing overheads, standard slides, or printing your presentation out, skip this part and use the time you save to sneak out to the movies. (Just tell your boss you're doing research on traditional mass-market presentation media!)

Part 4: Sharing the Presentation with Others

Designing your presentation is only half the battle. After designing it, you have to know how to show it to other people. This might mean knowing how to print it out, how to get it onto slides, how to turn it into a Web page, or how to engrave it in chocolate. Each of these (except the chocolate one, alas) and more are covered in Part 4. You only have to read up on the methods you're going to use. If you're not going to use PowerPoint to create Web pages, for example, there's no need to read the chapter on how to do so... even though I slaved for hours on end over a hot keyboard creating that chapter for you, checking each fact and carefully turning each phrase several times to make sure it was just right! Aw, go on, skip it!

Part 5: Getting the Most Out of PowerPoint

This last part is a bit of a weird one, because it has less to do with how to use PowerPoint and everything to do with why you're using PowerPoint. Although there is a chapter on using information from Microsoft Word and Excel with PowerPoint, the other chapters are about what makes for a good presentation. A presentation that looks good but doesn't make a lot of sense is like a date who looks good but doesn't make a lot of sense; it may be fun for the thrill of it, but it's not going to do you a lot of good in the long term. There's a chapter on what you should put in your presentation and one on how to speak to people as part of your presentation. You don't have to read any of this stuff, but it's all there if you want it.

The Rest of the Book

There's a table of contents in the front and an index in the back, both of which are handy if you need them, but I doubt you'll just be sitting down and reading them. If you're fairly new to Windows or aren't fully comfortable with the terminology, the appendix tells you about how to use Windows and what the various parts of it are called.

Further back is a section called Speak like a Geek, which is a glossary full of techno-terms you might run into and what they mean to regular people. That's a handy reference if you need it. And before Part 1 there's an introduction, and it's too late to decide whether you want to read that, because you're already most of the way through it!

The Language of the Book

A few standard tricks are used in this book to make things clear. If I tell you to press a key, click a button, or select a command, for example, the command name, button name, or key will be printed like this. If I want you to hold down the Shift, Alt, or Ctrl keys and press another key, it will look like: press Shift+G to get a capital G.

If I tell you to type something, the phrase that you type will look like this. When I'm giving you a definition to a word, we'll put the new word in italics (slanty letters).

If you look around this page, you will see a number of sidebars, gray separate sections that are not part of the normal reading. The ones on this page explain about the sidebars you'll run into later in the book.

Check This Out! Sidebars

Sidebars with this picture are used to tell you about special features and other little bits of information that it might be handy to know. This is where you'll find shortcuts for doing hard tasks and other ways of saving time.

Techno Talk Sidebars

This picture means that the sidebar is letting you know some technical details about how something works. You don't need to know this stuff to use PowerPoint. If you understand the technical side of computing, it may be interesting, and if you don't understand technical jargon, this is a good place to learn. Don't let this symbol scare you away!

New in PowerPoint 2000

This picture is used to let you know when there's a new useful feature that was not in older versions of PowerPoint.

Part 1

Running Start

You've got this absolutely great computer on your desk, with 3D sound, 3D video, and a 3GB hard disk (and it's all held together by 3M tape). You're all ready to play Revenge of the Space Bunnies IV in all its multimedia splendor, but someone wants you to do something useful (yawn) with the machine and get it to put out a presentation!

This part gets you going. You learn the most important things about PowerPoint and about using Windows, and then zoom! you're making a simple presentation. After that's got your confidence up, we tell you about what to do when things go wrong!

Chapter 1

What the Heck Is PowerPoint Anyway?

PowerPoint sounds like the name of the superpower belonging to the villainous Human Finger. "Do not dare stop my nefarious scheme, Lady Power, or I shall be forced to PowerPoint your helpless boyfriend right into oblivion!" But if I could teach you that, I wouldn't. You might use it for your own nefarious schemes, and besides, I'd rather spend the time using it for my own nefarious schemes. ("Give me all your chocolate donuts, or I shall be forced to PowerPoint your jelly ones into an unsightly mess!")

PowerPoint is a software tool that lets you create presentations. That opens up the question: "What is a presentation?"—a question that is so important that it needs to be put in great big letters.

What Is a Presentation?

When someone is standing up in front of a group of people, using slides and over-head projectors to display various reasons why you should invest in his new fast-food franchise, Lotsa Lard, *that's* a presentation.

When you are watching the local access cable TV channel, and they are showing an endless loop of fancy screens listing when last month's bake sales and fund drives were, *that's* a presentation.

If you are in a motel, and it has a computer screen displaying a list of local attractions on which you simply touch the name of the local amusement park to see a short film clip about how great and wonderful the rides are, *that's* a presentation.

When you are on the World Wide Web, and you find a Web site that is nothing more than a bunch of pages telling you how wonderful that Web site is, *that's* a presentation.

When the moon hits your eye like a big pizza pie, *that's* not a presentation. It's painful, that's what that is.

What Is the Point in PowerPoint?

If you think about an overhead projector presentation, you might not see that much point to PowerPoint. Sure, it can put text onto the sheet, but so can a word processor. PowerPoint can put a picture on the sheet, but so can a modern word processor. PowerPoint can help create charts and graphs, but some of that stuff isn't too hard to cut and paste from a spreadsheet into your word processor. And PowerPoint can create nicely designed, consistent backgrounds for your overheads that, well, your word processor can't.

PowerPoint also has built-in capabilities for creating *speaker's notes*, cheat sheets that let you see the slide along with some notes of what you want to say to the audience. It also prints out handouts, with all the overheads reproduced, several to a page, that your audience can refer to later, after they realize that they spent the whole presentation trying to fish the pen cap out of their pants pockets without standing up.

MultiMedia in PowerPoint Is Really Good and Really Effective

If you are showing a presentation using something that can show motion (such as on a computer, or on video tape), then you get to use a whole passel of pleasing PowerPoint properties:

➤ Your text can move, slide, and scroll.

➤ You can have fancy transitions where one display fades away while another appears.

➤ You can put digitized film clips into your presentation. You can incorporate sound, either just little highlights of sound or a complete narration.

➤ Your presentation can even start and stop an audio CD in your CD-ROM player. That way, if you have a boring part in your presentation, you can suddenly start playing the National Anthem, and everyone will have to stand at respectful attention while your presentation continues!

Interactivity: What We Used to Call "Doing Stuff"

If the person seeing the presentation is seeing it on a computer screen, your PowerPoint presentation can be interactive. Basically, this means that the user clicks something (or, if you have a touch screen, touches a point on the screen), and something happens. You can have a screen where you click one place to learn more about the brand new luxury time-share condominiums in scenic Siberia, for example, or click another place to learn *much* more about the condominiums.

If you are letting people see your presentation via the World Wide Web, you can have words, buttons, or pictures to click that take the viewers out of this presentation and show them things on other Web sites.

Better Webber

PowerPoint 2000 turns out much better Web sites than previous versions, but that's not saying much. If your main goal is to design a Web site, PowerPoint isn't the best tool for that (programs like Microsoft FrontPage are better). PowerPoint's features are great, however, for letting you take a presentation created for something else and also use it on the Web.

PowerPoint Does the Work

PowerPoint can't do all your work for you—only you know the information that is going to be in your presentation. What it can do is take care of many of the little things that go into making the presentation nice, and let you worry about the big things. PowerPoint has templates waiting for you, already structured like good presentations. All you have to do is fill in the information. If you are doing a sales presentation, for example, you can use a template designed for sales presentations, broken into sections where you talk about the strengths of your product, how it meets customer needs, where it beats the competition, and so on. After you put in the information ("Diggity Donuts have the biggest hole in the industry, for easy holding;" "Diggity Donuts fit precisely into the customer's stomach," whatever), you have a complete presentation, with nice backgrounds and transitions already selected for you.

But you aren't stuck with doing things the way PowerPoint wants. You can start your presentation from scratch, or you can use a template and then change around whatever you want. You are in control. PowerPoint is a smart tool, but it is still your tool (as opposed to that artificial intelligence-powered lawn mower that got too smart and is now ruling a small nation).

Don't Let the Power Make You Forget the Point

If you saw an advertisement for Brougham's Amazing, Wonderful, Ultra-Fine, Classy, Improved, A-1 Recycled Gallstones, would you buy them? Not even if they were half off? Of course not. All the fancy packaging in the world can't save a bad concept. PowerPoint gives you many great tools you can use to fine-tune your presentation, but it makes it easy to spend all your time fine-tuning the look of things (making it dangerously easy to overlook the actual information you are presenting).

Your goal should be to communicate information, and all of PowerPoint's tricks are just tools to that end. You can spend a lot of time adding all the latest bells and whistles (not that bells and whistles are new, but it's easier than saying "all the latest multimedia doohickeys and interactive thingamaboobles"), but if that doesn't leave you time for figuring out what has to be in your presentation and how to make it clear, your presentation will be bad. Spend more time on the information than you do on the details of the presentation.

But the Nifty Stuff Is Still Useful

If your presentation is so poor that it doesn't communicate the information, your good concept will get lost. Your words and concepts should hold attention on their own, but wise use of design and multimedia can effectively carry the information. Staying totally wrapped in your content and not paying any attention to how to present it will leave you with a long, boring presentation few will choose to pay attention to. Try to achieve a balance between the substance of your presentation and the gift-wrap you put it in.

Chapter 2

A Quick and Easy Presentation

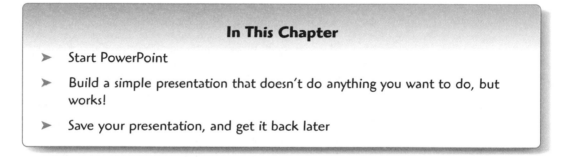

In This Chapter

➤ Start PowerPoint

➤ Build a simple presentation that doesn't do anything you want to do, but works!

➤ Save your presentation, and get it back later

Experts will tell you that the proper way to start any new activity is to study what you are to do carefully, read up on all the materials, and proceed in tiny steps as you learn. This is why experts so rarely seem to be having any fun.

Fun is had by people who make the cake without the recipe, people who hop on their tricycle before learning the proper hand signal for a left turn, people who don't study the fine and historic art of crafting fiction and instead just make something up! Let's throw caution to the wind and jump in with both feet! (And if you think it's easy to jump feet first into the wind, you haven't tried it!)

In this chapter, I show you how to quickly make a simple presentation. It won't be a presentation that you would ever actually want to show, and it sure won't show you every feature of PowerPoint. It will, however, give you a basic sense of what PowerPoint does and how it does it, and that will come in handy when we start talking about the steps of the presentation that you *do* want.

Jump-starting PowerPoint

A computer program is different from a car. (Surprise!) After all, a car is still useful even when it isn't running; you can just sit in the front seat and listen to the radio (although that will run down the car's batteries, and later you will have trouble getting a spark), or you can sit in the back seat and smooch (which will start you sparking all by itself). But until you start running the computer program, it's just a bunch of information on your hard disk.

To start PowerPoint, click the **Start** button. On the **Start** menu that appears, click **Programs**. Another menu appears to the right of the Start menu. If there's an entry on the menu marked **Microsoft PowerPoint**, that's the one you want to click. If there isn't, click the entry marked either **Office or Microsoft Office** (it will have a little picture of a folder next to it), and another menu appears. That menu will have the **Microsoft PowerPoint** command, which you can now click and start the program!

Ordering the Menu

The Program menu usually lists all the *folders* (which lead to another level of menus) first, in alphabetic order, followed by a list of commands, in alphabetic order. Finding the one you are looking for should be easy, if you have the alphabet memorized!

To Know the PowerPoint Window Is to Love the PowerPoint Window

You can tell that PowerPoint has started when its window appears. It's full of good stuff!

The top of the window has the same information as any main program window: a title bar and a menu bar. Below that are one or more rows of buttons, arranged in logically grouped sections called *toolbars*, with more toolbar space at the bottom of the screen. Keep working with windows, and soon you will have seen more bars than a worker on Hershey's assembly line! (Of course, they also get a lot of kisses....)

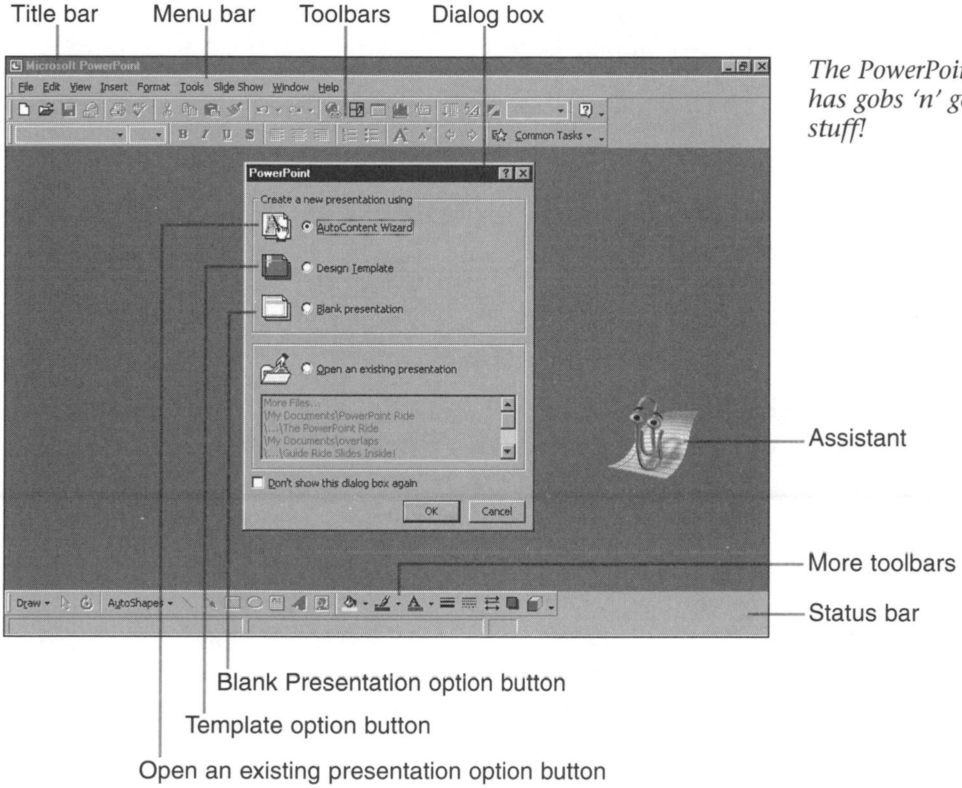

Title bar   Menu bar   Toolbars   Dialog box

The PowerPoint window has gobs 'n' gobs of good stuff!

Assistant

More toolbars

Status bar

Blank Presentation option button

Template option button

Open an existing presentation option button

You will see a funny-looking animated character (called the *Assistant*). If it's asking you what you want to do, click **Start Using PowerPoint** to get him out of the way for the moment. If it's not asking you anything, ignore it for now—you learn more about the Assistant in Chapter 3, "Help Is on the Way"—but if it makes a funny face at you, feel free to make one right back!

We're Off to Use the Wizard!

When the PowerPoint window appears, it has a dialog box in the center of it. PowerPoint knows that you want to be working on a presentation, but it doesn't know which presentation. The dialog box offers the choice of not one, not two, but three (not four, not five!) ways of starting a new presentation, as well as the option of continuing work on a presentation that you have already started.

In this dialog box, you notice that the AutoContent Wizard method of creating a new presentation is at the top of the list. *Wizard* is Microsoft's term for a procedure that takes care of a lot of little bits of work for you. *AutoContent Wizard* is an automatic system that puts together the basics of a presentation for you, so you only have to

13

put in the original material you want to present—it already has good designs and formats for a wide range of presentations. Letting the computer do the work is a wonderfully lazy way of getting something done. Click the **AutoContent Wizard** option button; then click the **OK** button to get the wizard working for you!

No Dialog Box?

If this dialog box does not come up after you start your copy of PowerPoint, that just means that someone working with your system has told this dialog box to go away and never come back. You can start the AutoContent Wizard by choosing **File**, **New**, selecting the **General** tab, and then double-clicking **AutoContent Wizard**.

If you want this dialog box to appear every time you start the program, choose **Tools**, **Options**, click the **View** tab on the dialog box that appears, put a check in the **Startup dialog** checkbox, then click OK.

Working with the Wizard

After you start the wizard, a window marked AutoContent Wizard appears. In the left part of the screen is a list of five steps that you will have to go through to get the wizard to do its job. The first step is just Start, and you accomplish that step by clicking the **Next** button at the bottom of the window.

Step Back, Jack!

If you make a mistake on any of the wizard steps and realize it while working on another step, just press the **Back** button. It will take you back to the preceding step.

Presentation Type-Casting

In this step, you have to pick a type of presentation to design. In the center is a list of categories of presentations that the Wizard can make. Click the button marked **Corporate**. At the right side of the window, a list of project-oriented presentations appears. Depending on the way that PowerPoint was installed, you may see a lot of different types of presentations that you may want to do some day (and others that you may never want to do, and can't even imagine anyone wanting to do). Click the one marked **Business Plan** to select that type of presentation, and it becomes *highlighted*—that is, it appears in a different color so that you can tell it from the rest of the list. Then, click the **Next** button to move to the next step.

The AutoContent Wizard holds your hand through the few steps it takes to put together a basic presentation.

Skipping up the Steps

The next step asks you to pick how the project will be presented. The computer will already have guessed what you want. Its guess is right, so you don't have to correct it. Click the **Next** button to move through this step. Zoom!

Making Your Presentation Feel Entitled

It's time to pick a title for your presentation, something that reflects what the presentation is about. Now, you may have some great ideas for presentations, but I have got one I have been aching to do, and you can help me with it!

When Que Publishing contracted me to write this book, they bought a lot of rights. They got U.S. rights, translation rights, book-on-tape rights, but they got something even more valuable: the theme park rights! That's right, if Que and their corporate partners want to, they can now make *The Complete Idiot's Guide to PowerPoint: The Ride!* Thrill to the attack of the giant buttons! Look out for the flying text! You are in for the presentation of your life!

So what I want you to type into the **Presentation title** field is Complete Idiot's Guide to PowerPoint: The Ride. Type an amusement ride proposal into the **Footer** field (*footer* is a term derived from the Latin for "more foot").

With this form filled out, you are ready to click Finish and let the Wizard do the work.

With all that information entered, click the **Next** button to move on to the final step. The final step is clicking the **Finish** button, which you can do with aplomb. (If you are all out of plombs, do it with a prune.)

Even Weirdos Can Have a Normal View

PowerPoint puts together the presentation for you. A PowerPoint presentation is made up of individual segments, called *slides*. Although they may end up being slides in a slide show, they might also become computer screens in an onscreen display, sheets of paper in a hand-out, overheads in a projected show, or Web pages. I suppose *slidesorscreensorsheetsoroverheadsorwebpages* was just too big a thing to call them! (And calling them *Morty* was just too informal.)

The presentation is shown to you in *Normal* view. In this view, the screen is broken into three portions (called *frames*). At the left is an *outline* of the presentation, a numbered list of slides. For each slide, you see the contents of that slide, including the main discussion point and the *bulleted* (dotted) list of other discussion points underneath it. To the right of that is a picture of one of the slides in your presentation, and below that is a space for notes about this slide. (You can use other views, which I will discuss in Chapter 4, "Sliding Slides into Place.")

Using the Normal View mode, you can see your presentation in three ways simultaneously, unless you close your eyes.

The text of your slides

A picture of the currently selected slide

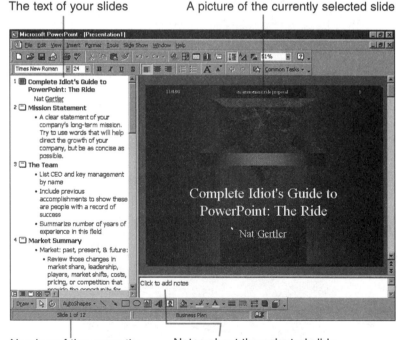

Number of the currently selected slide

Notes about the selected slide

Notice that except for the first slide listed on the outline (which has the title), the contents of the slides don't say a thing about the thrilling adventure that is *Complete Idiot's Guide to PowerPoint: The Ride.* The wizard isn't *that* smart. It doesn't understand what your title is about—it can't figure out what it means. (That doesn't mean that the wizard is stupid, of course, just illiterate. Just because a wizard can cast a spell doesn't mean that it *can* spell!) What the wizard has put in is some guideline text, which includes concepts and guidelines for the types of things that should be contained on each slide.

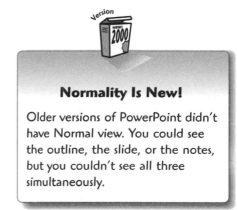

Normality Is New!

Older versions of PowerPoint didn't have Normal view. You could see the outline, the slide, or the notes, but you couldn't see all three simultaneously.

Replacing Words with More Words

At this point, your presentation is totally generic, except for the title. You will have to change it before you can really feel that it's yours. If you were working on a real presentation to show others, you would probably replace most of the text. In the interest of being efficient (or, if you are like me, lazy), just change it a little—just one line of text. Specifically, go to slide 2 in the outline (Mission Statement) and change the text of the first point (which starts with A clear statement...).

To do this, first you have to tell the computer what you are going to change. This is called *selecting.* Slide your pointer over to the line you are going to change. The pointer, at this point, will turn into a large capital I (called the *insertion point*). Slide that to the left of the first letter of what you are going to select, push down the left mouse button, and drag it to the end of the phrase. As you do this, the words will magically, mystically (well, electronically) change color to show you which words you have selected. Instead of black letters on a white background, the letters turn white and the background turns black. Also, when you select the text in the outline section of the window, PowerPoint will display that slide in the slide frame. Release the mouse button once the entire phrase is selected.

Selection Correction Directions

If you somehow end up selecting the wrong thing, don't worry! Click any unselected text to clear the selection. Then try selecting what you meant to select in the first place!

Type Finally, a ride as fun as crafting a presentation! When you start to type the words, the phrase you had selected disappears, and what you type appears in its place, both in the outline and in the picture of the slide. Now you have a custom presentation designed to sell the world on the greatest amusement ride ever conceived! It's now time to see this presentation in action.

Presenting Your Presentation!

Now that you have everything in place, it's time to put on a show. Click the **View** menu and select the **Slide Show** command. The screen goes blank, and the computer spends a little time thinking little computer thoughts ("I think, therefore, I am...a chipmunk!").

Then the title slide appears. There, in big letters, is the name of the ride we have all been waiting for! Sit and stare at it, with its big yellow letters and lovely colored background. You can stare for a long time, because it's not going anywhere. It's just staying there, staring back.

The title slide for this title's ride.

Sliding Through the Slides

There is, of course, a way to move on to the next slide. I asked my techno-geek friend how to do this. She said, "One begins by extending one's index digit. Place said limb attachment onto the most horizontally elongated entry device. Rapidly depress and release said rectangular solid."

But those of us who aren't so geeky can just *press the Spacebar*.

That's Not Me!

If someone else's name appears on the first slide, you can change it to yours after you finish viewing the presentation. It's the same as changing any other text. If you want to make sure your name appears on other presentations you design, choose PowerPoint's **Tools**, **Options** command, click the **General** tab on the Options dialog box, and type your name into the **Name** field. Click **OK**, and PowerPoint will now remember your name!

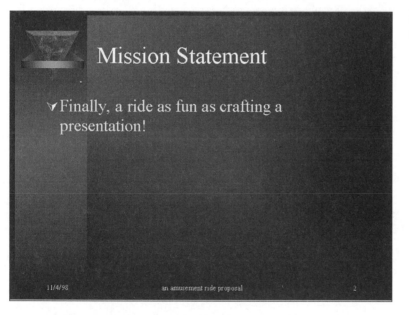

Hallelujah, the point we added is presented!

The new slide replaces the title slide with the next slide all at once. (This is just one way to get rid of the old slide and bring on the new one. The effects used when switching slides in computerized slideshows are called *transitions*. You will learn more about these and other special effects in Chapter 15, "Tricky Transitions and Terrific Timing.")

If you keep pressing the Spacebar, you will move through the 12 slides that make up the presentation. After the last slide, the display goes black. Push the Spacebar once more to return to Normal view. The quick, easy, and useless presentation is complete, and you can feel proud of your accomplishment.

And the good news is that making a slideshow that tells what you want it to tell, instead of just a bunch of preprogrammed slides, isn't much harder than that. Oh, you can make it hard, if you are one of those people who like to organize and fine-tune every little thing. ("Oh, it's all wrong! The red in that background is far too scarlet! I need a burgundy!") But you are closer than you probably realize to making presentations that get the job done.

Save the Show

Now that you have made your first show, you have to learn to *save* it, to store it on your hard disk. If you don't, when you leave the program, the computer totally forgets about your show. In this case, that might not be so bad; like the TV series *My Mother, The Car* proved, some shows are worth forgetting. But to do everything right, you should save it.

Click the **Save** button. A dialog box appears, with a name for the presentation (either the title of your first slide or **Presentation1**) already in the **File name** field. Type a name for the presentation (PowerPoint Ride should do fine); then press **Enter**. PowerPoint stores all the information about the presentation in a file called *PowerPoint Ride.ppt* (with *ppt* standing for PowerPoint.) I show you later how to get that file back, if you ever want to see that presentation again.

Leaving PowerPoint, and Returning to the Real World

Now that you have finished creating your presentation, it's time to leave the program. Just click the **Close** button (the X button on the title bar—that will be at the very top right corner of the PowerPoint window). The program *closes*, which means it stops running and leaves your screen. The program is still on your computer's hard disk, so you can run it again any time you want. It just isn't running now. And hey, it's earned the rest!

Presentation Regeneration Information

When you want to get the presentation back and look at it again (or even work on it further), here's what you do: Start PowerPoint. When it shows you the opening dialog box, click the **Open an existing presentation** option button; then click **OK**. Another dialog box with a list of presentations appears. Click the name of the presentation you want to bring back, click **Open**, and the presentation will be loaded again!

Loading Without Leaving

If you are using PowerPoint and have finished working with one presentation and want to work with another, you don't have to leave PowerPoint. Just save the work you have done on the first presentation, and then tell PowerPoint that you want to stop working on that presentation by clicking the **Close Window** button on the menu bar (not the one above it on the title bar!)

 Next, click the **Open** button. It will show you the list of presentations so you can select another one to load!

The Least You Need to Know

➤ You start PowerPoint by clicking the **Start** button, pointing to **Programs**, and then selecting **Microsoft PowerPoint** from the submenu that appears.

➤ The AutoContent Wizard can help you create a presentation quickly and easily.

➤ In PowerPoint, the term *slide* refers not only to an actual slide in a slide projector show, but also to a screen of information on a computer display, a printed page, an overhead for an overhead project, or a Web page.

➤ Normal View mode shows an outline with all the text from your slides, a picture of one slide, and a space to type notes into.

➤ To change text, first *select* the text you are getting rid of (drag the mouse across it with the left button pressed down); then type the text that you are adding.

➤ To start the presentation display on your computer, open the **View** menu and select the **Slide Show** command.

➤ Press the **Spacebar** to move from one slide to the next.

➤ To save a presentation, click the **Save** button.

➤ To get back a presentation you have saved, click the **Open** button.

Chapter 3

Help Is on the Way

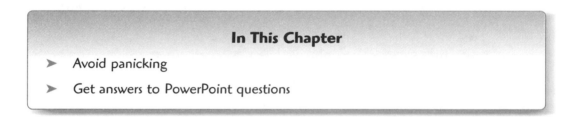

In This Chapter

➤ Avoid panicking

➤ Get answers to PowerPoint questions

While working on your presentation, you are likely to have many questions—ones like, "How do I make a black background?" or "What does this button do?" or "Isn't it lunch time yet?" If you are lucky, you have a nearby handy-dandy expert who can answer all your questions for you. (If you are *really* lucky, you will find a billion dollars, and you can hire a crew of people to make your presentations for you, as well as to bring cold sodas and warm pizza—but that's a little much to hope for.)

Unfortunately, we don't all have a handy-dandy expert, and even experts get time off. Besides, if you bother experts with every little question, they're likely to become annoyed, and annoyed experts can do some *really* nasty things to your computer.

The Author's Favorite Reference

You already have an easy-to-use, technologically simple source for answers right there by you. Just look around. Is it next to the book? No, check the other side. Maybe it's under the book? Wait, now I remember—it *is* the book! Yes, *The Complete Idiot's Guide to PowerPoint* is more than just a handy bug-squasher. It's very good at answering questions, because of the following advantages:

➤ It has a nice, big table of contents.

➤ It's broken into chapters by subject.

➤ There's a detailed index in the back.

➤ You can look up answers even when you are away from your computer.

You won't find all the answers here, however. PowerPoint has so many little features and options that there wasn't room to squeeze every little answer in. Also, you can get a quicker answer to some questions on the computer. In addition, you may not always have the book with you while using PowerPoint, particularly if you borrowed this copy from a friend or a library. (If you did borrow it, you probably shouldn't use it to squish bugs… at least, not big ones.)

What's This Button?

PowerPoint has many onscreen buttons, each of which displays a little picture that tells you exactly what the button does…or would do, if you could read the minds of the graphic designers. For example, one button has a picture of a star with speed lines coming out of it, making it look like a shooting star. Does pushing this button give you information about famous shooting stars, such as John Wayne and Annie Oakley? No, it just adds a toolbar full of animation control buttons to the display. (This is a curious design for a button, because John Wayne and Annie Oakley weren't animated; they were live-action!)

However, most of the people reading this book aren't interested in animating (or even reanimating) Mr. Wayne and Ms. Oakley. (At least, I hope not! I'd rather the audience was made up of people who want to use the book to squish bugs, because there's probably a lot of would-be bug-squishers out there.) For you, each button has a name that explains, basically, what it does. To see the name of a currently usable button, just point to it. After a second, the name of the button appears in a yellow box. This is called a *ScreenTip*. Point to the little star-with-lines button, for example, and you will see the button's name, *Animation Effects*. That certainly tells you more than the picture of the star did.

What Is "What's This?"

If you pull down the **Help** menu, you find a command simply known as **What's This?** Sounds mysterious, eh? If you select this command, the pointer changes into an arrow with a question mark. If that's all it did, it might be mysterious, but it wouldn't be useful.

If you use that pointer to click a button or select a command from a menu, the button or command doesn't take effect. Instead, a box pops open with a short explanation of the thing you clicked. Try clicking the button with the little picture of a star, and you will get this explanation: `Animation Effects adds or changes animation effects on the current slide. Animation effects include sound, text, and object movements, and movies that occur during a slide show.` Thankfully, it says nothing about bringing the dead back to life. Click the mouse, and this message disappears.

Your Onscreen, On-the-Spot Office Assistant

While using PowerPoint, you probably see a small animated character in it that doesn't seem to have anything to do with PowerPoint. (If you don't, click the **Help** button and it will appear.)

This animated fellow is your *Office Assistant*. The Assistant always has an eye on what you are doing and can answer your questions at any time. Sometimes it's just sitting still, sometimes it's bopping back and forth in animated motion, but sometimes it is offering advice—and it's always ready to answer questions.

Office Assistants Offer Assistance

Sometimes the Office Assistant realizes you might not know the best way to do something, or are doing it awkwardly. When this happens, a light bulb appears—the light bulb being the recognized international symbol for an idea. (However, it's a yellow light bulb, which means it's a bug light.)

Click that light bulb. A comic-strip–style word balloon with advice in it appears. In addition to written advice, the balloon may also hold some buttons that you can click to let the Assistant help you get the job done. The Office Assistant will only volunteer this particular piece of advice once, so pay attention!

(If someone else has been using this copy of PowerPoint, you can make sure that the Office Assistant doesn't skip the tips that it has already shown to the other person. Right-click the Assistant, select **Options** from the shortcut menu, click the **Reset My Tips** button, and then the **OK** button. The Assistant will suddenly have amnesia, forgetting that it ever told anyone anything!)

When the light is on, click Office Assistant for all kinds of useful information.

Ask Your Assistant

The Assistant is pretty good at answering "How do I...?"-type questions. If you have a question like that, click the Assistant and a word balloon appears. The Assistant's smart enough that the balloon may already have a list of topics it *thinks* you might want to know about. If you are interested in something that's on the list, simply click the topic, and a window of information pops up (often with a more-detailed list of topics to pick from).

Office Assistant Unleashed

In the previous version of PowerPoint, the Assistant was trapped in a separate window. Now he's right in front of everything, and you can move him by just dragging him with the mouse.

*The Office Assistant
really wants to help, but
it needs to know what
you need help with. It
gives you a whole list
of possible topics. If you
want something else,
you can just type it in.*

Whether or not the Assistant provides a list, it will provide a space for asking a specific question. Just start typing, and your question will appear in that space. Press **Enter**, and the Assistant will try to answer your question.

This is when you learn that the Assistant isn't very smart.

Cartoons are never very smart. Even Mister Peabody, genius inventor of the Wayback machine, never went back in time and invested in Microsoft in the early days. The Assistant will not come up with a specific answer to your questions. Instead, it will produce a list of topics that it thinks can answer your question. You get to click one of the topics and hope that it has the right information.

You see, the Assistant isn't smart enough to understand the question. Instead, it looks for certain keywords that tell it what topic is being talked about. If you ask, `How do I add a button to the toolbar?`, it will give you a list of topics, one of which is the right one (Add a button to a toolbar). If you ask, `How do I button my shirt?` or even `Button, button, who's got the button?`, however, that topic also appears. The Assistant just recognizes the word *button* and pulls up its list of button-related topics.

Changing Your Assistant

Depending on how your copy of PowerPoint was installed, you may have a choice of different Office Assistants. They all offer the same advice; the only difference is how they look. Some look more goofy and fun, and some look more businesslike—just like your real-life coworkers!

Short on Assistants?

Each Assistant installed on your system takes up a lot of disk space. That's why some of the Assistants that you see here may not be installed.

To change yours (your Office Assistant, not your real-life coworkers), right-click your Assistant to get a shortcut menu. From that menu, select the **Choose Assistant** command. A dialog box appears, with a tab named Gallery displayed. There are two buttons marked **Back** and **Next** that you can use to flip through all the Assistants on your system. After you find the one you want, click the **OK** button to use it. (If the Assistant tells you that it needs the Microsoft Office CD, get that CD, put it in your drive, and click **OK**.)

These are the different Office Assistants that are available with Microsoft Office. They may look different, but they all give the same advice!

Using What You Get

When the Help information appears, it may just be something that you read, and after you finish, you click the **Close** (**X**) button.

Some Help information has more than that, however. Some have a list of steps that you can leave open while you work on doing what it says. Others have *hyperlinks*, places to click on to get more information. You can recognize these hyperlinks because they have a gray button or a colored text. The pointer turns into a pointing finger when you pass over them (someone obviously never told your computer that it wasn't polite to point.)

Click a hyperlink and you might see a small, quick explanation of what you clicked appear in a box. Or the whole Help window might move to another page of information about what you clicked. If it moves on to another page, you can get back to the page you were on by clicking the **Back** button. (And here you were hoping the Back button would cause the computer to scratch your back for you! Boy, when computers can do that, they will be *really* user friendly!)

Back button

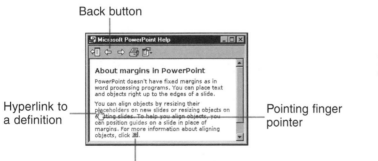

Hyperlink to a definition

Hyperlink to another Help topic

Pointing finger pointer

The Help display has a lot of things you can click for more help.

Contents and Index: A Whole Lot of Help

The Office Assistant's advice is handy if you just have a quick question to ask. If you want to do more in-depth research without constantly asking the Assistant questions, however, you can. This is a completely indexed reference work ready for you to use. And lucky for you, it's a reference work about PowerPoint! (At first, Microsoft was going to put *The Beginner's Guide to the Care and Feeding of Squished Bugs* into the system before they came up with this brainstorm.)

Help Printing Help

To print out a Help topic, right-click it and select **Print** or **Print Topic** from the shortcut menu. A Print dialog box appears. Click **OK**!

To access the table of contents and index for this reference work, ask the Assistant a question. Then, in the Help window, click the **Show** button (if you are using Windows 98) or the **Help Topics** button (if you have an earlier version of Windows).

Contents: They're Not Just for Breakfast Anymore!

The information in the Help system is organized like a book, but you aren't going to want to read it straight through. There are two main ways to find what you want: Look in the table of contents or look through the index.

The Help system, organized like a book with chapters and sections on various topics.

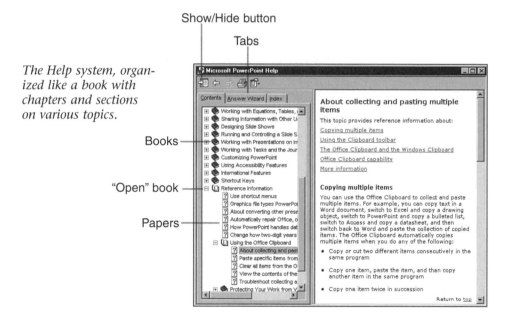

To reach the table of contents, click the **Contents** tab in the Help dialog box. A list of topics appears, each with a little book next to it. That book means that this is a big topic, and it is broken up into sections. Double-click the book, and the list expands to show all the sections in that book. Double-click the name of a section, and that section displays in the Help window.

If you want to know about how to add another button to one of PowerPoint's toolbars, for example, open the **Toolbars and Menus** book. In there is a paper marked **Add a button to a toolbar**. Double-click that. A display with the information that you want appears.

If you want to close a book that you have open, double-click it again. The list of sections of that book will disappear quicker than a bowl of mice at a python party.

Dexterously Using the Index

The index can find any article based on any important word in the article. To look something up using the index, click the **Index** tab in the Help dialog box. This tab has three areas: a text entry field, an alphabetic list of keywords, and a list area for help topics. If you have a good grasp of the traditional order of the alphabet, you can use the scrollbar to go through the list and double-click on a keyword that describes what you want help about.

If you want to find the topic faster, you can type the first word of what you are looking for into the text box. As you type, the part of the keyword list starting with that word will appear in the list section. You can type more than one word, click **Search** to find topics that have all the words.

When you find the topic you are looking for (or if you find a topic that you aren't looking for but sounds fascinating anyway!), double-click it. You might go right to the Help information you wanted, or you might be taken to a shorter list of related topics, from which you can select one topic.

If you want to use the index again, press the **Clear** button before selecting your words. That resets the index so that it won't limit you to just the articles with the previous words you entered.

Kill Your Assistant

If you find the table of contents and index handier than using the Assistant, right-click the Assistant, choose **Options**, and then clear the **Use the Office Assistant** check box. From then on, clicking the **Help** button will take you right to the Help window.

The World Wide Web Is a Huge Helpful Haven

The Help system is full of information that people need. Well, actually, it's full of information that the folks at Microsoft *thought* people were going to need when they were making up the Help system. That's close, but it's not quite the same thing.

After all, no matter how much effort you put into expecting how someone is going to use something, they will still surprise you. I remember one toy that our parents bought for us. It was a soft doll of a little old lady, one of those where you pull the string and it talks. It was a perfect gift for rambunctious kids: soft, nondangerous, engaging, respectful, and most of all, nonviolent. So what did we do with it? We used it as a hand grenade! Pull the string, count to three, and throw it into another kid's room. If the doll finished saying its phrase before being cleared out of the room, we considered the grenade to have "gone off," and the people in the room to have been "blown up."

Computer users are a lot like that. The people who design the programs spend a lot of time figuring out how you are going to use the program, and then you turn around and try to do something with it they never thought of. This can create two types of questions that can't be answered in the Help files: "How do I do such-n-such?" and "When I do such-n-such, why does the program stop working?"

Because new questions pop up, Microsoft has a Web site devoted to answering them. If you have your system set up to access the World Wide Web, you can get to it by pulling down the **Help** menu and selecting the **Office on the Web** command. When you pick this, PowerPoint loads your Web browser and gets it to display the Web site. (You may have to enter your Internet password information.)

Improving a Point

It's a good idea to check out the Office Web site from time to time, even if you don't have a question. Microsoft often offers additional files to add features to their products, available for free just by downloading them from the Web site!

PowerPoint 9-1-1

Sometimes, the answer just can't be found. You have checked the book, asked the Office Assistant, gone through the Help index, checked the Web site, asked the expert down the hall, asked the guy who was stealing a donut from the expert down the hall, and what you need to know just doesn't seem to be out there. What to do?

It's time to call up Microsoft! If anyone knows, they should! Microsoft has a whole flotilla of people just sitting by the phone, waiting for you to call. (Well, not just you. But I'm sure they would love to hear from you as well!) Microsoft's technical support staff is friendly, quick, and knows lots and lots of answers.

But that's why you should use them last. Oh, the problem is not that they know the answers, but that everyone knows that they know the answers, so everyone calls them. Sometimes you can get through to them very quickly; but other times, it takes quite a while, because everyone is trying to ask them things at once. You may spend a lot of time on hold, waiting to get through.

To get information on how to call them, pull down the **Help** menu and select the **About Microsoft PowerPoint** command. A window opens, giving you certain information about your copy of PowerPoint (the revision number and things like that). On the bottom of the window is a **Tech Support** button. Press that, and you will see a list of Help topics on how to contact Microsoft's helpful helpers! (Leave the About Microsoft PowerPoint window open, however, because the technical support people will need some of that information to help you out.)

The Least You Need to Know

➤ Clicking the **Help Button** icon causes the animated Office Assistant character to appear.

➤ When the Office Assistant has a light bulb with him, click it to get some suggestions about what you are doing.

➤ If you need help figuring out how to do something, click the Office Assistant and type in your question.

➤ The **Help, What's This?** command turns your pointer into an arrow and a question mark. Click the arrow or question mark on anything to find out what it is.

➤ Clicking the **Help Topics** or **Show** button in the Assistant's answer brings up a table of contents and an index for Help.

➤ When using the table of contents, double-click a book to see more information on that topic. Double-click a paper to see Help information on that topic.

➤ The **Help, Office on the Web** command brings up a Web page of Help information if you are properly connected.

➤ To find out how to reach Tech Support, use the **Help, About Microsoft PowerPoint** command and click the **Tech Support** button.

Part 2
Building Your Presentation

A presentation is like a salad. You can put a lot of things into it and make it fancy, or you can put a few things into it and keep it simple. And some people look at you weirdly if you give it to them without dressing.

In this part, you learn about putting the basics into your presentation salad—the lettuce, the croutons, those little cherry tomatoes that go squish in your mouth. We'll get to the fancy stuff, the endives and anchovies, later.

CHICK CHINK

Chapter 4

Sliding Slides into Place

In This Chapter

➤ Create new slides

➤ Get rid of old slides

➤ Slip a slide from one place into another

➤ View your slides several different ways (front, back, and slideways!)

A *slide* is a single part of a presentation. If you are dealing with a printed presentation, it's a single page. If you have an onscreen presentation, it's a single screen display. And if you are using a slide projector, a slide is a slide!

A *slideshow* is a group of slides, organized in a specific order or with a specific choice of paths from one slide to the next. A *presentation* is one or more slideshows, stored together, which may also contain notes on the slideshows. A whole bunch of presentations, organized together with a break for lunch, is a *long, boring symposium* (but those are, thankfully, outside what this book covers).

Looking Slideways

PowerPoint provides a number of different ways for you to look at slides. Each is good for some things and not so good for others, so it's a good idea to get used to them all. Popping from one way of looking at things to another is easy; you can change your view quicker than a politician changes an opinion. At the lower-left part of the PowerPoint screen is a set of buttons, each of which gives you a different view to your slides.

You have already run into Normal view, which you can bring up at any time using the **Normal View** button. Because it shows you the outline of the presentation and a picture of a single slide, this is handy view if you are working on the text and the adjusting the visuals simultaneously. Because it's trying to show multiple things at once, however, there's little room for each. It's like having one of those plastic plates with separate compartments for meat, mashed potatoes, and a sprig of parsley; it's very handy if you are having a full meal, but not so good if what you want is an entire plate full of parsley.

Slide View? Aren't They All Slide Views?

Clicking this **Slide View** button puts you into *Slide view*, where you can see the slides onscreen one at a time. Each slide appears about half the size it would be in an onscreen slideshow. You can move from viewing one slide to another by using the scrollbar at right to move up or down through your slideshow, or by clicking a specific slide from the numbered list at the left.

In Slide view, you get a good look at one slide at a time.

Slide numbers

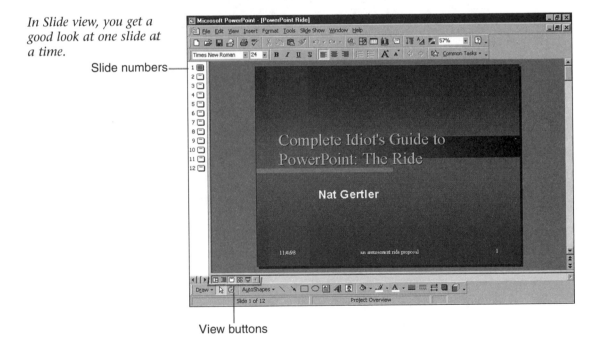

View buttons

The Slide view is good for changing the contents of a slide. This gives you the biggest view of a slide (about half the size that your slide will be in an onscreen presentation), making it easy to precisely place the text, graphics, movies, and other elements that make up your slide.

Slide view has its weaknesses, however. You can see only one slide at a time in this view, which means that it isn't very good for finding a slide, adding new slides, getting rid of old slides, or changing the order of slides. And because it does show you as much of the detail as it can, it can be slow if you are using complicated slides, particularly if you are using a slow computer. (Isn't it funny that you don't remember *buying* a slow computer? You remember buying a lightning-fast, state-of-the-art machine! Yet over the years it has somehow been replaced with a slow computer....)

Viewing the Outline Isn't Out of Line

The *Outline view*, which you can see at any time just by clicking the **Outline View** button, is a lot like Normal view. The main difference is that it shows the slide very small, leaving space to show a lot more of the outline.

Selected slide   Small version of selected slide

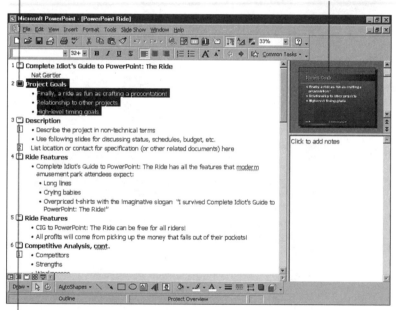

With the Outline view, you get a sense of the entire presentation.

Unselected slide

You will use Outline view often because it shows a lot at once and you can do a lot with it. For each slide, it shows you a little icon of a slide followed by the text of the slide. This is great for getting the sense of the entire presentation at once, because you can see the text from a number of slides at the same time and in easy-to-read form. You can also make quick text changes, delete slides, and move slides around. (Outline view isn't any good for adding pictures, sounds, charts, animation, or exotic Caribbean spices, however.)

Use Slide Sorter for the Slides' Order!

The *Slide Sorter view* is great for rearranging your slides. Click the **Slide Sorter View** button and you will see small versions of your slides, several of them onscreen at a time. The slides are arranged in rows, with the first slides going from left to right on the first row, the next slides on the second row, and so on. You can use the scrollbars to see slides further on in the show.

Slide Sorter view is great for rearranging slides and for finding a specific slide in the set. You can't change what's on any of the slides here, but you can rearrange the slides to your heart's content (if rearranging slides makes your heart content).

In Slide Sorter view, you can see many slides at once—and quickly shuffle them.

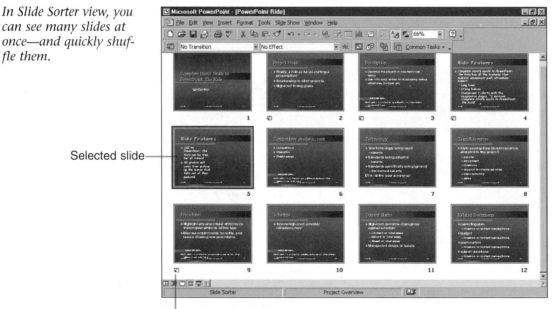

Selected slide

Transition indicator

Check This Out

Automatic Transition

In Slide Sorter view, if you see a little slide icon underneath one of the slides, try clicking it. Right there on the mini version of the slide, you will see how the transition takes place from the preceding slide to this one! This appears only if a transition has been chosen. (You will learn more about transitions in Chapter 15, "Tricky Transitions and Terrific Timing.")

Note the Notes Page View

PowerPoint can print out a cheat-sheet, so you can have a listing of notes about each slide to refer to while making your presentation. The Notes Page view is designed just to let you work on these notes, displaying one slide and a place to edit the notes for each page. To see this view, choose **View, Notes Page**.

To learn more about making the notes for the Notes page, check out Chapter 20, "Reaching a Crowd: Slides, Overheads, Projection Screens, and Network Presentations." (No, don't check it out *now*! Wait until you learn about creating slides before you try adding notes to them.)

The Notes Page view is very good for adding notes, but not much good for anything else. Some consider being good for just one thing *specializing*; others consider it *being lazy*.

Slide Show: The Show-Off View

Clicking this button starts showing your slideshow. There are also commands for starting the slideshow on the View menu and the Slide Show menu, but this button has one important difference: It starts the slideshow with whatever slide you are currently working on. If you are in Notes Page view and are looking at the third slide in your show, for example, clicking this button shows the slideshow starting at the third slide. To move to the next slide, press the **Spacebar**.

This is the clearest display of how your final presentation will look, because it's basically your final presentation. However, it's no good for changing things. Trying to change things while the slideshow is going would be like trying to change your tires while driving.

Selecting Slides

Before you start changing, moving, or otherwise mutilating slides, you have to tell PowerPoint which slide you are working with. The different views have different way of doing this, just to keep you on your toes:

Show-Stopping

To stop the slideshow, right-click, and then select **End Show** from the shortcut menu, or just hit **Esc**.

➤ In the Slide view and the Note Pages view, you don't have to select slides. Because each displays only one slide at a time, PowerPoint figures that the slide displayed is the one you want to work with. And it's right!

➤ In the Normal view or the Outline view, click the little slide icon to the left of the slide text. The text of the slide you have selected will reverse colors.

➤ In the Slide Sorter view, just click the picture of the slide you want to select. You can't make it any easier than that! (Well, you could hire an entire staff of slide-selecting personnel, but you probably have better uses for your money. If you don't, could you send me some?)

Selecting More Than One Slide

If you want to select more than one slide at a time (if you want to move or delete a whole group of slides, for example), and you are in Slide Sorter view, hold down the **Ctrl** key while selecting. You can keep selecting as many as you want (but leave some room for dessert). In Normal or Outline view, select a group of them by clicking the first one and then holding down **Shift** and clicking the last one. In either view, to select them all, press **Ctrl+A**.

A New Slide to Start With

If you want to add a new slide as the very first one in your slideshow, you have to add it somewhere else, and then move it into the first position. (You will see how to move it later in this chapter.)

Adding a Slide

You can add a new slide in any view except the Slide Show view. To add a new slide, first select the slide you want the new slide to appear after. Click this **New Slide** button and a dialog box appears.

The resulting dialog box offers different possible layouts for your slide. Some of these layouts contain places for charts, pictures, or movies. Double-click a layout that looks like how you want your slide to appear. Don't worry if it isn't exact; you can rearrange things as much as you want later.

The New Slide dialog box shows small pictures of the different slide layouts you can add. Selecting a picture brings up a description of the slide on the right of the dialog box.

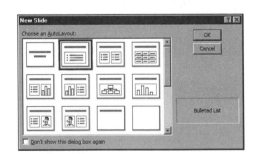

Don't worry now about adding the text or other contents of the slide; I show you how to do that in the next chapter.

Slide Deleting

To delete a slide, go into the Slide Sorter view, select the slide, and press **Delete**. Boom! It's gone, never to be seen again!

Never Say Never?

If you delete a slide that you didn't mean to delete, just click on the **Undo** button! It's good for undoing all sorts of mistakes! You can even click repeatedly on it to undo the last few steps, one at a time.

Sliding a Slide Around

Sometimes, you want to rearrange your slideshow to get things in a more logical order. Other times, you want to rearrange other people's slideshows, just so they get really confused when they are doing their presentations. Let's face it: You are mean!

To do this, go into Slide Sorter view, because sorting your slides is sort of what this view is all about. Select the slide (or slides) that you want to move, and then drag them. The slides don't actually move as you drag them, but you will see a vertical line moving in-between slides, following the pointer as well as it can. Get that line in front of the slide that you want to move these slides in front of, and then release the mouse button. The slides will be rearranged just as you want them to be!

Sliding into Second: Duplicating Your Slide

To make a copy of a slide, select the slide, and then pull down the **Edit** menu and select **Duplicate**. (If **Duplicate** does not appear on your **Edit** menu, click the double-arrows at the bottom of the menu to see a longer menu.) The second copy appears immediately after the first. Then you can move it to where you want it.

Why would you want to do this? Sometimes, you just want to have a slide appear more than once in your slideshow. You might want to end your show with a copy of the title slide, for example, so that people leave with a reminder of what this presentation was all about.

Sometimes, however, you may want to just create nifty effects. Say, for example, that you have a computer-based presentation with a slide that says Complete Idiot's Guide To PowerPoint: The Ride is the world's fastest. Make two copies of that. Now you have three identical slides in a row. Replace the word fastest with biggest on the second slide, and with best on the third. Now when you step through the slideshow, it will look like it's one slide, with just the last word changing. Keen, eh?

Sliding into First, and Then Stealing Second

If you want to steal a copy of a slide from another presentation and put it into yours, you can do it! (Make sure you get permission from whoever made the slide.) You can reuse all the slides you want. You can even put on a "greatest hits" retrospective of your favorite slides.

To do this, first select the slide that you want the new slide(s) to appear after. Then pull down the **Insert** menu and select the **Slides from Files** command. The Slide Finder dialog box appears. Click the **Browse** button. A list of your presentation files will appear. Select the one that has the slide(s), and then click the **Open** button.

Now, the name of the presentation you selected appears in the File text box on the Slide Finder dialog box. The first three slides in the presentation appear in the lower half of the display (if they don't show up instantly, click the Display button). You can scroll through the presentation with the scrollbar beneath the slides. Select the slides that you want by clicking them. (You can select more than one, and you don't even have to hold down the **Shift** key.) Then click the **Insert** button, and the slide (or slides) will be added to your presentation!

The Slide Finder dialog box shows you the slides in the presentation that you are copying from. If you want to copy them all, click on the **Insert All** *button.*

The Least You Need to Know

➤ There are six different slide-viewing modes:

Click for Normal view. To select a slide in this mode, click the small slide icon on the outline.

Click for Outline view. Selecting is the same as for Normal view.

Click for Slide view. The slide you are viewing is automatically considered selected.

Click for Slide Sorter view, and then click a slide to select it.

To use the Slide Show view starting from the currently selected slide, click the **Slide Show View** button. You cannot select slides in this view.

For Note Pages view, choose **View, Notes Page**. The slide you are viewing is automatically considered selected.

➤ To add a slide, select the slide you want to appear before it, and then click the **Insert New Slide** button.

➤ To delete a slide, select the slide and press **Delete**.

➤ To move a slide, use Slide Sorter view. Select the slide, and drag it until a vertical line appears before the slide you want to put this slide ahead of.

➤ To copy a slide, select the slide, and then select **Edit, Duplicate**.

Chapter 5

The World of Words

In This Chapter

➤ Put words on your slides

➤ Make words bigger and smaller

➤ Make words bold and italic

➤ Create lists so that you will no longer be listless!

➤ Correct misspelled words (and mess up correct ones, if you want!)

Words are very important. Sometimes, they are very, very important. If you get paid by the word, they can be very, very, very, very, very, very, very important. (That's 75 cents worth right there!)

It's possible to create a presentation without any written text. Most of the time, however, not only do you use text, you use a lot of it.

Brave New Words for Brave New Slides

If you have just created a new slide, the best view to add words in is the Slide view. In that view, you will see that your new slide has the phrase Click to add text wherever text is going to be on the slide. That phrase is so full of depth and meaning, which boils down to this: To add text, click there!

But you have to do more than just click there! That was too easy! After you click there, you have to type the text. As you type, what you type appears onscreen. If you make a mistake, press the **Backspace** key to get rid of it, and keep typing. (If you decide not to add any text at all, press the **Esc** key and escape out of it!)

Some text areas are specifically designed for lists. If you start typing in one of those, a *bullet* (a dot) will appear before what you type. Every time you press the **Enter** key, a new line will start with another bullet.

Reworking Your Words (or Rewording Your Work)

Select Tricks

To quickly select a word, double-click it. To select a whole paragraph, triple-click. And if you click a hundred times on the word, you get... a tired clicking finger!

Sometimes, you want to change words on one of your slides. Perhaps you have discovered better words, or maybe you have just discovered that you are allergic to the word *agenda*. Whatever the reason, changing what you have typed is easy.

First, *select* the text you are going to change. (Remember, this is done by pointing to the start of the first word you want to change, holding down the mouse button, and dragging to the end of the last word you want to change.) The selected words will show up in a different color. Start typing the new text; the old text, feeling unwanted, will leave immediately.

Word-Do's: Styling Your Text

Remember that way back, in your great-grandmother's day, they had a device called a *typewriter*. This method of putting words on paper created letters that all looked alike. A typed shopping list looked the same as a contract, which looked the same as a love letter. Really important words such as *One-Third Off* looked the same as unimportant words such as *heretofore*. This was a great way to be understood, but an absolutely horrible way to look hip and fashionable.

Luckily, PowerPoint has a full set of tools to make your words look fancy. Now you can make your words so heavily designed that they are as hard to read as one of those modern magazine ads! You can even create the sort of teeny tiny text that they use to tell you that use of this product may lead to spontaneous human combustion.

Leapin' Letters: Bold, Italic, Underline, and Shadow

You can quickly add some basic effects to your text. Select the text you want to emphasize, and then click

B   To get **bold** text (or press **Ctrl+B**)

I   To get *italic* text (or press **Ctrl+I**)

U To underline text (or press **Ctrl+U**)

S To give the text a small shadow, as if it were hovering over the page.

You can combine these effects by clicking more than one button. If you want to get rid of the effect, just select the text and click the button again. The button will pop out, and the text will be back to normal.

Buttons, Buttons, Who's Got the Buttons?

If you don't seethese text-formatting buttons on the screen, it could be for one of several reasons. Someone may have told PowerPoint to hide the toolbar. Right-click the buttons you do see, check to see that **Formatting** has a check mark next to it on the menu that appears. If it doesn't, select it, and the Formatting toolbar appears. (You now have the ability to make toolbars appear and disappear—but it's not as fun as making chocolate bars disappear.)

Font-astic Formatting

Use the **Format**, **Font** command to get a dialog box which you can use to make text *embossed* (raised), *subscript* (smaller and below the rest of the text), or *superscript* (smaller and above the rest of the text).

» If the Formatting toolbar is on the screen but is missing some of the buttons, try clicking the **More Buttons** button at the end of the toolbar. A set of buttons appear that there wasn't enough room for; click the one you want.

If you don't see the button you want on the More Buttons list, click **Add or Remove Buttons** at the bottom of that list. Another list appears, showing all the possible buttons for the Formatting toolbar. Select the button you want to see, and it will be added either to the displayed buttons or to the More Buttons list. (These techniques work for any of the toolbars, not just Formatting.)

If you still don't see the button you are looking for, check to make sure your eyes are open.

Colorful Language

There's little that can make your text stand out more than color. Red is a particularly good one; that's why we have terms like red letter days, red ink, and *The Scarlet Letter*. PowerPoint automatically uses a color that shows up well against the background, but you can change that color at any time.

When buttons are missing from a toolbar, use that toolbar's More Buttons button to see additional buttons.

More Buttons list

Formatting toolbar   More Buttons button

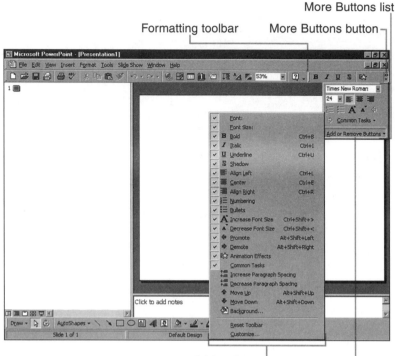

Add or Remove Buttons list

Add or Remove Buttons button

More Buttons Butting In

Choose **Tools, Customize,** and on the **Options** tab clear the **Standard And Formatting Toolbars Share The Same Row** check box, and PowerPoint will put those two toolbars on separate rows. This shows you more buttons, so you won't need to use the More Button list.

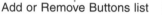 To change the color of text, first select it. Then head down to the bottom of the screen and click on the small drop-down arrow to the right of the Font Color button. A small menu pops up, which has a bunch of little colored squares on it. Just click the square of the color you want. If you want to change more text to that color,

you can select that text and click the **Font Color** button. (If you don't see this button at the bottom, right-click on any button you do see, and select **Drawing** from the menu that appears. The button will now be seen.)

Invisible Text

A neat trick is to turn shadows on, and then make your text the same color as the background. The text will seem to disappear, with only the shadows visible, but that's enough to be clearly readable. Try it!

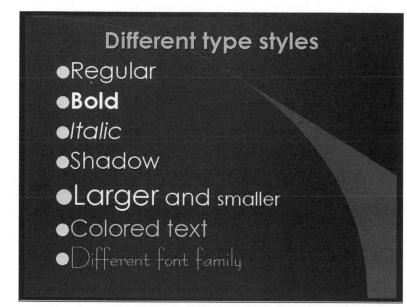

Don't actually use all the different style options on the same slide. If you mix more than three on a slide, it becomes as hard to read as a bowl of alphabet soup!

Sizing Up (and Down) Your Words

Some concepts call for huge words, like *I love you!* or *Free donuts!* Others call for a mite more delicacy, like *I only love you because you give me free donuts*. By changing the *font size* (the size of the letters), you can create a sense of importance and make sure that the most important thing is seen first. Keep clicking the **Increase Font Size** and **Decrease Font Size** buttons until the selected text is as big or as small as you want it.

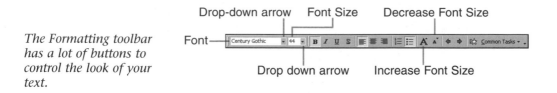

The Formatting toolbar has a lot of buttons to control the look of your text.

The Font Size field shows you how big your letters are (measured in *points*, 72ths of an inch). You can fine-tune the size by changing the number there.

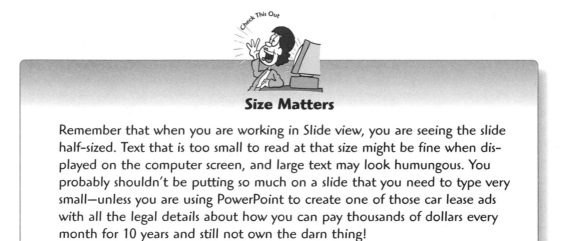

Size Matters

Remember that when you are working in Slide view, you are seeing the slide half-sized. Text that is too small to read at that size might be fine when displayed on the computer screen, and large text may look humungous. You probably shouldn't be putting so much on a slide that you need to type very small—unless you are using PowerPoint to create one of those car lease ads with all the legal details about how you can pay thousands of dollars every month for 10 years and still not own the darn thing!

Just Put One Font in Front of Another

There are a lot of different *fonts* (type designs), ranging from the boring to the unreadable. Somewhere in between, there are some you should actually think about using. Click the drop-down button next to the font field, and you see a list of fonts on your system. Select a font from the list, and the selected text appears in that font.

The Youth of Fontin'

A new feature in this version of PowerPoint is that the font list has each font's name in that font, making it easy to tell what sort of font it is. Some of the fonts that look ugly on the font list will look better on your slide, where it will be larger and more detailed.

If you aren't familiar with the fonts you have, you should spend some time getting friendly with them. When you have some time to spare, select a sentence and see what it looks like with each font on your system. Some will look better than others. Some of the fancier ones may only have capital letters and will replace all of the lowercase letters with squares. Remember which ones look good, so you can get them back when you need them. You can use the ugly ones when you put your competitor's name on the slide!

Founts of Fonts

There are plenty of fonts available for download from the Internet. You can also get CD-ROMs with hundreds or even thousands of fonts on them. Many are considered *display fonts*, which are too fancy to write letters with but can be good for titles.

Speling Is Emportent

All the pretty letters in the world won't do you any good if they don't form words. Misspelled words are hard to understand, and they make you look both stupid and sloppy. And someday, your old grade-school English teacher may be watching your presentations, and it would be horrible to have her drag you back into third-grade spelling class at that point!

PowerPoint has a *spell checker*, a program feature that will go over all the words on your slides and make sure that they are all indeed words, showing that you didn't make a major typo and that your cat didn't trundle across the keyboard while you weren't looking. (I was once filling out my Township Pet Registration form when my cat jumped on the typewriter, bringing the cat, typewriter, and my last bottle of white-out smashing to the floor at once. Poor little fejo;lwwq/'vv!)

You don't even have to tell PowerPoint to check your work. As you type, PowerPoint is constantly looking over your shoulder, just waiting for you to make a mistake so that it can point out the mistake and laugh at you. Okay, it doesn't laugh out loud, but you know that somewhere, deep inside, it's laughing. When you type something that it thinks is a mistake, it will underline the word with a wavy line.

Fixing the Misteak

If you recognize your mistake, you can just fix it, and the wavy line will go away. If you don't know what the right spelling is, or if you think you do have the right spelling, right-click the word and a menu will appear.

Right-clicking on a typo brings up a list of suggested fixes.

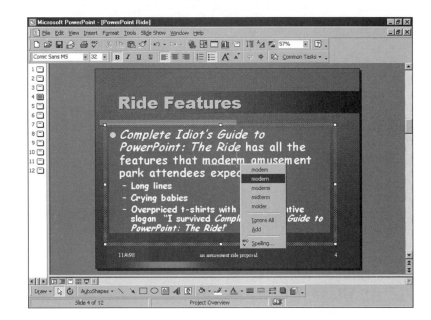

At the top of the menu is a list of words that it thinks you might have meant. If the right word is there, just select it from the menu. PowerPoint will take away your wrong word and slide in the right one, and no one will be any wiser! If PowerPoint doesn't recommend the right word, try replacing it with another guess at the right spelling. Even if you don't get it right, you might get close enough for PowerPoint to make the right suggestion.

My Spelling Is Ryght, Dadgummit!

PowerPoint is a know-it-all. It thinks that just because it doesn't recognize a word, it must be misspelled. Sometimes it's right, and sometimes it's wrong. There are a lot of things that PowerPoint doesn't know, including a lot of names. If PowerPoint incorrectly corrects you, feel free to laugh at it.

If PowerPoint calls something a typo, and it isn't, you can do three things:

➤ Ignore the wavy line. (Don't worry, the wavy line won't show up in the finished slide show!) The problem is that if you ignore the wavy line when it isn't a misspelling, it's hard to notice it when there really is one.

➤ Right-click the word and select **Ignore All** from the menu. This lets PowerPoint know not to count that same word as a mistake again in this presentation. (It will still count it as a mistake if you use it in another presentation.)

➤ Right-click the word and select **Add**. This tells PowerPoint to add the word to its dictionary, so next time it will not count it as a mistake.

Missed Mistakes

You can make mistakes that PowerPoint has no way of noticing. That's because many typos accidentally turn one word into another. If you put, say, `Compete Idiom's Glide` on a slide, PowerPoint will not complain a bit, because everything in it is a word. PowerPoint is not smart enough to recognize that none of them are the right words. Congratulations! You are smart enough to outsmart the error-catching technology!

These mistakes are best battled with the power of the human brain. Read over your presentation or, better yet, get someone else to read it over. Murphy's Law says that any mistake you don't catch will be seen by every member of your audience!

One Dictionary for the Whole Office

All Microsoft Office products use the same dictionary file to check spelling. If you add a word to the dictionary in PowerPoint, Word (for example) will also recognize it!

Alignment Assignment

Usually, we see text where each new line starts right below the preceding line, but each line's end is in a slightly different place, depending on the length of the words on the line. This is the easiest thing for most people to read. But dagnabbit, we have put a lot of work into designing this presentation, so maybe it should be just as much work to read it!

You have three different choices for how your lines of text will line up. While you are working on a block of text, you can click

 To get *left alignment*—the text lines up the usual way.

 To get *center alignment*—each line of text is centered across the text area, giving it a balanced look). This is good for titles.

 To get *right alignment*—the ends of the lines are stacked neatly, but the beginnings of the lines don't line up. This creates a new-wave look for short lists, but isn't very useful.

Lust for Lists!

Lists are very popular in presentations. There's nothing like saying that your product will make the customer:

➤ Rich

➤ Healthy

➤ Irresistible to members of the appropriate sex

Many of the slide layouts that PowerPoint's AutoLayout feature offers have list areas. You can recognize them in the layout pictures in the New Slide dialog box because they show lines of text that start with a *bullet* (a dot).

Entering text into a list works just like regular text, except that every time you press **Enter**, a line is skipped and a bullet is put in front of the line. Soon, you will have more bullets than the Tombstone medical examiner's office in the Old West!

Demotion of De List

Individual items on your list may have their own lists that go with them. When the preceding list tells your customer that your product will make him healthy, you may want to list the individual health benefits (a healthy glow, washboard abs, and the end to cavities). This sublist should be indented more than the normal list.

 Click this, the **Demote** button, to get the indent effect and to show you are working on a less-significant list. After you click it, everything you enter will be indented more.

 After you finish entering the sublist, press **Return** to get to the next line, and then click the **Promote** button to show you're working on the most significant list.

Bite the Bullet

Lists don't have to have bullets. To remove bullets from a list, select the list, and then click this button. The bullets disappear. Click the button again, and they reappear.

If you want to use a different-looking bullet, you can do that too! Select the whole list, and then pull down the **Format** menu and select the **Bullets and Numbering** command. The Bullet dialog box displaying a half-dozen other bullet styles appears. You can click the one you want. If you don't see any you want, there's a Character button that you can click to select any symbol character from any font to use as a bullet. There's also a Color drop-down button that you can click to pick the color of the bullet, and a Size field where you can enter the caliber ... er, *size* of the bullet! After you have selected your bullet, click the **OK** button to use it!

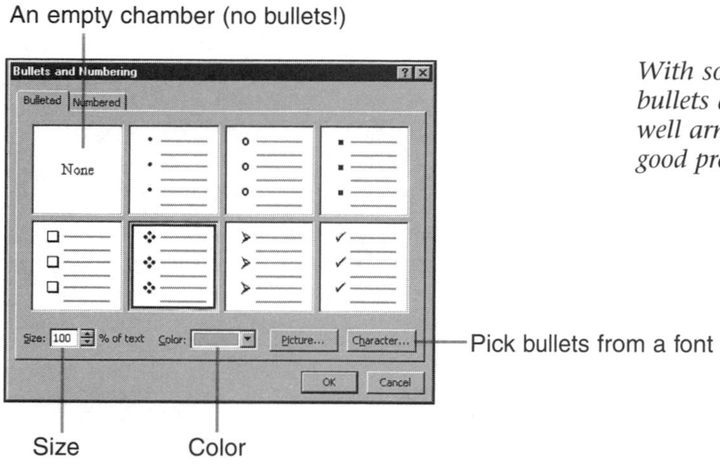

An empty chamber (no bullets!)

With so many different bullets available, you are well armed to make a good presentation.

Pick bullets from a font

Size   Color

Numbering Your Million Points of Light

Select your bulleted list, and then click the **Numbering** button. Instead of being bulleted, your list, your points, and even your days will be numbered!

The Least You Need to Know

➤ To start putting text on a new slide, click where it says Click to add text.

➤ To change text on an existing slide, select the text that you want to change, and then type over it.

➤ If you don't see the Formatting toolbar, right-click any other toolbar and select **Formatting** from the menu that appears.

➤ The Formatting toolbar buttons are used to format and manipulate text.

➤ The drop-down arrow at the right end of the Font field opens a drop-down list from which you can select a completely different typeface.

➤ If you type a word that PowerPoint doesn't know, a wavy line will appear under it. Right-click on the word to see a menu that will let you pick the correct word, or to teach PowerPoint this word.

➤ When entering a list, each time you press enter you start a new item on the list. Each item starts with a bullet, unless you click the **Bullets** button to stop the bullets.

Chapter 6

Layout: Not Just Something You Do in the Sun

In This Chapter

➤ Arrange boxes of text and other slide contents

➤ Change each box's size

➤ Overlap boxes

➤ Add boxes, remove boxes, and even group boxes!

Learning how to lay out your slides is very important. Extremely important. The fate of civilization may depend on it.

Well, okay, it's not *that* important. Heck, with all the nice built-in slide designs that PowerPoint provides, you may not need to know it at all. But still, knowing this could help you make your presentation look that much better—and isn't that more important than civilization?

Boxes in Slides? I Thought Slides Went in Boxes!

The design of a slide is broken down into areas called *boxes*. Each box holds one *object*, one piece of your slide. If you have a slide with a title, a list, and a chart, for example, you will have three boxes: one for the title, one for the list, and one for the chart. You could have a slide with no boxes, but that would be a blank slide.

Each box is a rectangular shape, even if it's holding something that isn't rectangular, such as a circular picture or New Jersey. (Not that you can actually put New Jersey itself on a slide, but if you could, it would be in a rectangular box.) On the slide designs that PowerPoint starts you off with, none of the boxes overlap, but you can overlap them if you want.

Selecting and Moving Boxes

To select a box, go into Slide view and click on the box's contents. (You can also do this in Normal view or Outline view, but the slide is smaller and harder to work with there.) When you do this, eight little white squares will appear around the edges of the box, one at each corner and one at the center of each edge. These white squares are *sizing handles*, which you use if you want to change the size of the box. On some boxes, an edge line appears around the box as well.

Use these sizing handles to change the size of a box.

The line and white boxes around the list show that it's selected. Don't confuse that with the dotted line around the space for a chart, which is just there to show you where it goes.

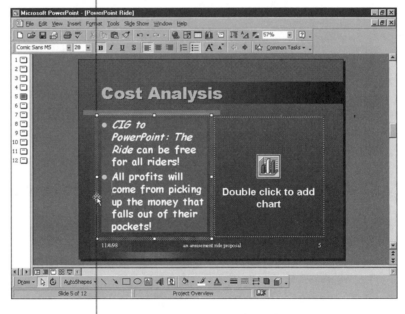

Point to a box edge, and your pointer takes on the Move pointer shape.

Moving boxes is easy. Just point to an edge of the box, and your pointer should turn into an arrow with arrowheads pointing in all four directions (useful, I suppose, to very clumsy hunters). Push down the mouse button and drag the rectangle wherever you want it to go! You can even drag it off the edge of the slide; but if you do, it won't be in your slide show! (Although you can make some nifty effects by dragging it just over the edge of the slide so that *part* of it shows up in the show.)

Sliding It from Slide to Slide

If you want to move a box from one slide to another slide, a different method comes into play. Just follow these easy steps:

➤ First, select the box you want to move (if you are doing a text box, reselect it by grabbing the edge so that PowerPoint doesn't think you want to select just some of the text).

➤ Then, click the **Cut** button, which will *cut* the box off of the slide, storing a copy of it in an area of memory called the *Clipboard*.

➤ Finally, go to the slide that you want to put the box on, and click the **Paste** button, which takes the last thing stored on the Clipboard and *pastes* it onto the page. Then you can move the box into place.

Supercuts and Superpastes

The Clipboard now stores up to 12 items, not just one. Right-click any menu and select **Clipboard** from the pop-up menu. A Clipboard toolbar appears, with icons representing the last 12 items cut or copied. Point to an icon, and a description of the item appears. Click it, and the item is pasted on your slide.

Resizing Boxes: When Size Matters

Sometimes, you find you want a bigger box, such as when you have more text than will fit in the box you have. Sometimes you want smaller box. Let's face it, you are just never satisfied!

Make a box that is wider or narrower   Grab one of the sizing handles on the middle of the sides of the box. Use the handle to drag the size to where you want it.

Make the box taller or shorter   Grab the handle on the middle of the top or bottom of the box and use it drag that edge where you want it.

Shrink or grow the whole box   To do so and keep the same basic shape and proportion, hold down the **Shift** key and drag one of the corner handles. PowerPoint will make sure that the ratio between the width and height remains the same.

Feel free to experiment with resizing your box. After all, if you don't like the new size, you can just click the Undo button to erase your changes! (The same goes for experimenting with other things as well!)

Time to Play Spin the Box!

Just because a box has to be a rectangle does not mean that it has to be a straight up-and-down. You can tilt the box, or rotate it, to put your title at a jaunty angle, or just to tilt a chart a little bit to get on the nerves of precise people (you know, the sort that wander around your house, straightening your paintings).

To do this, first select the box that you want to take for a spin. Click the **Free Rotate** button on the lower edge of your screen. The sizing handles on the box will disappear, and you will start to see green dots before your eyes. Don't worry, these dots are *rotation handles*. Grab one of those handles and drag it around. An outline will show how the box rotates, turning around the box's center, which stays still. When you have the outline where you want it, release the button. The box will tilt into position. The contents of the box become tilted as well, so you get tilted words, tilted pictures, tilted New Jersey, whatever.

After you have tilted it, click the **Free Rotate** button again to return to a normal pointer.

Precisely Tilting

If you hold down the Shift key while rotating the box, it will rotate in precise 15–degree steps so that there are only 24 different positions you can rotate it to. This is handy if you want to rotate several things the same amount.

The Box Is a Pushover

If you want to quickly push the box over on its side, click the **Draw** button. A menu will pop up. Select **Rotate or Flip**, and a submenu will appear. From that menu, select either **Rotate Right** or **Rotate Left**, and the object will be rotated 90 degrees. To turn it upside-down, just do this twice. And if you do it four times in a row, the box will be back where it started and you will have successfully wasted 20 seconds!

Boxes on Top of Boxes

You can create some interesting effects by *overlapping*. No, overlapping doesn't mean licking the cone after all the ice cream is gone—it means putting one box on top of another box. By doing this, you can put text on top of pictures, text on top of other text, pictures on top of each other, or even New Jersey on top of Idaho (if you could get them into boxes).

Getting a box on top of another box is no problem: Just move it over. The real question is how you choose which box goes on top and which goes on the bottom.

The order in which things are piled makes a big difference. These two piles have the same objects overlapping; in the bottom one, however, the circle is on top, hiding the text.

Boxes Going Up and Down (Aren't Those Called Elevators?)

To move where a box is in a stack, first select it. Then right-click it, and a shortcut menu will appear. Select **Order** from this menu, and you will see a submenu with four commands on it.

If you only have two boxes in your pile (now that's not much of a pile, is it?), you will select **Send to Back** (which takes the selected box and puts it at the bottom of the pile) or **Bring to Front** (which makes it the top of the pile).

If you have a real serious pile, a couple of other commands come in handy. Selecting **Bring Forward** moves the selected box up the stack by one. So if you have the third box in the pile selected, it brings it up so that it's the second. **Send Backward** does just the opposite, lowering the item in the pile by one.

Search for the Missing Box

To work with a box, you have to be able to select it. Usually, this is easy, but if you have a small box buried under larger boxes, there may be no visible part to click. New Jersey may be completely buried under Alaska. The trick is to select the box on top, and then start pressing **Tab**. Each time you press Tab, a different box becomes selected. Eventually, the box you want will be selected!

Groups: Boxes Full o' Boxes

Sometimes you will want to take several boxes and treat them as one, just like you might want to squish a bunch of marshmallows together and treat them as one big megamarshmallow. This is very handy if you have a mixture of text and pictures that you want to copy or move together, or if you are making megas'mores.

To do this, first you have to select several boxes to show what you want to pull into a group. That's a trick worthy of its own little headline, so here it is:

Selecting Multiple Boxes at Once

First, select one of the boxes. Then while holding down the **Shift** key, click the other boxes. The sizing handles on each box will appear, showing that it is selected.

Quickly Select a Bunch

If all the boxes you want to select are close together, and there aren't any other boxes mixed in with them, you can select them all in one smooth motion. Point to a spot up and to the left of the boxes, hold down the mouse button, and drag to below and to the right of the boxes. Release the mouse button and you will see sizing handles on all the selected boxes.

Bringing the Group Together

When you have all the boxes selected, it's time to make a group out of them. Click the **Draw** button, and select the **Group** command from the menu that appears.

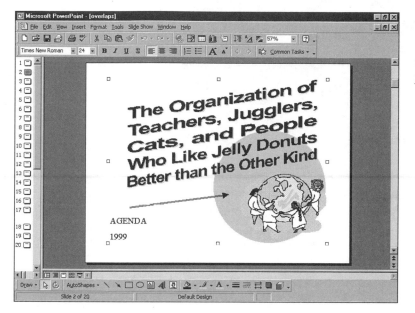

If we can put words, pictures, shapes, lines, and logos into a single box, why can't we have world peace?

Kazowie! Suddenly, all these boxes are one big box! Instead of having a bunch of different handles, they have one set of handles. Everything that you can do to individual boxes, you can now do to this one big box.

Bringing Loners into the Group

Any box that PowerPoint's AutoLayout feature built in to the slide won't want to join in the group. If you have one of these selected, you won't be able to use the group command. However, you can fool PowerPoint into forgetting that a box was put there by AutoLayout. To do this, choose Format, Slide Layout. In the Slide Layout dialog box, double-click the blank slide image.

Next, select the problematic object. click the Cut button, then the Paste button. The box should now look the way that it originally did, but PowerPoint has now forgotten that it is a special box. If you select the pieces for your group again, you will be able to group them just fine! (And don't worry that you don't know what that AutoShape feature is yet. I will be teaching you about it in Chapter 8, "Lines and Shapes: Good Things in Variable-Sized Boxes.")

Driving the Group Apart

There's always a way to drive any group apart. You could become the Yoko Ono of the PowerPoint box set with this capability! Select the group, click the **Draw** button, and select **Ungroup**.

Unkazowie! All the boxes in the group are their own selves again, each with their own handles. If you want to do something with just one of these boxes, click off the side of the slide (to clear the selection), and then select that box.

The Big Reunion Tour: Bringing the Group Back Together

Theoretically, you should never put your group together until you are absolutely sure that every piece of the group is perfect. In the real world, however, if you wait until everything is perfect to do something, you will never get anything done!

If you do discover that part of the group needs to be changed, resized, or moved, you will have to take the group apart using the Ungroup command described earlier. After making the change, however, you don't have to go to all the trouble of selecting everything. Just click the **Draw** button and pick the **Regroup** command. All the boxes from the group will rejoin!

Giving the Group a New Member

If you already have a group, and you want to add another box to it, you don't have to break up the group. Just select both the group and the new box, and then select **Draw**, **Group**.

The Least You Need to Know

➤ The items on a slide are called *objects*. Each object has its own *box*.

➤ To select a box, click on it. To select several boxes at once, hold down the **Shift** key and click them each in turn.

➤ To move a box, select it, click its edge, and drag it.

➤ To change the size of the box, click one of the *sizing handles* (white squares) and drag it into position.

➤ Selecting a box and then clicking the Cut button will cut the box from the slide, storing a copy of it on the Clipboard.

➤ You can paste a copy of the last thing you cut on any slide by going to that slide and clicking the Paste button.

➤ To rotate a box, click on the **Free Rotate** button, and then drag one of the green dots at the corner of the box.

➤ *Grouping* turns a bunch of boxes into a single box. To do this, select the boxes, and then click the **Draw** button and select the **Group** command. The **Ungroup** command on the same menu breaks a group back into separate boxes.

Chapter 7

WordArt: Your Low-Calorie Logo-Making Friend

In This Chapter

➤ Create colorful fancy logos and titles

➤ Stretch and shape your words

➤ Give even shallow phrases visual depth

➤ Fire half of your art department

A good logo or an impressive-looking title can really set the stage for a good, impressive presentation. PowerPoint's WordArt feature makes such impressive logos a snap. It's an excellent tool for when you are trying to pass off your teeny little company as a huge conglomerate.

Instant Logo

You can throw together a logo in a few seconds, which is particularly good if you already told the boss it would take all week.

To get started, go into Slide view and get the slide where you want your logo to appear. Click the **WordArt** button on the Drawing toolbar, and a grid of 30 different logos appears. They all say the words *WordArt*, but they all look different. There are curvy WordArts, shiny WordArts, rainbow-colored WordArts, more different WordArts than you would ever thought you would see or, frankly, than you would ever want to!

WordArt Is EveryWhere

The WordArt function is not only available in PowerPoint, but also in other Microsoft programs such as Word and Excel. The things you learn in this chapter serve with those programs as well, and the designs you make in any one of these programs can be used with the others.

The WordArt dialog box offers you 30 different designs to work with.

Immediately, you think this is a great tool to use if you are creating a logo for a company called WordArt, but otherwise.... But never fear: You can change the text to anything you like. Double-click the style of logo that you want, and a dialog box pops up asking for the text that you want to use. The text field says either Your Text Here or whatever words are currently selected on your slide and if you really want your logo to say this, just go ahead and click the **OK** button now.

Of course, if your company doesn't happen to be named *Your Text Here* (and why not? It's a name no one else seems to be using!), you can type the company name, the title, or whatever words you want to be a work of art. If you want your logo to have multiple lines of text, just press **Enter** between lines. (The text box has automatic word wrap if you type long lines, but the new lines it starts appear only in the text box, not in the finished logo.)

Click the **OK** button, and your WordArt logo masterpiece appears! And wow, it is impressive looking, isn't it? And would it be even better if it were another color? Or a little wider? Or the letters were spaced a bit farther apart?

WordArt Adjustments

Moving and resizing your WordArt are done just as with any other object. When you change the size of the box, the logo will automatically redraw to reflect the new size. But the logo doesn't necessarily fit inside the box; the box is the size that the WordArt would be if it were flat. Because a lot of WordArt is angled and three-dimensional, however, the logo may extend beyond the edges of the box.

Sizing handles

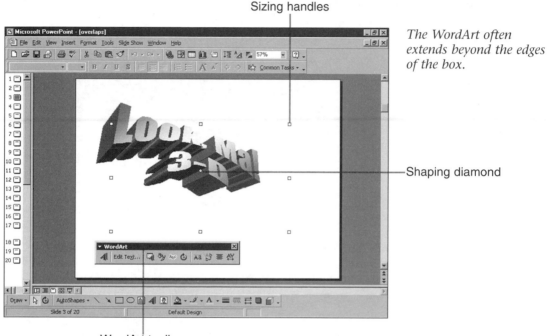

The WordArt often extends beyond the edges of the box.

Shaping diamond

WordArt toolbar

In addition to the white squares around the edges of the art, you should also see one or two yellow diamonds. Dragging these diamonds around changes the shape of your logo. Exactly what it changes depends on the type of design that you chose. If you experiment with a diamond, you quickly see what it does (or, if you don't, you can remain ignorant, which is supposed to be blissful).

Buttons for the Indecisive

When you select the WordArt object, a WordArt *toolbar* (group of buttons) appears on the screen. Two of these buttons are for redoing things you have already done. These buttons are only useful if you don't do everything perfectly the first time. Just in case there are any imperfect people out there, I will tell you a bit about them.

69

If you click the **WordArt Gallery** button, the gallery of 30 different designs reappears. Double-click any design to change your words to that design. If you look at all the designs and decide that you were right in the first place (and had merely underestimated your perfectness), click the **Cancel** button.

The **Edit Text** button brings up the Edit WordArt Text dialog box again. Of course, you can use this to change the words in your logo, but that's not all. Now that we are not rushing through it in an attempt to break the World Logo-Making Speed Record, we can check out some of the other features that this dialog box has to offer.

The Edit WordArt Text dialog box lets you change your words and their basic appearance.

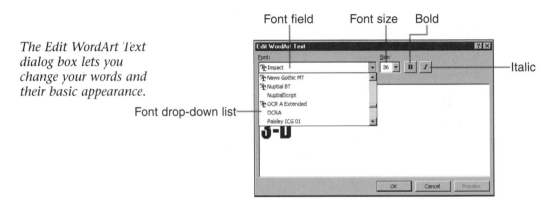

A pair of buttons lets you make your text bold or italic. The italic is a little tricky because italic normally makes your words slanty, but some logo designs will straighten them back up. Italic versions of letters are a little more ornate than the plain version in some fonts, such as Times New Roman, so it may be worth trying the change to see what effect it has.

The real powerhouse here is the Font drop-down list. Open it and you see a list of fonts that you can use for your logo. Select a font, and your text appears in the font in the Text field. (Your logo looks better if you select a font with a TT next to the name than one without.) Click the **OK** button, and that font is twisted, stretched, and colored to make your logo.

If you have a very fancy logo style, with a lot of curves or 3D or other tricks, you are probably better off using a fairly simple font. A fancy font can be hard to read after you do all that stuff to it.

WordAerobics: Getting Your Logo in Shape

The WordArt Shape button is used to change the shape of the face of your logo. You may not be able to get your logo ship-shape, but you can make it wave-shape, bridge-shape, or any of dozens of other shapes. Click this button, and a visual menu will appear, with pictures of all the different shapes. Click the shape you want, and your logo will be stretched into that shape.

TrueFacts About TrueType

When a letter is shown on the screen or printed out, what you see is a pattern of dots that make up the letter. Some fonts are stored on disk in files that have dot patterns for all the letters in each of a number of sizes. With TrueType fonts (marked with a TT) and other outline fonts, one precise mathematical description of the outline of each letter is stored. When Windows displays text using an outline font, it stretches the outline to the size it wants, and then figures out which dots it takes to fill the outline. The outline is very easy for the computer to resize, stretch, warp, and work with in other ways that would be hard to do with a dot pattern. This is why WordArt looks better with outline fonts.

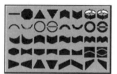

Choose your WordArt shape from these 40 fine forms.

Free Rotate: Spinning at No Cost

The Free Rotate button on the WordArt toolbar is the same as the one on the Drawing toolbar. It has a bit of a different effect in WordArt than you might expect, however. Dragging one of the green dots doesn't rotate the whole image of the logo. Instead, it rotates the basic design of the face of the logo. If you take a look at the next picture, you see the difference this makes. The lower version of the logo is just a rotated version of the top one. Notice that the lower version has the 3D perspective effect still pointed toward the top rather than pointed toward the bottom as you might expect after turning it upside-down. Notice also that the color fade still goes from top to bottom, even though what had been the bottom is now the top. Finally, notice that an upside-down logo is a really dumb idea, unless you are planning to give your presentation in Australia.

Turning the logo upside-down doesn't just give you the same picture, upside-down. (But if you put both logos on the ride, people watching it could still read it while the ride is doing a loop-de-loop!)

Fit to Print

There's an old Egyptian saying about how a person sizes their letters. Unfortunately, I don't know any old Egyptians, so I don't know what this saying is, but I'm sure it's pithy and wise.

Here are a few buttons on the toolbar that can be used to adjust how the letters fit in the shape:

 The WordArt Same Letter Heights button stretches all the smaller letters on a line (such as lowercase letters) to be the same height as the biggest letter. This looks pretty cool if you are designing a logo for a 1960s rock band (although if they don't have a logo by now, it may be too late!), but it looks kind of silly for most things. In addition, it stretches things like periods, commas, and apostrophes until they become unreadable.

The WordArt Vertical Text button switches the logo between running the letters horizontally and stacking them vertically. Horizontally is usually better. If you need a tall logo, it's usually better to make a wide logo and rotate it. That's what most publishers do for the titles that go on the spines of books. (Of course, if you take a look at the spine of this book, you will realize that I couldn't make up my mind *which* direction the words should go in, so you have to wiggle the book to read it!)

Closing Space

Stretching all the letters to be the same height as the biggest does have one side-effect that can be useful. If you have a logo with more than one line of text, this will decrease the space between lines. If you have a multi-line logo in all capital letters with no punctuation, try this button and see how it looks!

 In a multi-line logo, one line is always going to be shorter than the others and won't make it all the way across the space provided. If you don't want that uneven look, click the **WordArt Alignment** button to choose how to deal with that problem. It brings up a menu listing six ways of dealing with this. The first three options move the shorter lines to the left, the middle, or the right of the logo, respectively. The **Word Justify** option expands the size of spaces between words on the short line, pushing the first and last words to the edges. (This doesn't do any good if you only have one word on the line.) The **Letter Justify** option increases the size of the spaces between letters on the short line, stretching the line to fit the space. The last option is usually the best one: **Stretch Justify**, which stretches out the letters themselves to fit the space.

 Finally, the WordArt Character Spacing button is for adjusting how much space is between letters. When you click this button, a menu appears, listing five levels of closeness. Choosing **Very Loose** creates a very open, formal look. On the other end of the scale, **Very Tight** closes up the space so much that letters may actually overlap, creating a very energetic effect. It's a lot easier getting your letters tight now than before WordArt was invented; back then, it took a fifth of scotch to get them really tight.

Color Commentary: Filling in the Letters

So far, we have mostly worried about the shape of your logo, but there is more to a logo than just shape. After all, would rainbows be as impressive if they were all gray rather than the colors of the lovely trout from which they get their name?

To fill your letters with your choice of colors, click the down arrow to the right end of the Fill Color button on the Drawing toolbar. A menu will pop up. This menu has about 8 to 16 little colored boxes. Click one of those boxes, and your letters will become that color.

But hey, what's all this 16 color stuff? The *cheap* box of crayons always had 16 colors. You should demand more to choose from! And you will get it, too, because on that menu is also a selection marked **More Fill Colors**. Select that, and a Colors dialog box appears with two tabs. The first tab shows hundreds of colored hexagons that you can select from. Double-click the one you want, and that color will fill your text.

You can pick from all the colors of the spectrum. Well, all the colors of the hexagon.

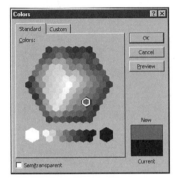

If you don't see just the right color there, try the **Custom** tab, which has thousands of different shades spread out across a rainbow-like grid. The color you click will appear in a band at the right, in a range of brightness from very dark to very bright. Click that band at the brightness level you want, and then click the **OK** button. Between the color setting and the brightness setting, you actually have over 16 *million* colors available. Now *that's* a lot of crayons!

Frilly Fills for Fabulous Fun

Having 16 million colors at your fingers is dissatisfying when you can only use one at a time. If you click the down arrow to the right of the Fill Color button and select the **Fill Effects** command, you will find where the really powerful stuff lurks! The Fill Effects dialog box appears, listing four tabs that contain even more stupefying fill options:

➤ **Gradient** creates fades from one color to another color. To use this, first click the **Two colors** radio button. To the right, two drop-down menus will appear, marked Color 1 and Color 2. Open **Color 1** and select a color from those displayed. (If you don't like any shown, you can select **More Colors**; this brings up the same Color dialog box described in the preceding section.) Repeat this with Color 2.

Color selections

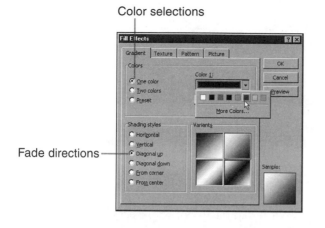

The Fill Effects dialog box is filled with effects!

Fade directions

The lower left of the dialog box has a list of directions in which the fade can take place. You can pick a horizontal fade, which will give you a sunset-like effect, or a fade from fade from the center, which creates sort of a glow. Fades from the corner are "in" right now; that's what you call a fade fad! When you select a fade, you will see two or four variations of that sort of fade in the squares at the right. Click the variation you want, and then click the **OK** button. You will see that fade in your work!

➤ **Texture** is the next tab on the list. Click it to give your logo the trustworthy look of solid marble, the powerful look of the mighty oak, or the wimpy look of a crumpled shopping bag. An assortment of textures is displayed. Double-click any one of these, and your text will take on that appearance.

Fancier Fades for Fade Fanciers!

Click **Preset** for access to the Preset Colors drop-down list of predesigned color combinations, including some like Gold and Chrome designed to look like metal. Silence may be golden, but if you want your words to be golden, this is the route to go. (Selecting the direction of the fade and the variation are done the same way as before.)

Putting the *Yours* into *Textyours*

The Textures tab has an **Other Textures** button for adding your own *textures*. Textures are just images that repeat well (that is, if you put one right next to another or one on top of another, you don't see where one ends and another begins; it looks like a continuous picture.) Use any art program to create such an image. (You can also borrow them from sets of web backgrounds.) Clicking the Other Texture button brings up a Select Texture file navigator for selecting the file with the image. Select the image and click the **OK** button. That image will be added to the group of textures you can choose from.

➤ Use the **Pattern** tab to fill your logo with a two-color pattern, such as stripes or checkerboards. At the bottom of the tab are two color selection drop-down lists: one for **Foreground** and one for **Background**. Use these two lists to select two different colors. You will see an array of patterns using those colors above the menus. Double-click the pattern that you want, and it will fill the letters.

➤ The **Picture** tab is for filling your logo with any picture you want. Just think: Your logo could have a picture of you in it! You have always been a person (or alternate life form) of your word, and now you will be a person *in* your word! To do this, you will need to already have the picture stored in digital form (as a JPEG file, for example) on your hard disk. Then just follow these steps:

1. On the Picture tab, click the **Select Picture** button. A Select Picture file navigator will appear. Click the drop-down button at the end of the Look In field to get a list of disks on your system.

2. Select the disk that has the file. A list of folders on that disk appears below that. Double-click the folder that has the picture file.

3. When that folder opens up, a list of files will be displayed. Double-click the name of the picture file. The file navigator goes away, and your picture appears on the tab.

4. Click the **OK** button, and the picture you selected will be stretched and shaped to fill your logo!

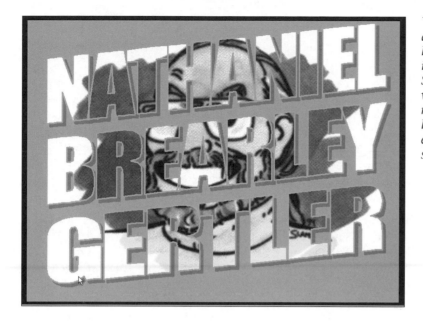

When you fill a logo with a picture, remember how large the logo will appear in the actual presentation. Small pictures look bad when blown up. Even this medium-sized picture looks fuzzy when expanded to fill the screen.

Outlinear Thinking

You can put an outline around all the letters of your logo. This is particularly neat when you have a fancy logo against a fancy background; it creates a clean edge between them.

 To pick a color for your outline, click the down arrow at the right of the Line Color button on the Drawing toolbar. A color selection menu will appear, enabling you to pick from several colors or select **More Line Colors** to get the Color dialog box. After you select a color, PowerPoint uses all its brain power in figuring out that if you want an outline color, you must want an outline, and the outline appears! (To get rid of the outline, click the **Line Color** button and pick **No Line** from the menu.)

To set the thickness of the line, click this button. A menu showing different thicknesses of lines appears. Pick the one you want. (You can pick the one you don't want, if you want, but I don't know why you'd want to.)

 You can even turn the line into a dotted line by clicking this button, but dotted lines usually look ugly as outlines for WordArt lettering. Then again, sometimes ugly is hip! (Or so I have kept trying to convince my dates.)

Who Knows What Shadows Lurk in the WordArts of Men?

Shadows are cool. That's because the sun is blocked from them.

To build such coolness into your logo, click this button. A menu of green boxes with gray boxes under them appears. Some of the shadows make it look like the logo is hovering just over the page, casting a shadow on it. Others make it look like the logo is standing vertically, casting a shadow on the ground. Click the shadow design you like, and that type of shadow appears on your logo. If you want to get rid of the shadow, click **No Shadow** on that menu. (Of course, the only thing that doesn't cast a shadow is a vampire. Do you really want a vampire logo?)

To fine-tune the shadow, click the **Shadow Settings** button on that menu. A new toolbar appears. This has four buttons with pictures of green boxes with arrows, one with an arrow in each direction. These are used to move the shadow, as if you were moving the light. (It's much easier to move the sun on a computer than in real life!) Click the button at the right end to select the color of the shadow; this works like all the other color-selection menus. It also has an added option called **Semitransparent**. Click that, and your shadow looks like a shadow in a well-lit room, one that only darkens things a bit instead of blocking things out altogether!

3D or Not 3D, That Is the Question

The 3D features of WordArt enable you to do two things: *extrude* your logo so that it looks like it has physical depth as well as width and height, and to *rotate* your logo. Of course, you can already rotate your logo in the same plane as the slide (the same sort of direction that the hands move on a grandfather clock). Using 3D, you can also rotate it against the vertical axis (like when you turn a clock around to fix it) or against the horizontal axis (like when you push a grandfather clock forward, so that it smashes to the floor).

2-Don'ts of 3D

There are two things that don't work when you are 3D-ing your logo: shadows and outlines. Both disappear when you turn your logo into 3D.

3-D 4-U

To quickly shove your logo into 3D, click the **3-D** button on the Drawing toolbar, which is the master button for all 3D operations. A menu will pop up, showing a square turned into 3D with various rotations and extrusions. Click the way that you want your logo to be 3D-ized, and PowerPoint will leap to work. (If you have a lot of text in your logo, it may take a few seconds for the logo to draw. Remember, Rome wasn't made 3D in a day!)

Rotation Creation Station

Rotate the logo

The Fill Effects dialog box is filled with effects!

Extrusion and lighting controls

If you click the **3-D** button and select **3-D Settings** from the menu, a new toolbar will appear on your screen. This toolbar has all the tools you need for fine-tuning your logo's 3D aspects. On it there are four buttons with pictures of arrows wrapping around poles. Click any one of these buttons to rotate the logo a little in the same direction as the arrow.

Extrusion and Intrusion

The five buttons on the right of the 3-D Settings toolbar control the extrusion. Clicking on the **Depth** button brings up a menu of different lengths for the extrusion. You can pick various sizes from zero to infinity! Yes, your words can go on forever!

Clicking the **Direction** button brings up a menu for picking the direction of the extrusion. It can go straight back, or head off in any of eight directions. This menu also has two commands called *Perspective* and *Parallel*. These affect how the farther-away parts of the 3D object look. If you choose **Parallel**, the faraway parts look the same size as the close parts. If you choose **Perspective**, things get smaller as they get farther away. Usually, Perspective is better. (Why, all things look better after you put them in perspective.)

PowerPoint pretends that a lamp is shining on the extrusion, creating light and dark areas. To move the lamp isn't hard; after all, it's light work! Just click the **Lighting** button and you can then pick from eight lamp directions. There are also three choices for the brightness of the light.

Clicking the **Surface** button brings up a menu with four choices of what your extrusion is made of. All this really affects is how shiny it is. Matte is not very shiny, Plastic is somewhat, and Metal is quite shiny. The fourth choice is Wire Frame, which just shows the edges of your entire logo.

The final button, **3-D Color**, is the color of the extrusion. Clicking the arrow at the right of this button gives you the normal color selection options. It will not, however, let you select any gradients, patterns, or textures; extrusions have to be solid colors.

Why a Wire?

Very few logos look good in Wire Frame mode. A logo in this mode gets displayed very quickly, however, because the computer has less to figure out. If you have a slow computer, you may want to use this mode while you work on getting the rotation just right, and then switch to one of the solid modes.

Logo A-Go-Go

Watch out! Now that you know how to do it, you will be tempted to write all your letters in 3D metallic perspective lettering with marble fronts!

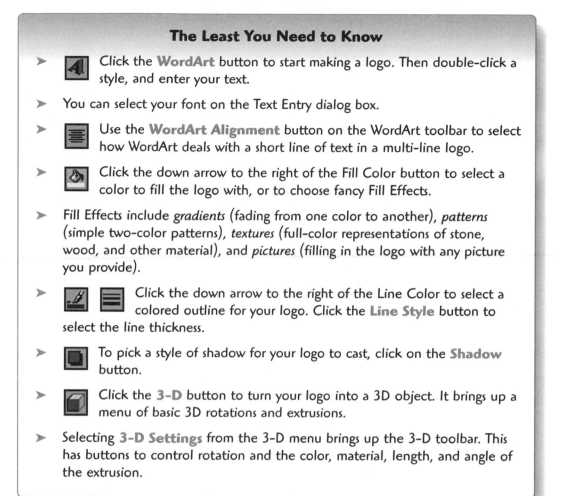

The Least You Need to Know

➤ Click the **WordArt** button to start making a logo. Then double-click a style, and enter your text.

➤ You can select your font on the Text Entry dialog box.

➤ Use the **WordArt Alignment** button on the WordArt toolbar to select how WordArt deals with a short line of text in a multi-line logo.

➤ Click the down arrow to the right of the Fill Color button to select a color to fill the logo with, or to choose fancy Fill Effects.

➤ Fill Effects include *gradients* (fading from one color to another), *patterns* (simple two-color patterns), *textures* (full-color representations of stone, wood, and other material), and *pictures* (filling in the logo with any picture you provide).

➤ Click the down arrow to the right of the Line Color to select a colored outline for your logo. Click the **Line Style** button to select the line thickness.

➤ To pick a style of shadow for your logo to cast, click on the **Shadow** button.

➤ Click the **3-D** button to turn your logo into a 3D object. It brings up a menu of basic 3D rotations and extrusions.

➤ Selecting **3-D Settings** from the 3-D menu brings up the 3-D toolbar. This has buttons to control rotation and the color, material, length, and angle of the extrusion.

Chapter 8

Lines and Shapes: Good Things in Variable-Sized Boxes

In This Chapter

➤ Put circles, stars, squares, arrows, and other marshmallow cereal shapes on your slide

➤ Color in these shapes, outline them, and make them look three-dimensional

➤ Build pointers and callouts to call attention to things

➤ Fill the shapes with words

Remember how I told you that you could pick and choose which chapters to read? (What? You didn't read the introduction? *Nobody* ever reads the introduction!) Whether you saw that or not, when I told you that, I lied. If you are going to read this chapter, you should read the preceding chapter first.

Why? The AutoShape feature works much the same way as the WordArt feature. So, much of the stuff that I put in the preceding chapter also applies here, and I didn't want to waste your time by telling it to you twice. (Okay, I didn't want to waste *my* time by typing it twice!)

The Simple Shapes

Things that are simple you use all the time. You use a kitchen knife several times a day, whether it's for chopping chicken, opening the plastic packet of hot dogs, or affixing a "You ate all my Krunchy Puffs!" note to your roommate's headboard. On the other hand, the Amazing Electro-Deluxe Avocado Peeler with 37 Attachments sits gathering dust on the pantry shelves, a stark reminder of Aunt Edna's bad taste in presents.

With shapes, it's the same thing. The simple ones (rectangles, ovals, lines, and arrows) you will probably use all the time, so they each have their own handy-dandy button on the bottom row of buttons (the *Drawing toolbar*).

Lines and Arrows and Bars, Oh My!

Straight lines are very useful, and not just to set up punch lines. With PowerPoint, you can quickly draw more lines than you can shake a stick at. (Although shaking a stick at lines seems like quite a waste of time to me.)

➤ To draw a line, click the **Line** button. Point to where the line starts, and then drag the mouse to where the line ends; your line will appear.

➤ Arrows are just lines with pointy ends. Hunters may not realize that, but PowerPoint does. Draw a line with an arrow just like a line without one: Click the **Arrow** button, and then drag on the slide.

➤ After drawing a line (with or without a pointy end), you can decide whether it's a line or an arrow by clicking the **Arrow Style** button. A menu of different arrow styles appears. You can pick an arrow with a number of different types of pointy ends. You can pick an arrow with both ends pointy. (Hunters hate arrows like that, because you always prick your finger while shooting them.) You can even pick an arrow with no ends, in which case it turns back into a line.

➤ To change the thickness of the line, click the **Line Style** button and pick a thickness.

➤ To make a dotted line (or a dotted arrow!) click the **Dash Style** button and pick a dotting style.

➤ Finally, you can set the line's color by clicking the down arrow next to the **Line Color** button.

Jumpy Line?

If the end of your line seems to jump as you draw it, you have the *Grid* feature turned on. This feature treats the slide like a piece of graph paper, keeping all your points and corners at the intersections of lines. You can turn this off by clicking the **Draw** button and selecting **Snap**, **To Grid**, or you can override it by holding down the **Alt** button while you draw shapes.

Un-Awful Ovals and Cor-Rect-Angles

Use the Rectangle and Oval buttons to draw rectangles and ovals, respectively. Click one of them, point to where you want one corner of the rectangle to be, and then drag to the opposite corner. If you are drawing an oval, it will be an oval that goes to the edges of the rectangular area you dragged.

A square is just a rectangle designed by someone who couldn't make up his mind which side should be longer. A circle is just an oval that forgot to stretch. Drawing a square or a circle is the same as drawing a rectangle or oval, only you hold down the **Shift** key while you do it. PowerPoint will make sure that it's equal on all sides.

The Center for Correct Centering

Sometimes you may need a rectangle or an oval with its center at some precise point. Now, if you are very good at drawing these objects the normal way, you can center them yourself. But if you aren't a self-centered person, try drawing them by pointing where you want the center to be, and then hold down the **Ctrl** key as you drag the mouse to an outer corner.

Colors, Lines, Fills, Shadows, and Other Frilly Things

Now that you've got your shape in place, you want it to have the right color and the right outline and maybe you even want shadows or 3D effects. The way that you do all of that stuff is exactly the same way that you did it with WordArt! That's right, just back up a few pages, the instructions are all there. I will wait here while you go back and reread them.

(Tumm-tadiddle, toodley-tum, tummy-doodly-doodly-doot!) You are back? Good! Now on to:

Fancy Shapes: They Aren't Just for Marshmallows Anymore!

Circles and squares are fine for everyday use, but you have company coming, and you need something fancier! You need squiggles and arrows and happy faces! Is PowerPoint equipped? You betcha! Just click that **AutoShapes** button on the

Drawing toolbar, and you will get a menu of types of shapes. Each type has its own submenu, showing you all the shapes it has to offer! Let's head down the list one by one.

One hundred fifty-one shapes at your fingertips, grouped by type.

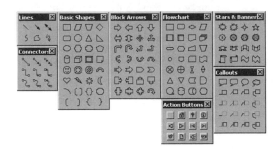

Lines

The top row of the Lines submenu shows you straight lines, but heck, we already know how to do those. But under those, we get curvy lines of various sorts, and those are a lot more exciting. The first of these makes smooth curves: Just click where you want some key points of the line to be (double-clicking the last point), and PowerPoint will shape the curve to match. Use the other two to draw any line you want—at least, any line you can manage with your mouse, which is not the world's easiest-to-use drawing tool. Just select one of them, and then hold down the left mouse button as you draw.

Line Altering

If you create your own line, and you want to make adjustments to it, right-click the line and select **Edit Points** from the shortcut menu. The key points on your line will show up as black squares. On a straight line, there are only two: one at each end. You can click anywhere on the line and drag to create a new key point, however, and then move it where you want it. Using this method, you can turn a simple straight line into a zigzag of any proportions you like.

If you want to make your own object shape, use any of those non-straight line choices, and end your line at the same place that you started. PowerPoint will assume that you are making a shape, and will let you fill it in.

A shape

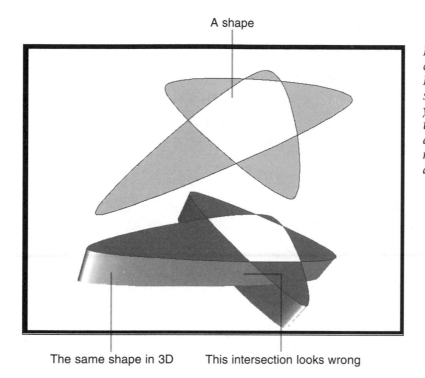

If you cross lines while creating a shape, PowerPoint considers some areas to be outside your shape, as seen at the top. The intersections don't look right when you make the shape three-dimensional.

The same shape in 3D   This intersection looks wrong

Connectors

Charts are very important in an organization. Without an organizational chart, the only way to tell who is boss is to see who can be late without getting yelled at. Many charts need connecting lines to show how things are related. The Connectors sub-menu has a variety of these. Some of these are basic straight lines; others are angled or curved lines. You use them all just like straight lines: Point to the starting point, and drag to the end point. Unlike a regular line, connectors "snap" to existing objects on your slide, so the connectors neatly tie one object to another. You can even make a dotted line or change arrowheads by using the appropriate buttons.

Many connectors will show yellow diamonds in the middle when they are selected. Dragging this yellow diamond will change the path that the connector takes, which is very handy when you are trying to route it around other objects on a diagram.

Basic Shapes

This is a collection of various shapes. A couple of them have built-in shading for a 3D effect without using the 3D features. If you choose one of those, remember that they look best without any outline. Most of these have yellow diamond controls that let you change them in interesting way. My favorite is the happy face (an odd choice for a "basic shape" to begin with!) where you can use the yellow diamond to turn the smile into a frown. What a feeling of power!

Block Arrows, Flowchart, Stars, and Banners

These three menus have the sort of standard shapes that their name describes. Block arrows are big, thick, decoratively styled arrows. The Flowchart submenu has all the special figures you will need for computer and process diagrams. Stars and Banners has scrolls, banners, and stars—not real stars, which are great flaming gas bags, but nice precise little foil-medallion-type stars. Some of the images of stars on the menu have numbers inside them; those numbers indicate how many points the star will have. The number will not appear on the shape itself.

Callouts

Callouts are special members of our little AutoShape family, because they are designed to hold text within the shape. Callouts include not only simple boxes with lines pointing from them (useful for explaining part of a picture), but also comic book-style word and thought balloons (useful for showing that part of your picture is thinking).

Three types of callouts: a word balloon, a callout with a visible box, and a callout without a visible box.

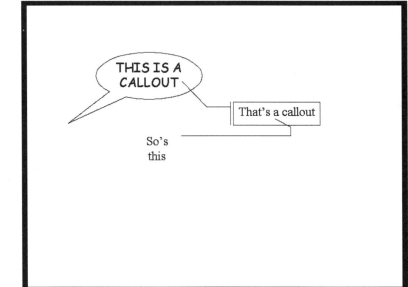

After you draw your callout, you can start typing, and it will appear in the text area. Callouts are like other text boxes; you can resize them, justify the text, use different fonts, and so on.

Keep Callouts Flat

As with any other shape, you can use the 3D features on the callouts. However, the 3D will not affect the text in the callout. If you are just extruding the callout, that's not a problem, but if you rotate the callout, the text won't rotate with it. If you want rotatable text, you need to use WordArt, described in the preceding chapter.

Action Buttons

Action Buttons are designed specifically to be used with interactive presentation features, which is something that doesn't show up in this book until Chapter 13, "Click Here for Interactivity." I explain this stuff in there, where it will make more sense.

More AutoShapes

The final entry on the AutoShapes menu is **More AutoShapes**. Select this, and a dialog box opens displaying more shapes, mostly special-purpose things like pictures of phones and chairs and such. Right-click on one of these shapes and select **Insert** to add it to your slide, and then click the **Close** (X) button on the dialog box.

The good news is that you can add shapes to the More AutoShapes display, either downloaded shapes or ones you got on disk. This is because this is part of the *ClipArt Gallery*, an expandable collection of images, sounds, and videos. You will learn about using this gallery in Chapter 9, "Putting Pictures in Their Places."

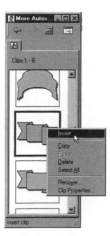

The More AutoShapes feature gives you access to lots and lots of outline pictures… or is that locks and locks? Depending on your installations, the shapes you see may vary.

The bad news is that most of the shapes here aren't as good as the usual AutoShapes. With almost any of the main AutoShape selections, you can rotate it, color it, turn it 3D, or adjust it with a diamond. With most of the selections in More AutoShapes, however, you can only do some of those things, if any. They show up automatically where they feel like appearing and in the size they feel like appearing in, instead of letting you draw them into place, sticking you with moving and resizing them. All in all, you probably won't be using More AutoShapes very often; you will have to settle for the 151 shapes you already have.

Getting Your Text into Shape, Literally

You can put text into any of these shapes, except for lines (which don't have any space for text). To do this, click the **Text Box** button first, and then the shape. The rectangle around the shape turns into a text box, and you can start typing.

The big difference between this and a normal text box is that the text starts in the middle of the box rather than at the top. This way, it's more likely to end up in the shape rather than on its edge. If you add more text, PowerPoint keeps the text centered in the rectangle.

Changing Shape: I Never Metamorph I Didn't Like

If you change your mind about the shape you want, you can change it without having to redo all the outlines, colors, and text that you chose. Just click the **Draw** button and select **Change AutoShape** from the menu. There you will see a menu of all the standard shapes (except for Lines and Connectors—this process doesn't let you work with Lines and Connectors at all) and will be able to pick the one that you want.

Remember: You can also rotate and flip the shapes, just like any other box. All the commands are in the **Draw** menu.

The Least You Need to Know

➤ Drawing a shape involves just selecting a shape from the toolbar or AutoShape menu, and then dragging the mouse from one corner of where you want the shape to another.

➤ If you hold down the **Ctrl** button while drawing the shape, the place where you started dragging will be considered the center of the shape rather than the corner.

➤ If you hold down the **Shift** key while drawing an oval, it will be a perfect circle.

➤ If you hold down the **Shift** key while drawing a rectangle, it will be a perfect square.

➤ Many shapes show yellow diamonds when you select them. These can be dragged to fine-tune the shape in different ways.

➤ The colors, fill effects, outline, shadows, and 3D effects work the same on shapes as they do on WordArt.

➤ Callouts are shapes with pointers and text areas. After you create a callout, you are expected to enter the text.

➤ You can put text on any shape by clicking the **Text Box** button, and then on the shape.

➤ If you draw a line or an arrow, click the **Arrow Style** button for a menu where you can select which ends have arrowheads and what type of arrowheads they have.

Putting Pictures in Their Places

In This Chapter

➤ Put pictures on your slides

➤ Trim the pictures down to size

➤ Cast a shadow for your picture (No, I don't mean "In this movie, Alec Baldwin will play The Shadow.")

➤ Fill the shapes with words

They say that a picture is worth a thousand words, but have you ever tried to trade one in? Where do you take that old photo of Mara Friedman eating cake at your cousin's bar mitzvah to get, say, a thousand choice adverbs? Once again, *they* don't seem to know what they are talking about.

A picture *is* worth paying attention to. By putting the right picture in your presentation, you will not only get that attention, you will make good use of the attention you get. Once you have their attention, you can achieve your main goal: selling them time-share condo space in prime Florida marshland.

Where Do Pictures Come From?

To put a picture on your slides, you need to have a picture, and it will have to be stored on a file that your computer can read. By *picture*, we don't necessarily mean a photograph. It could be a drawing, a logo, a ray-traced rendering; any flat visual item is considered a picture. (Computer people often refer to these as *images* and editorial people call them *graphics*, but we will be genuine human people and call them pictures.)

Get Pre-Made Pictures

A lot of pictures are already out there in computer format. Many folks sell CD-ROMs full of photos and drawings specifically meant for people like you (and even people shorter than you) to use as part of their own computer creations. In addition, the Internet is full of pictures that you can download to your PC and use. (Just because you *can* download and use it doesn't mean that you are *allowed* to. If the creator says that the picture is in the *public domain*, that means that the copyright on it has been waived, and it is free to use. Otherwise, you have to get permission.)

PowerPoint even comes with a library of drawings called *clip art* that you can use in your presentation. Clip art works a little differently from other pictures. I explain how to use the clip art pictures later in this chapter.

PC: Picture Creator

Plenty of programs out there let you create your own pictures. There's even a basic one that you got for free with Windows, called Paint. (You will find it in your **Programs Accessories** menu if you click the **Start** button.) Some of these programs let you paint a new picture using the mouse. Others let you create imaginary objects or areas in the computer's mind, and then let you pick a point to photograph the object from (these are *3D rendering* or *ray-tracing programs*).

If you use one of these programs, you have to make sure that it can save files in a graphic format that PowerPoint can use. Hundreds of different formats are out there. The good news is that almost everything these days stores in a format that PowerPoint understands. If the program creates files that end in .bmp, .cgm, .cdr, .dib, .drw, .emf, .eps, .fpx, .gif, .jpeg, .jpg, .pcd, .pct, .pcx, .png, .rle, .tga, .tif, .wmf, or .wpg, PowerPoint can read them. (If you can pronounce that last sentence in one breath, give yourself a pat on the back!) If you have files that aren't in those formats, translation programs (such as Graphics Workshop) may be able to take your file and turn it into a file type that PowerPoint can read.

Which Format Is Best?

Many programs let you choose which format to save a file in. If you have a simple drawing with only a few different colors, the Graphics Interchange File format (.gif) is the best. If you have more colors and want an exact reproduction, use the PC Paintbrush format (.pcx). If you have a lot of colors (particularly if you are working with a digitized photograph) and you are worried about how much space your file will take up, use the Joint Photographic Experts Group format (.jpg or .jpeg).

Copycat-Scans: Using a Picture from Outside

If you have a drawing, a photograph, or any sort of document that isn't in computer format (you still have paper? How old-fashioned!), you can put it on the computer by using a *scanner*. A scanner takes a picture of your picture and stores it on the computer. Scanners have become a real bargain lately, and even the ones that are under $100 should meet your PowerPoint needs.

If you already have a scanner, you don't have to start another program to do your scanning. Just click the **Insert** menu, select **Picture**, and then from the submenu select **From Scanner or Camera**; PowerPoint will start your scanner software. (How your scanner software works depends on which scanner you have. Check your scanner's manual for details.)

Getting the Picture: Get the Picture?

To get an existing picture from disk and put it on the slide, select the **Insert** menu and from the **Picture** submenu select **From File**. The Insert Picture dialog box will open, showing you a list of files. Click the drop-down arrow at the end of the Look In field, and select the disk with the file from that list. A list of folders and picture files appears. If your picture files are in a folder, double-click the folder. Keep navigating until you find your files. Then click the file you want and click the **Insert** button.

Now, if you are perfectly organized, your files probably have all these nice long names that tell you exactly what they are, and you can find the folder easily. For the rest of us (and we are in the majority folks, so don't let those goody-goody types get on you!), you will find yourself faced with a list of filenames like *test3.gif*, *feb273.jpg*, and *other.pcx*, without a clue as to what pictures they contain. Don't worry, PowerPoint has a quick picture preview feature for people like you.

To preview pictures, click the drop-down arrow next to the **Views** button, and select **Preview** from the list that appears. The file list area breaks into two panes. Click a picture file in the file list (the left pane), and a preview of that picture appears in the preview area (the right pane). This way, you can keep clicking files until you find the one you want, and then click **Insert**.

Click a picture file, and the picture will be displayed. Make sure you don't have pictures of me in your directories (like this one by Ted Slampyak), as they may scare small children and pets.

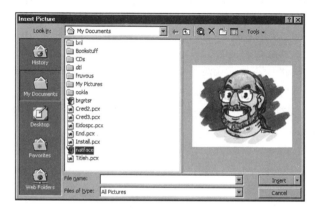

Sizing Up the Scene

The size of a computer picture is measured in *pixels*, the small squares that make up the image on a computer screen. The computer picture is made up of a gridwork of dots, and PowerPoint assumes that you want your picture to be displayed at its *natural* size, one picture dot per screen dot. But that might not be the size that you want it.

When you insert the picture on to your slide, it has sizing handles (white squares) at all four corners and the center of all four sides. Just drag one of those handles to change it to the size you want. Drag a handle in the center of a side to change that side, or drag a corner to change two dimensions at once.

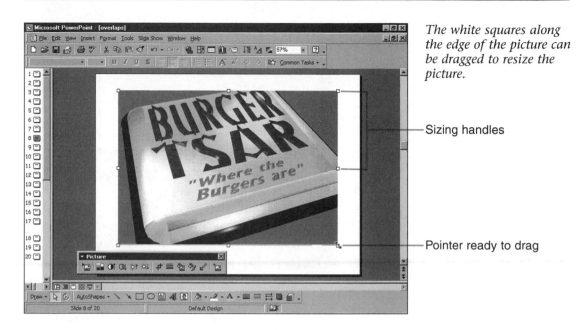

The white squares along the edge of the picture can be dragged to resize the picture.

Sizing handles

Pointer ready to drag

Natural Is Good

Pictures look best at their natural size. Shrinking the picture means there won't be room to display some of the picture dots, and detail gets lost. Enlarging it means that picture dots are stretched to cover several screen dots, which makes the picture grainy.

The Picture Toolbar: A Row of Pictures for Working on Pictures

If you want to make major changes to the picture such as drawing a moustache and glasses on everyone in the shot (or, in the case of a picture of me, erasing the moustache and glasses), PowerPoint is not the place to do that. Start up your favorite art program and work on it there before you add it to your slide.

However, if you just want to trim the picture or adjust the colors, there's no need to reach for another program. You can find most of the tools you need on the Picture toolbar. To see this toolbar, just right-click the picture and select **Show Picture Toolbar**.

The Picture toolbar.

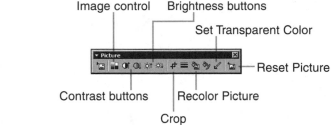

Image control   Brightness buttons
Set Transparent Color
Reset Picture
Contrast buttons   Recolor Picture
Crop

Picture Diet: Trim Your Picture Down

Microsoft must figure that more graphic designers than farmers will be using PowerPoint, because its *cropping* tool is used for shrinking rather than growing. Cropping is what you use when you have a picture of a whole donut and what you want is a picture of a donut hole.

To do this, click on the **Crop** button on the Picture toolbar. Your pointer will change to match the picture on the button. Use the pointer to drag one of the sizing handles toward the middle of the picture. When you release the handle, all of the picture outside the new rectangle disappears. (These missing picture parts are off in the same invisible land as the dirty words that they cut out of movies on TV.) By cropping from all four sides, you can isolate the one part of the picture that you want.

Scheming to Change the Color Scheme

PowerPoint gives you a number of ways to mess with the colors, to get them more like you want them. Sometimes, colors that look good when a picture is standing alone don't look so good when the picture is sitting in the middle of your slide, surrounded and harassed by other pictures, shapes, and backgrounds.

One of the keenest color changes that you can do is to make one color from your picture invisible (or, as Microsoft calls it, *transparent*). Now, why would you want to do this? If you have a picture that's so ugly that you don't want to see it, you just don't put it on the slide, right?

That's not what it's for. The main reason to make some color invisible is that it lets you have a picture that doesn't look rectangular. If your picture is of a donut, and everything outside the edge of the donut is red, you can make that red invisible by clicking on the Set Transparent Color button, and then on a red part of the picture. Suddenly, you don't see the red anymore; wherever the red was, you see through to the next thing on the slide! You can only make one color invisible on each picture, and only those pixels that exactly match that shade disappear. (Be careful! In trying to make one part of your picture invisible, you may make other parts that are the same color. You may have to use a paint program to change the color of the part you want invisible, to make sure it's not the same color as anything else.)

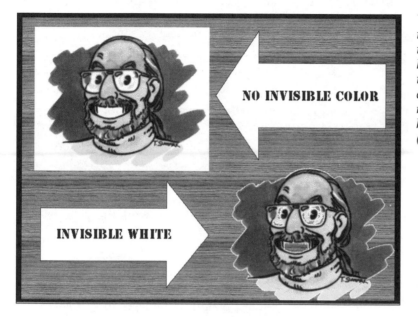

With the white color turned invisible, the picture loses its rectangular border. However, because the same color is used elsewhere in the picture, my teeth and my eyes are knocked out as well (ouch!).

If you think there's too much color overall in the picture, try clicking the **Image Control** button. That brings up a menu of different coloring styles. By clicking **Grayscale**, you can get rid of all those pretty colors and turn the picture into a black, white, and gray version. If even gray is too fancy for your liking, try **Black & White**. Or, if you just want something a lot lighter, select **Watermark**; you will get a pale version of your picture. (Watermark is really useful if you want to use the picture as a backdrop for words or other images, because the pale colors aren't likely to distract from what you put in front of it.)

Four other buttons on the Picture toolbar let you fiddle with the picture to your heart's content (not to be confused with your heart's *contents*, which would be blood):

➤ **More Brightness**   Makes all the colors in the picture brighter.

➤ **Less Brightness**   Makes all the colors darker.

➤ **More Contrast**   Makes the bright parts of your picture brighter while making the dark parts darker. This can make some things stand out better.

➤ **Less Contrast**   Clicking this button decreases the contrast.

If you want to increase the brightness colors or decrease the contrast (or whatever) a lot, you have to keep clicking the button—you can't just keep it pressed down.

Framing Your Picture

Framing your picture in PowerPoint is easy, and it costs a lot less than framing the picture of a purple cow your kid painted for you at summer camp! The following buttons on the Drawing toolbar can help you perfect your picture presentation:

➤ Use the **Line Style** button to put a border around the picture.

➤ Use the down arrow to the right of the Line Color button to select the color for the border. However, the line will always be rectangular. (The line doesn't know whether you set one of your colors to be invisible.)

➤ On the other hand, if you use the **Shadow** button to create a shadow, only the visible portions of your picture will cast a shadow. The Shadow knows!

➤ You can also use the **Fill Color** and **Fill Effects** tools to replace the invisible color with another color, a texture, or a pattern. The tools work the same as they do with shapes.

Rotating Your Picture

You can't. Pictures don't rotate. However, you can open some images in a program that supports rotation, like the Microsoft Photo Editor that comes free with some versions of Office, and do your rotating there.

Clip Art: Resizable, Reusable, but Not Refundable ('Cause It's Free!)

With PowerPoint, Microsoft gives you a bunch of already made pictures, which they call *clip art*. When Microsoft says clip art, however, they mean something a little more specific than when other people say clip art. Clip art is generally used to refer to any piece of art that you are allowed to use in your work. Microsoft uses it to refer to pieces of art in a certain, special format, one that is quite useful.

Microsoft clip art pictures are not defined as a series of dots. Instead, mathematically defined lines and curves define them. Because of this, a clip art picture doesn't have a natural size. You can take a clip art picture and make it any size you want, and the computer will draw the lines and curves to that size. This way, the picture doesn't look grainy, and unless you make it fairly small, it doesn't lose details.

Clip Art, Oh Clip Art, Where Art Thou?

To find the clip art, click the **ClipArt** button on the drawing toolbar. The Clip Art Gallery dialog box opens, with tabs for pictures, sounds, and videos. If you have been paying attention to the topic at hand, you can probably guess that you want the Clip Art tab, and you would be right!

Search field   Clips Online button

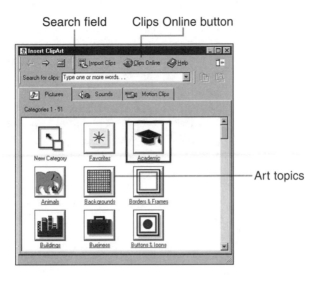

The Clip Art dialog box lets you see all the pictures by category and pick the one you want.

Art topics

The main part of the dialog box is a list of subjects. Click any of these, and the dialog box will display the pieces of clip art that have to do with that topic. Or, if you want, you can type words about the sort of picture you are looking for into the search field, and pictures having to do with those words will appear. Not only is this free art, it's organized!

You can scroll through the images if there are too many to be displayed simultaneously. After you find the piece that you want, just right-click it and select **Insert**. Boing! It appears on your slide, ready to work with.

Check This Out

Free Clip Art on the Web

If you have an Internet connection, try clicking on the Clips Online button on the menu bar. It will hook you up to Microsoft's database of free clip art!

Clip Artery

Two different formats of clip art are mixed together in the Clip Gallery. Some can be rotated, and some can't. To find out if clip art you've added can be rotated, click on the Draw button. If Ungroup is grayed out, this cannot be rotated. Otherwise, to rotate, choose Ungroup. Click Yes on the dialog box that appears. Then choose Draw, Group. Finally, click the Free Rotate button and rotate away!

You can change all the colors in the same type of clip art that can be rotated, but you have to recolor it before you ungroup it. Click the **Recolor Picture** button on the Picture toolbar. (Remember, if you don't see the toolbar, just right-click the object and select **Show Picture Toolbar**.) The Recolor Picture dialog box appears with a drop-down button for each color. Open a drop-down list to see a menu of colors that you can replace it with. (You can select **More Colors** from this menu to see more colors if none of the listed ones please you.) A preview window lets you see how the colors effect things. After you have the colors you want, click the **OK** button.

Picture colors   Preview of recolored image

The Recolor Picture dialog box works only with certain clip art pictures.

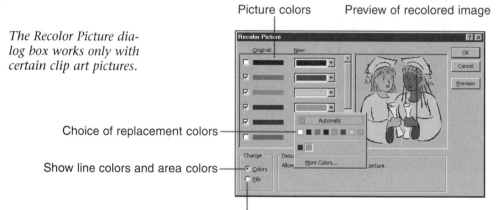

Choice of replacement colors

Show line colors and area colors

Show only area colors

The Least You Need to Know

➤ PowerPoint can put pictures from most computer art programs on your slides.

➤ To get the Insert Picture dialog box, pull down the **Insert** menu and select the **Picture, From File** command. On the Insert Picture dialog box, click the name of a file to see the picture in that file. If it's the right file, click the **OK** button.

➤ Right-click the picture and select **Show Picture Toolbar** to get the Picture toolbar.

➤ Use the buttons on the toolbar to crop your picture and change the colors in various ways.

Chapter 10

The Art of the Chart 101: Numerical Charts

In This Chapter

➤ Enter numbers to chart on a chart

➤ Chart the numbers you entered

➤ Change the chart of the numbers you entered

➤ Assign a design, and then refine it 'til it shines!

Charts are Mother Nature's way of making numbers look pretty. By putting your figures into a bar chart, a graph, a pie chart, or any of a dozen other types of charts, you can turn a bunch of boring numbers into a quickly understood image. And, a graph can show you patterns in your numbers that might otherwise go overlooked. Also, they are great fun at parties.

The chart capabilities of PowerPoint are very powerful. A few years ago, the chart part alone could have been sold as a separate program, and would have been considered a very good one. There are so many chart-enhancing tools that a full book this size could probably be written on the chart program, and we would offer that book if we thought we could sell it for a lot of mon…er…if we were convinced that there was a real need for one. Luckily, you can learn to make charts pretty quickly, which is what this chapter covers. After that, you should explore the various features on your own, to see what more you can find.

The Part Where You Start the Chart

 Starting the chart is easy: Just click the **Insert Chart** button on the Standard toolbar.

Entering Chart Information in Formation

When you start work on your chart, a grid that looks like a spreadsheet appears. It's not actually a spreadsheet—it can't calculate anything for you. It's just a grid to hold numbers and words. But the amazing thing is that the grid already has all the information needed for a chart, and the chart is automatically put on your slide! The computer must be psychic! You don't have to enter anything.

There are places in the data sheet for all the information that you are charting.

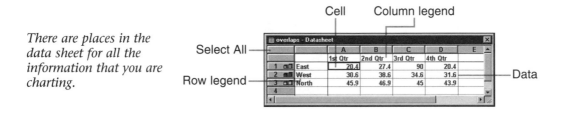

And then you realize that the figures you see aren't for your chart. They are just for an example chart. Your dreams of having the computer do everything for you while you head down to the video arcade to play *Deluxe Space Bunnyball* are shattered.

The grid has a bunch of numbered rows and lettered columns. The numbers and the letters are on buttons at the start of each row and column. The buttons on the rows with numbers in them have colored bars on them, which show you what color each respective row of data will be on your chart.

The top row and the first column are unlabeled. Use the top row to give each column a name (this will be the legend that goes across the bottom of your chart) and the first column to give each row a name (this will be the legend for each different item that you are charting). Just replace the sample text that's there by selecting a cell (click it) and typing.

Get This Example out of My Face

To clear the datasheet so that you can start entering your own data, click the **Select All** button, which is the unmarked button where the row-numbered buttons and column-letter buttons meet. All the *cells* (the rectangles where the rows and columns meet) turn into white letters on a black background, to show that they are selected. Right-click the selected area to bring up a shortcut menu, and choose **Clear Contents**. The example numbers and legends disappear faster than cookies in a kindergarten!

Entering the Information

Now it's time to put your own data into the cells. To pick the first cell to work with, just click it. Then, type the information that you want in that cell. To move to the next cell, just use the *cursor keys* (the four arrow keys on your keyboard), or select the cell of your choice by clicking it with the mouse.

Changing the Look of Your Data

If you want to change the lettering style, just use the standard Font and Font Size drop-down lists and the Bold, Italic, and Underline buttons on the formatting toolbar. Be careful that you don't pick a font that's hard to read at a small size (unless, of course, this presentation is about how you single-handedly messed up the company's finances, in which case the harder to read, the better).

If you want your numbers to look a certain way, such as to be shown as a percentage or with a fixed number of decimal points, click the **Select All** button to select all the cells. (If you're using numeric column or row headings and don't want them changed, just select the cells you want changed.) Then

➤ Use the **Currency Style** button to have the numbers appear (both on the datasheet and on the chart) as dollars and cents.

➤ Use the **Percent Style** button to have the numbers appear as percentages.

➤ Click the **Comma Style** button to put commas into long numbers (like 3,769,400 donuts).

➤ The **Increase Decimal** button increases the number of digits to the right of the decimal point.

➤ The **Decrease Decimal** button decreases the number of digits to the right of the decimal point.

(Remember, if you don't see these buttons, click the **More Buttons** button at the end of the Formatting toolbar.)

So Where's the Chart Already?

After you have your datasheet in shape, it is time to work on the chart that represents the data. Click the datasheet window's **Close** (X) button to make the datasheet disappear. You will now be in *Chart Editing mode*, which looks like Slide view, but has different menus and toolbars designed for working with the chart. (Any time you're in Slide view, you can enter Chart Editing mode simply by double-clicking your chart.)

If you want to bring up the datasheet again, choose **View**, **Datasheet**. (If there is no Datasheet command on the View menu, then you aren't in Chart Editing mode; double-click the chart and then look for it again.)

Chart Standard toolbar

*While you are working
on your chart, it looks
like you are in Slide view,
but you see different
toolbars and menus.*

Chart Formatting toolbar

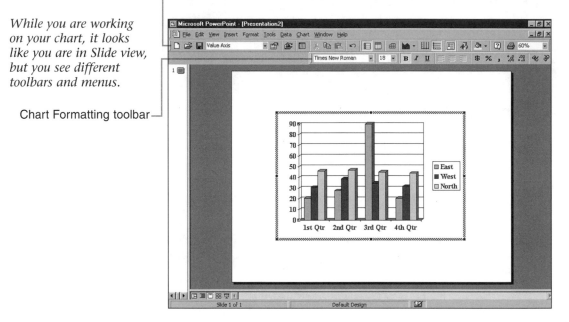

Choosing a Chart Type: So Many Choices, So Many Wrong Ones

To pick a chart type in Chart Editing mode, pull down the **Chart** menu from the menu bar and select the well-named **Chart Type** command. A dialog box appears. Down the left is a scrollable list of chart types. When you select the type of chart you want, pictures of several subtypes of that type appear to the right. Click the one you want.

This dialog box also has a great button marked **Press and Hold to View Sample**. Point to and hold this button down to see what your data would look like in the subtype of chart that you selected! It will look a little squished because it only has a small area to show it in, but it really gives you a sense of what to expect.

After you have found a chart type and subtype you are happy with, grin a little grin and press the **OK** button.

There are about as many different types of charts as there are types of donuts, and, like donuts, the wrong chart type won't communicate anything.

Give Me My Usual Chart

If there's one chart subtype that you use most of the time, you can tell PowerPoint to make that your default, so you don't have to pick it every time. Select that subtype in the Chart Type dialog box, and then click the **Set as default chart** button before clicking **OK**.

The pictures of chart sub-types don't reflect your data. But click down on the Press and Hold to View Sample button, and you will see your numbers in action.

Bar and Column Charts

A *bar chart* is one where there are bars, and their length indicates some quantity—the bigger the number, the longer the bar. Where PowerPoint says bar chart, it specifically means a chart where the bar goes side-to-side. When the bar goes up and down, it's a *column chart*. PowerPoint also offers bar charts with different shapes besides a bar, called *cone, cylinder,* and *pyramid charts.*

Bar charts are very good for comparing the quantity of a number of things. For example, one bar might represent how many chocolate donuts you have sold, and another raspberry-filled, and a third for glazed. If you have totals to compare as well as types that make up the total, you should try the *stacked bar* chart. On a stacked bar chart, you might have one bar for each of the five donut stores in your chain, showing total donut sales. Each store's bar would be broken into different-colored sections, showing how much of that store's total was chocolate, how much was glazed, and so on. If you want to make one of these, don't bother entering the totals in your datasheet; the chart will automatically show the totals just by stacking the individual components.

A bar chart.

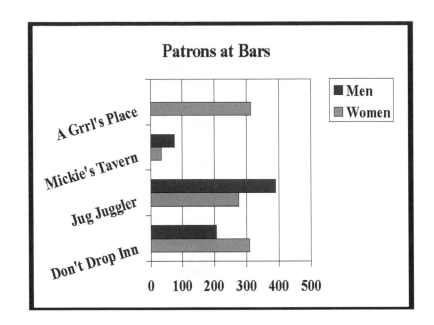

(In case you hadn't guessed, this chapter is underwritten by *The Hole-Sale Warehouse*, a top-notch donut shop at the corner of Third and Main. They are paying big bucks to get me to mention donuts until you get hungry enough to buy some. Okay, it's not big bucks, but they did give me a dozen.)

Line Charts

Line charts have a series of points that show the quantity of something in different conditions, and a line connects those points. Line charts are probably the most mis-used charts yet devised. They should *only* be used when your different conditions have some natural order, such as when you are showing how long a piece of metal gets over a range of temperatures, or how many donuts you are selling each month. In those cases, you can expect some sort of pattern to emerge in the order (sales go up in the summer and down in the fall, for example).

You shouldn't use a line chart for how many donuts are sold in each of a list of stores, for example, because that list doesn't have a natural order. You could totally rearrange the order in which the stores are listed, and the line would end up looking very different without meaning anything different. People would try to look for meaning in the line, and would be distracted from the real information.

If you are using something that's right for a line chart, but you also want the totaling effect of the stacked bar chart, try *stacked area* charts, which you will find under the Area type selection.

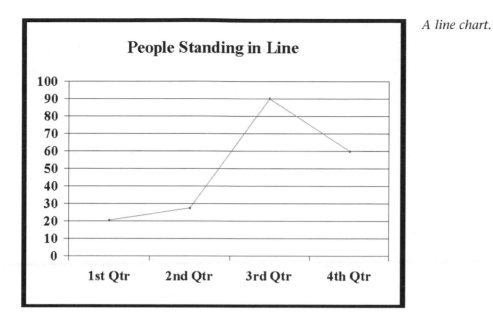

A line chart.

Pie Charts

Pie charts show a circle broken up into pie-piece–shaped sections. They are used for comparing a fairly small number of quantities. Pie charts are very popular, although some people find it hard comparing the size of the pie slices, because each slice is at a different angle.

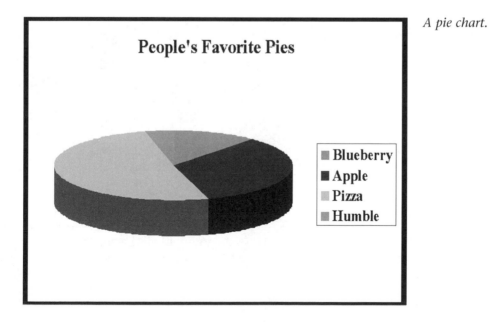

A pie chart.

A pie chart can show only one column of data from your datasheet. If you want to show the same sort of breakdown for several columns, you can either have several pies, or you can try a (believe it or not) *doughnut chart*, which has a series of nested circles, broken up into wedges. Most people aren't accustomed to doughnut charts, however, and may have trouble understanding them.

Fancier Chart Types

PowerPoint can make a lot of cool-looking chart types that you may never have heard of before, with names like *radar chart* or *bubble chart*. A good rule of thumb is that if you are unfamiliar with a type of chart, you shouldn't be using it! This isn't because you wouldn't be able to figure out how the chart works—you probably could do it fairly quickly. But if you don't know about the chart, your audience probably won't know about it either. You will end up spending a lot of time explaining how the chart works instead of discussing the information that you made the chart to present.

The Top-Five Chart-Busting Chart Features

You can make number of quick enhancements to your chart in Chart Editing mode. You don't always want to throw all these things in, but it's nice to know that they are there. To find these enhancements, choose **Chart**, **Chart Options**. A dialog box with a number of tabs appears. The exact tabs shown differ depending on the type of chart, because some of these features are only for certain types of charts. This dialog box has a small picture of your chart and will show you the effect of your changes as you make them.

The Chart Options dialog box lets you set all sorts of options and see their effect on the chart.

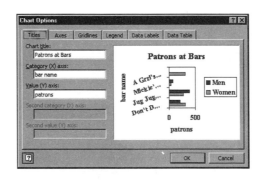

Titles

A chart with just colored bars and numbers doesn't really tell you anything—you have to know what it's a chart of! Pick the **Titles** tab, and you will be able to enter three primary titles. The name that you put in the **Chart Title** field is a title for the whole chart, and it goes at the top. For most charts, what you type in the **Category (X) axis** field goes across the bottom of the chart and names what the different points across the chart mean. If you have a column chart of donut sales by month, for example, a good thing to put in this field would be month. The **Value (Y) axis** field is the place to name the values you are measuring, such as number of donuts sold. (3D charts and some of the fancier chart types make different use of the Y axis and even have a Z axis.)

Gridlines

If you have a big chart with a lot of things on it, it can be hard to quickly see across and tell which points stand for which values. That's why PowerPoint offers you *gridlines*, lines that go across or up and down your chart, making it easier to see how things line up. On the **Gridlines** tab, you find two check boxes for the **Category (X) axis**. Checking **Major gridlines** gives you vertical lines on most chart types, and checking **Minor gridlines** as well doubles the number of lines. Similarly, the same two check boxes in the **Value (Y) axis** area set up horizontal lines.

Legend

The *legend* of your chart is not a tale about how your chart slew five dragons, only to die in its lover's arms, killed by a poisoned donut. Instead, it's a guide to what each of the colors in your chart means. Click the **Legend** tab to not only be able to turn the legend on or off, but to pick where around the chart the legend will appear.

Data Labels

Data Labels enable you to put the value you are charting or the name of the column right by the point. Usually, this is used to give the value, which allows the viewer to see the exact number in addition to the visual representation. On the **Data Labels** tab, check **Show value** to show the value or **Show label** to show the name.

Legendary Speed

To quickly turn the legend on or off without opening the dialog box, just click the **Legend** button on the Standard toolbar!

Data Table

You put all that work into filling in your datasheet, and now all you have to show for it is this chart. Don't you want people to see all the work you did? Well, if you do,

Data Table in Double Time

To quickly turn the Data Table on or off without opening the dialog box, just click the Data Table button on the Standard toolbar.

Data Table is the tab for you. Click **Show data table**, and your datasheet appears with your chart, showing your audience all the raw figures. If you have the Data Labels on, you shouldn't also use the Data Table, because it just ends up giving the same information twice.

The second option, **Show legend keys**, makes your datasheet double as a legend. If you turn this on, you should turn your legend off.

After you have made all your changes using the dialog box, click the **OK** button and they will be applied to your chart. (Click **Cancel** instead if you decide not to make the changes.)

A Fine-Tune on the Charts

Now that you have the pieces of your chart basically in place, you could sit back and be pleased with what you have accomplished. Or, you could be paranoid about it and spend a ton of time fine-tuning the chart. But there is something worthwhile about paranoia; if there wasn't, why would everyone but me be paranoid? (It must be a conspiracy!)

Every little piece of your chart has a name, and each part has a control panel that enables you to meddle and fuss with it. You can change the fonts of the text areas, change the colors of just about anything, turn lines into dotted lines, and make lines thicker or thinner.

To choose the part of the chart that you want to change, click the down arrow button at the end of the **Chart Object** field (the big drop-down list on the Standard toolbar in Chart Editing mode). A list of parts of the chart appears. Click the one that you want to work on. Square dots appear on the ends of the part of the chart that you selected, so you can tell what you are working on.

After you have selected the piece, click the **Format** button, and a dialog box appears that lets you change the attributes of that item. Depending on what object you have selected, you will have a number of tabs that you can select to change all sorts of things. Explore this a bit, and see what you find! (If the Format button is grayed out, you cannot change any attributes of the item.)

Also, while selected, some parts can be resized by using the black boxes as sizing handles, or moved by dragging the whole object!

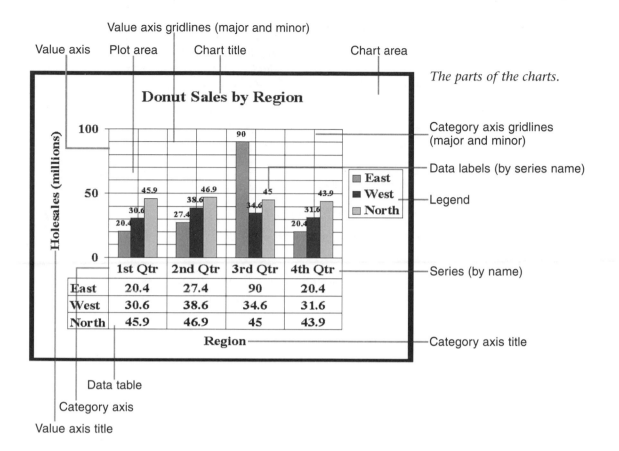

The parts of the charts.

Value axis
Plot area
Chart title
Chart area
Value axis gridlines (major and minor)

Donut Sales by Region

Category axis gridlines (major and minor)

Data labels (by series name)

Legend

Series (by name)

	1st Qtr	2nd Qtr	3rd Qtr	4th Qtr
East	20.4	27.4	90	20.4
West	30.6	38.6	34.6	31.6
North	45.9	46.9	45	43.9

Region
Category axis title

Data table

Category axis

Value axis title

Section Selection

You can double-click any part of the chart to bring up its dialog box. This can be trickier than it sounds, because there are so many pieces overlapping that it can be hard to tell just what you are pointing to. However, if you rest the pointer on something for a second, a box appears telling you what you are pointing to.

115

Gettin' Outta Here... and Gettin' Back

To leave the Chart Editing mode, just click outside of the chart, and you go back to the usual PowerPoint Slide View mode. In Slide View mode, you can resize the entire chart by using the sizing handles.

If you decide that you want to change anything about the chart later, just double-click the chart. You are brought back into the Chart Editing mode.

The Least You Need to Know

➤ Charts let you visually display numeric information.

➤   To start making a chart, click the **Insert Chart** button.

➤ Enter column and row names and data values by clicking one cell of the datasheet, typing in the information, and then using the cursor keys to get to the next cell.

➤ To select a chart type, pick **Chart Type** on the **Chart** menu. Select a chart type from the left column and a subtype from the pictures at right, and then click the **OK** button.

➤ Avoid using chart types that you are not used to seeing. They will just confuse your audience.

➤ After you finish working with the chart, just click outside of the chart area to go back to normal PowerPoint editing.

➤ To return to editing your chart, double-click it.

The Art of the Chart 102: Organization Charts

> ## In This Chapter
>
> ➤ Build an organization chart
>
> ➤ Enhance the chart with fancy lettering and pretty colors
>
> ➤ Rearrange the chart so that you are the boss!

Organization charts are used to show who reports to whom in a company. They tend to be loved by the people whose names are near the top of the chart ("I may be just a paper folder, but I report directly to the Assistant Vice-President in Charge of Origami!") and snickered at by those who dwell at the bottom. If you are the one making the chart, however, you can arrange it so that you are near the top. (Of course, your boss may wonder why the Deputy Presentation Assistant ended up above him.)

Charting the Path to Success

To get the whole thing rolling, find the slide that you want the chart to appear on in slide view, and then pull down the **Insert** menu and from the **Picture** submenu select the **Organization Chart** command. PowerPoint opens a new window with the beginning of an organization chart in it, if the feature is installed. (If Organization Chart is not installed, PowerPoint asks you if you want to install it. Insert your Office or PowerPoint CD-ROM and click **Yes**. The feature will be installed and will open up the window.) This window is actually a completely separate program designed just for organizational charting.

Organization Chart Program

The charting program is a version of a program called *Org Plus for Windows*, put out by IMSI. If you find you want to do more advanced, complex organizational charts, look into buying Org Plus, which has a number of features that were not included in the PowerPoint version.

The chart that you start with has four boxes: one top box for a boss (the program refers to bosses as *managers*, but employees usually call them bosses, and so will I), and three boxes for people working for him (they say *subordinate*, but I'll call 'em *employees*, just like real people do). The boss box looks different from the others, with the first line in red and four lines of text (so much that it overlaps the box below it). It doesn't look different *because* it's the boss box, but because it's currently selected for editing. You can change what's in each box, and in fact, you have to, unless everyone in your company is named *Type Name Here*.

In this shot, the chart program has been expanded to take up the whole screen, which you can do by clicking on the Maximize button.

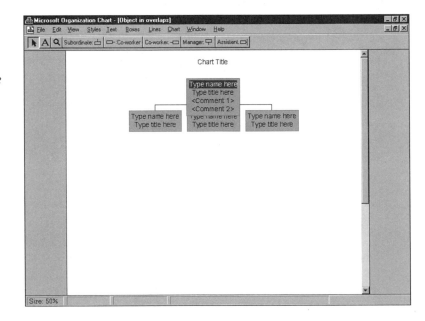

Editing a Box: More Fun Than Boxing with an Editor!

To edit the contents of a box, first you have to select it. That's as simple as clicking the box. In fact, it *is* clicking the box. When you do this, the text in the box turns to white on a black background.

Now that you have a black background, press **Enter**. The first line gets a colored background, meaning it's ready to be edited. The first line is for the name of the person. Type in the name to make the words *Type name here* disappear.

After you finish typing the name, press **Enter** again, and the red highlight moves to the next line where you can enter the person's title, such as *President* or *PowerPoint Ride Designer* or *Deputy Donut Eater*. After that, pressing **Enter** again takes you to the first of two lines for comments, which you can use for whatever you want. Use it for further descriptions of people's jobs, for their phone extension, or for comments on their hairdo. ("Nice blonde hair, why are the roots dyed black?")

Grow Your Company by Adding Boxes

If your company has only four people, you might never have to add any boxes. Then again, if your company has only four people, you probably don't really need an organization chart to begin with!

To add a person to the chart, first click one of the five buttons at the top of the window (**Subordinate**, **Co-worker** with the box on the left, **Co-worker** with the box on the right, **Manager**, or **Assistant**). When you do this, the pointer changes to a little box with a line coming from it. Then click the box that you want to connect the new box to. For example, if you want to add the Assistant to the Deputy Donut Eater, click the **Assistant** button on the box for the Deputy Donut Eater.

The two **Co-worker** buttons create new boxes next to the box that you click, connected to the same boss. The difference between the two buttons is that the one on the left adds the new box to the left of the existing one, and the one on the right adds the new box to the right of the existing one.

When you add a box, it is automatically selected, and you can press **Enter** to start filling in the name and position.

At the Top of the Chart Is... a Title!

When you start a new chart, it says Chart Title at the very top. Leaving that there would be a certain sign that you rushed through your work. To get rid of it, select the text by pointing to the start of the text and dragging to the end of the text. Then, type the title that you want to give it.

Frank Lloyd Chart: Fancier Structures

There are a number of different ways to change how people's boxes connect to each other—some let you reflect cases where employees have more than one boss; others are there just to make the chart look more organized.

If you click the **Styles** menu, you see a group of buttons with different chart diagrams on it. The top few are for groups, and there is one for assistants and one for co-managers.

The style menu.

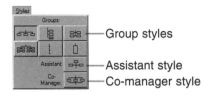

Groups

A *group* is a set of employees with the same boss. Using the buttons under the Style menu, you can group these employees so that they are all next to each other, or all stacked vertically, or even are all in the same box. To do this, first select all the people you want to organize. (You can do this by clicking the first one, and then holding down the Shift key and clicking the rest.) Then pull down the **Style** menu and click the button that shows how you want the group to appear. (Pick one of the six buttons toward the top; the lower two are used for other things.)

Selection in a Snap

To select a bunch of boxes all at once, point to above and to the left of the bunch, then drag to below and to the right.

Assistants

To change a subordinate into an assistant, invite him into your office and say, "Stop subordinating to me, and start assisting me!" To reflect this change on the chart, select the employee's box, and then pull down the **Style** menu and click the one Assistant style button.

Co-Managers

Co-managers are what you call the bosses when a group of employees have two or more equal bosses. To get the chart to show that these employees have this group of bosses, select all the bosses' boxes, pull down the **Style** menu, and click the **Co-managers diagram** button. The lines coming down from the co-managers boxes join and go to the employees group.

An assistant

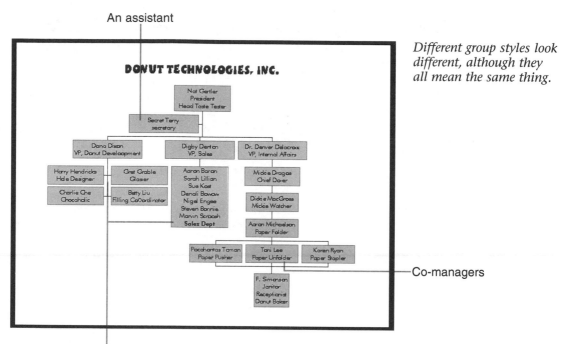

Different group styles look different, although they all mean the same thing.

Co-managers

Two different types of groups

The Job Shuffle: Rearranging the Chart

An organization chart is going to keep changing. People join the firm, quit, or are promoted, and that means that the chart has to be changed. Because you made the chart, you are going to be the one stuck rearranging it, until *you* quit or get promoted.

To get rid of someone, just select that person's box and press **Delete**. Anyone working under the deleted person will now be shown as working for the deleted person's boss.

To move a person from reporting to one boss to reporting to another, drag that person's box (a red outline follows as you drag). Drag it until your pointer is below his new boss's box, and then slide it up. When the pointer turns into the diagram on the Subordinate button, release the mouse button. The box is moved over there, and any employees of the person in the box are also moved, so they are still his employees.

If you drag the box in from the side rather than from below, the pointer becomes an arrow. If you release the mouse button then, the box you're dragging becomes a coworker of the box you're pointing to.

You Have Got It Organized, Now Make It Pretty

Now that you have got your chart all organized, it's time to mess with the colors, fonts, line thickness, and all that other stuff that can make your presentation more attractive. Some of this stuff can also help make the chart more informative.

Demotion Dilemma

If someone's position changes so that his old employee is now his boss, just dragging that someone down won't work. Instead, move the old employee up to the new boss, and then drag the old boss into his new position.

We'll Have Fonts, Fonts, Fonts ('Til Our Daddy Takes the Text Bar Away)

To change the look of any text, select the text (you can select the whole box, or even multiple boxes), and then pull down the **Text** menu. There you find commands to align the text at the left, right, or center of the box. You also find a Font command, which brings up a dialog box that enables you to pick the font, the size, and whether it's a bold, italic, or normal. There is also a Color command that brings up a dialog box showing squares of various colors—double-click any of them to make the text that color.

Every Company Needs a Colorful Background

Pull down the **Chart** menu and select the **Background Color** command (which shouldn't be hard to find, because it's the only command on that menu). This brings up a dialog box displaying various colors. Double-click the color you want, and it fills the chart background.

However, this only lets you have one of a handful of colors. The chart program does not have the wide range of colors or the nifty fill tools that the main PowerPoint program has. If you want something fancier, don't set the background color. Instead, after you finish making the chart, select the chart in PowerPoint, and then use the PowerPoint fill tool to set the background. (If you have already set a background color in Chart and decide that you want to use a PowerPoint fill instead, double-click the chart to get back into the chart program, do the **Chart**, **Background Color** command, and select the rightmost square on the bottom row. This resets the background color, and the PowerPoint fill now works.)

Colorful Co-workers

Changing the color of the boxes can be more than just decoration. For example, you might want to have all your administrative people (accountants, secretaries, and so on) show up in blue, your sales people in green, and your technical people (donut bakers, advanced donut-design engineers, and folks like that) show up in purple. To do this, select the boxes that you want to change, and then pull down the **Boxes** menu and select **Color**. You'll get the same sort of color dialog box that you get with fonts and with the background color, except this one controls the box background.

Also in the Boxes menu are commands that let you add a shadow under the box and change the color and style of the border line around the box.

Define the Line

You can change any line to any thickness and style you like. To change the look of a line, first you have to select the line. You can select any single line by clicking it. The line changes color when you do so, although the color change is minor and can be hard to see. You can select a bunch of lines at once by pointing to a spot on the chart's background and dragging diagonally. A rectangle appears, with one corner where you started dragging and the opposite corner wherever the pointer is now. When you release the mouse button, everything within in the rectangle gets selected. (Don't worry about the fact that boxes have been selected as well, because the Line commands won't affect them.) The selected lines turn gray. However, with the standard thin line, this color difference can be hard to see.

The commands on the Line menu let you set the thickness, style, and color of all the selected lines. The Thickness and Style commands let you just pick one from a submenu, while the Color command brings up the Organization Chart program's Color dialog box.

Again, these aren't merely decorative. For example, dotted lines are good for showing proposed changes to the organizational chart.

Adding New Lines

Sometimes you need more lines than just the ones from bosses to employees. You might want to use a different color line to show how information runs through the organization, or you might want to draw a big rectangle around a branch of the chart that makes up a single division.

If you type **Ctrl+D**, four additional buttons are added to the toolbar. The first, with a plus sign on it, is the Horizontal/Vertical Line button. The second (with a diagonal line on it), is the Diagonal Line button, used for drawing lines at any angle. These work when you click on the button, and then drag the mouse from the line's starting point to the line's ending point.

The third button is the Auxiliary Line button. This is the most useful one, as it lets you add new lines from one box to another. Click this button, and then point to the edge of one box and drag the pointer to the edge of another box. The program automatically routes the line around the boxes to connect the two edges.

123

Better yet, this line keeps the two boxes connected even if you move the boxes! (You can adjust the path of this line by grabbing hold of one of its edges and dragging it.)

The fourth button, Rectangle, lets you make new boxes. Using this, you can make boxes that aren't connected to anything, and you can make them any size you want. (Normal boxes are designed to fit tightly around the text they hold.) You can use this tool to put a title or a legend in a box, or to create a square highlighting one area of the chart. This box always appears *behind* other boxes and lines so that it won't cover them up.

Text to Go

You can put text anywhere you want on the chart; this lets you annotate things beyond what's said in the boxes. To do this, click the **Enter Text** button, and then click the chart where you want the text to appear. Then, type! (To edit the text later, just double-click it.)

Other Little Chart Tricks

The Organization Chart program has a number of other features that you can take advantage of. Because it is a separate program, it doesn't have all the same features as the main PowerPoint program—the animated Office Assistant, for example—but it does have its own tools to meet your needs (it still has Help information, which you can get by pressing the **F1** key).

Zooming in a Zoom

You can change how close a look you get at your chart. You can shrink it down so that you can see the whole chart at once, or you can zoom in on it so that you get a really close look at each dot in the dotted line. Change your view by pressing **F9**, **F10**, **F11**, or **F12**, with **F9** being the farthest view and **F12** making it so close that you'll think someone glued the chart to your eyeglasses. (Don't worry; this doesn't change the size of the chart on the slide.)

Selection Shortcuts

You can quickly select all of something (all the lines, all the boxes, all the co-manager boxes, and so on) by pulling down the **Edit** menu and selecting the **Select** submenu. There you find 10 different quick-selection possibilities (such as Group or All Co-Managers), which is handy if you are making big changes to a whole group.

Chart Trivia

Pull down the **Help** menu and select **Chart Info** to get a display telling you how many boxes are on the chart, how many are currently selected, and other information about your chart. You can use this to quickly count how many people are in your organization, or in some department. Just select the people you want to count, then use this command!

Returning to Uncharted Territory

After you finish working with your chart, click the **Close** (X) button. A dialog box appears, asking whether you want to update the object in your presentation. Click Yes, and you can go back to working on your PowerPoint presentation; there you find the chart on a slide.

If you want to make changes to the chart after it's on the presentation, just double-click it; this returns you to the Organization Chart program. If you find that your boss keeps asking you for changes, just change his title to Executive Bunnybrain and see how long it takes for him to notice! You'll be chuckling about that one while standing in the unemployment lines!

The Least You Need to Know

➤ To start making a chart, pull down the **Insert** menu, and from the **Pictures** submenu, select **Organization Chart**.

➤ To select a box on the chart, click it. To select additional boxes, hold down the **Shift** key and click them.

➤ To add a box, click the button for the type of box you want to add (**Subordinate**, **Co-Worker**, **Manager**, or **Assistant**), and then click the box you want to connect it to.

➤ Change to whom a subordinate reports by dragging the subordinate's box below a different boss's box, and then dragging up onto the box.

➤ [A] You can add text by clicking on the **Enter Text** button, and then clicking where you want the text.

➤ After you finish working with the chart, just click the **Close** (X) button for the Organization Chart window and select **Yes** from the dialog box that appears.

➤ To return to editing your chart, double-click it.

Chapter 12

Backing Up Your Words: Beautiful Backgrounds

In This Chapter

➤ Use a background designed by genuine Microsoft employees

➤ Design your own background

➤ Create a look for your presentations

"Behind every great man is a great background." Truer words have never been said. Well, *certain* truer words have never been said, but a lot of words that have been said have been truer. You can't expect deep philosophical insight from a computer book. What you *can* expect is to learn how to give your words and pictures a nice backdrop, and to pick the basic design look for your presentation. What could be more fun than that?*

The Lazy Way: Using a Pre-Made Design

PowerPoint comes with an assortment of design *templates*—files which have nicely designed backgrounds and layouts all ready for you. These are good for saving you time and effort. The one risk is that everyone else who has PowerPoint has the same templates; so if you use one of these, there's a reasonable chance that members of your audience will have seen them already and will somehow relate your presentation to the one they have seen before.

Answer: Dropping a thousand superballs off of a tall building.

To start a new presentation using one of these backgrounds, pull down the **File** menu and select the **New** command. A dialog box appears, with three tabs. Select the second tab (**Design Templates**), and you see a list of different designs.

View a list of filenames.

View each file as an icon. View full details about each file.

The three buttons above the preview change the way that the list of designs is organized.

New Presentation

General	Design Templates	Presentations

Artsy · Expedition · Network Blitz
Azure · Factory · Notebook
Bamboo · Fireball · Post Modern
Blends · Gesture · Pulse
Blue Diagonal · Global · Radar
Blueprint · High Voltage · Ribbons
Bold Stripes · Japanese Waves · Ricepaper
Cactus · LaVerne · Romanesque
Capsules · Lock And Key · Sakura
Checkers · Marble · Sandstone
Citrus · Mountain · Soaring
Construction · Nature · Straight Edge
Dads Tie · Neon Frame · Strategic

Preview

Lorem Ipsum

OK   Cancel

Preview of the selected design.

Check This Out

Doesn't Look So Good?

If the design you opened up doesn't look so good, click the **Close Window** (**X**) button on the menu bar to get rid of it, and then start again.

Click once on any one of the designs, and you see a small version of what a typical slide would look like in the Preview area at the right of the dialog box. The slide won't look very good. This isn't because the design is bad, but because the colors are simplified for the preview display, and the resolution is low, so just about any design will look bad. Still, it should give you some idea of what the slide will be like.

When you find one you like, click the **OK** button. PowerPoint starts the new presentation for you, and the New Slide dialog box appears, from which you select an AutoLayout for the first slide. If you choose the slide from the New Slide dialog box that's highlighted by default, you find that it's arranged visibly differently from the one you selected. It probably has the same pieces, but in different places. This is because every template actually has *two* slide designs. This design is used just for the title slide; the one you saw earlier is used for all the other slides.

Color My World, Differently!

If you like the basic look of the background, but you aren't happy with the color, change it! You can change the color for all the slides, or you can change just one to make it stand out.

To do this, pull down the **Format** menu and select the **Slide Color Scheme** command. A Color Scheme dialog box appears, showing a series of little slides. Each slide has a title in that color scheme's default title color, some bulleted text in the scheme's bulleted text color, a shape in the scheme's shape colors, and a chart using the scheme's chart colors. Click the scheme you like, and then click the **Apply** button to make it the color scheme for the current slide, or **Apply to All** to make it the color scheme for all the slides in this presentation!

Don't Get the Overcolored Blues

When the color changes from slide to slide, it takes your audience a little while to adjust. So it's okay to change the color on one slide to grab special attention to that slide, or to break a long presentation into chapters with a different color scheme for each chapter, but don't change the color scheme frequently.

Use the Standard tab in the Color Scheme dialog box to choose a pre-designed scheme, or use the Custom tab to create your own.

Design Yourself a Rainbow

If you want to roll your own color scheme, pick the color scheme that's closest to what you want, and then click the **Custom** tab. This displays the eight slide elements that get their own color in the scheme (such as backgrounds or shadows) and the currently-selected color for each element. Double-click any one of these colors, and a Color dialog box appears. This dialog box lets you select a new color for that element.

After you have selected a new color, click the **OK** button to close the Color dialog box and return to the Color Scheme dialog box. After you have changed at least one color, an **Add as Standard Scheme** button becomes available. Clicking this adds the color scheme to the list on the Standard tab. You can then use it on other presentations. What could be a better lasting legacy than that?*

Coloring for Clarity

For onscreen presentations, bright letters on a dark background look best. For overheads and slides, use dark letters and bright backgrounds.

As you change the various colors, you see the colors on the sample slide in the lower right of the dialog box change. After you have changed the color scheme to what you want, click **Apply** to apply it to the current slide, or the **Apply to All** button to change your whole presentation at once.

The eight colors you select will become the eight colors shown on the selection menu whenever you choose colors for anything in the presentation. If you later use this dialog box to change the colors on your slides, anything that you colored using those eight colors will change as well.

The Less-Lazy Way: Design Your Own Background and Slide Style

Some people like to design their own backgrounds. I know someone who said that he had been a serviceman stationed in the Gulf, when his real background was being a man at a Gulf service station.

If you want to design a *slide* background, it should probably be the first step in building your presentation. After all, what color you make everything else depends on what they will appear against. To get started with a new, thoroughly blank presentation, pull down the **File** menu and select **New**. From the dialog box that appears, select the **General** tab. On this tab, double-click **Blank Presentation**. The New Slide dialog box appears, asking you to choose a layout. Click the **OK** button to pick the default (Title Slide), and a basic title slide form appears, in plain black text on a white background. (Make sure you are in Slide view to see it.)

Master View: No, It's Not for 3-D Reels

For each presentation, PowerPoint has a *slide master*, a special slide never seen in your presentation that holds the basic design for the slides that *are* seen. To see this slide master, pull down the **View** menu and select **Master**, and then select **Slide Master**

*Answer: Finding a cure for hangnail.

from the submenu. The slide master appears in your Slide view. It has five boxes of text, including descriptions of what each box is for. Anything you add or change on the slide master will be added or changed on all your slides.

In the lower right of each text box on the Slide Master, there is a phrase which tells you what that box is used for.

Changing the Text Styles

Changing the text styles on the Master will change the automatic styles used on all the slides in the presentation. For example, if you click the text that says `Click to edit Master title style` and then click the **Italics** button, not only will the text on that line of the Slide Master be in italics, but so will the titles on all the slides you make. You can adjust the font, the size, and the color all in the same way you would change text in a text box, as you saw in Chapter 5, "The World of Words."

The largest box contains five lines of text. The first of these affects the main list on each slide. The second (which says `Second level`) affects sublists, the third affects sub-sublists, and so on. (If you are actually using fifth level on any of your slides, it's time to rethink your presentation! You don't need sub-sub-sub-sublists!)

Each level's style can be changed separately. You can even change the bullet style for each by right-clicking the line and selecting **Bullets and Numbering** from the pop-up menu, just like you would with text on a normal slide.

131

WordArt Won't Work

You cannot make your default text style WordArt. If you select the Master style area and then click the WordArt button, all you end up with is a fancy WordArt presentation of the words `Click to edit Master text style` on all your slides!

Changing the Text Areas

If you click any of the Slide Master's five text areas, sizing handles appear. At this point, you can resize or move any of the areas just like a normal text box. This will affect all the slides created with the AutoLayout tool. For some AutoLayouts, the main text area is divided in half (one half for text, the other for graphics), and this will still be true no matter how you resize it. You can even delete an area by selecting it and pressing **Delete**, but you shouldn't delete the title area or main text area. It's okay to delete the smaller areas, however, such as the Date or Footer areas, if you don't want them on your slides.

Changing the Basic Slide Color

The first step in designing your background is to choose the basic background color to fill up the slide. (Actually, the first step is to read this section of the book, but I would guess that you are already doing that.) Pull down the **Format** menu and select **Background** to get the Background dialog box. Click the drop-down button and select one of the colors from the list that appears, or select **More Colors** to go to a standard Color dialog box, or select **Fill Effects** to go the standard Fill Effects dialog box that you learned about in chapter 7, "WordArt: Your Low-Calorie Logo-Making Friend." You can fill it with gradients, textures, patterns, or pictures, just like with anything else.

Decorations: Deck the Slides!

To decorate your background with pictures, boxes, logos, whatever, do it in just the same way that you would decorate a regular slide. After you put that stuff on, it may appear to overlap the text on the master slide, but don't worry; the text on the actual slide will go in front of everything that you add.

Even so, you may want to be careful of adding things that overlap where the text is, because things that you add there can end up distracting from the text and making the text hard to read. It's usually better to add highlights at the edges of your slide, where you won't have text. You don't want something so busy that you can't see it; otherwise, trying to read your slides will be as hard as trying to listen to someone while people stand right behind you, whispering. If you are going to use light text, keep all your background elements fairly dark, and vice versa.

How'd They Do It?

If you see something you like in one of the prepackaged backgrounds, just load up that background, select the Slide Master view, and see what pieces they used. (You may have to select the background and Ungroup it to see what the individual pieces are.)

How to Earn the Title "Master Title Masterer"

If you only make one Slide Master, your title slides will have the same background as the rest of your slides. To make a separate Master for the title slide, pull down the **View** menu and click **Master**. If the command **Title Master** is selectable, there already is a Title Master for this presentation, and selecting that command will let you edit it.

If Title Master is grayed out, however, select **Slide Master** instead. Then pull down the **Insert** menu and select the first item, **New Title Master**. This will copy all the background elements you added to your Slide Master onto a new Title Master for you to work with.

Title Masters have different text boxes from Slide Masters. You can make your Title Master a bit busier than your Slide Master. After all, the text will be bigger, making it easier to read.

After you have made the Title Master, you can pull it up at any time by pulling down the **View** menu, selecting **Master**, and then selecting **Title Master** from the sub-menu.

Save and Save Again!

After you have designed a background for your presentation, you should save it twice, as described in the next couple paragraphs. The first time you save it, you are saving it as a template (so you can reuse the design with other projects); the second time, you are saving it in a normal presentation file for this project. You could save it a few more times if you wanted, but why would you waste time like that?*

Answer: Because you get paid by the hour!

133

First, pull down the **File** menu, and select **Save As**. The Save As dialog box appears. Click the drop-down arrow at the end of the Save As Type field, and select **Design Template** from the list. The file list will display the content of the folder where your design templates are stored. Type a name for your background design into the File Name field, and then click the **Save** button.

The Save As dialog box lets you save your backgrounds as a template as well as letting you save your presentation.

Now that you saved it, you can reuse your own design in the same way that you use the Microsoft-provided designs, except that when you start your presentation with the **File**, **New** command, you'll select your designs from the **General** tab rather than the **Design Templates** tab.

Quick Save

In the future, you can save additional changes to the presentation just by clicking the **Save** button.

Now, it's time to save your presentation for the first time. Give the **File**, **Save As** command again and select **Presentation** in the Save As Type field. Use the file browser to find the folder where you save your presentations (if you aren't certain where that is, try clicking the **My Documents** button.) Then, type a name for this presentation into the File Name field, and click the **OK** button. Now your presentation has a name!

Now that you have finished working with your Slide Master, click the **Close** button on the Master toolbar to resume working on the individual slides in your presentation!

Slide Nonconformist: Making One Slide Different

Sometime, you might find yourself needing just one slide that's different, one slide that doesn't have the same background as the rest of the slides in that presentation. You don't know whether there's some mystical command that will remove the background, or perhaps a mystical incantation that will cause it to disappear. You are faced with the problem of just how you make the background go away.

You don't make it go away. Instead, you do what you used to do when you had to clean up a big mess in the five minutes before your parents got home. You cover it up. Just draw a big rectangle over the whole background, and fill it with whatever you want the background of this slide to look like, then use the **Draw, Order, Send Backward** command to put it behind any text you've created. This is a much more effective cover-up than the time you threw the tablecloth over the grape juice stain on the rug.

Does "Footer" Mean It's More Foot Than Something Else?

A *footer* is just some information that goes at the bottom of something, below the main content. In this book, for example, the page number is a footer.

You can easily set up to three footer items on any presentation (assuming that you didn't delete the boxes for them while designing your master). They can be used to hold a date, a slide number, and one other piece of text that can be anything you want.

To do this, pull down the **View** menu and select **Header and Footer**. When the Header and Footer dialog box appears, make sure that the **Slide** tab is selected.

The dialog box says Header and Footer, but for slides, it only has Footers. That's the best place for things on a slide anyway.

The dialog box has three check boxes in the Include On Slide area to lets you choose which footers to show. If you check the **Date and Time** check box, you have to choose whether you want the current date to always appear (**Update Automatically**), or whether you want to set a **Fixed** date. If you pick Update Automatically, the date on the slides will be the same day that the person is watching the computer-based slide show or the date that the overheads were printed. When you pick Update Automatically, pull down the menu below it and pick the format for the date (such as choosing between **April 30, 1999** or **4/30/99** or any of a dozen different formats, some of which include the time as well).

To get the slide number to appear, just click the **Slide Number** check box. Do you want a slide number? If you are only doing a computer-based presentation, probably not, because that will just be additional information to clutter up the screen. However, if you are producing overheads, real slides, or printed handouts, you do want the numbers. Who out there hasn't at some time accidentally dropped a pile of papers or a tray of slides, and watched them scatter in various directions with little hope of ever getting them back in order?* Also, if you are using handouts, having the onscreen slide numbered makes it easier for the audience to find that slide in their handouts.

➤ To get the whatever-text-you-want footer, just click the **Footer** check box and type the text you want into the field.

➤ If you don't want the footer information on the title slide (and you probably don't), check the **Don't Show on Title Slide** check box.

➤ After you have set it all up, click the **Apply to All** button, and the footer will be added to all the slides! (Remember, if you're not happy with where the footer ends up on the slide, you can change it on the Slide Master.)

The Least You Need to Know

➤ To choose a pre-made background, use the **File**, **New** command, select the **Design Templates** tab, click the design you want from the list, and then the **OK** button.

➤ To start with a new, totally blank design, use the **File**, **New** command, select the **General** tab, and double-click **Blank Presentation**.

➤ To create your own background design, start with a blank design, and then select the **View**, **Master**, **Slide Master** command.

➤ Any drawing, shapes, or text that you add to the Slide Master will appear on all the slides as background, behind anything you add on the slide.

➤ The Title Master starts with all the elements that you put on the Slide Master. However, changing them or removing them does not change the Slide Master.

➤ To save your design as a template, use the **File**, **Save As** command, pull down the **Save As Type** menu, and select **Design Template**. Then type a name for your design, and click **Save**.

➤ To add footer information (including date and slide number), select **View**, **Header and Footer** to get the Header and Footer dialog box.

Answer: My mother. She's too perfect for something like that.

Part 3
Fancy, Flashy, Fabulous Features

Sound and movement are very important. Without them, we wouldn't be able to tell real flamingoes from the plastic ones. Without sound and motion in your presentation, it could be a flaming (or even flamingo) failure.

In this part, you learn about putting sound and motion in your presentation, along with making the presentation interactive. With properly set-up interaction, the user can skip over all the material you took so long putting together!

Chapter 13

Click Here for Interactivity

In This Chapter

➤ Make your presentation interactive

➤ Start other programs and bring up Web pages from your presentation

➤ Make nice-looking buttons for users to click

Interactivity is very useful in an onscreen presentation. With an interactive presentation, the users can choose which information they want to see, which means you can put a lot more information in without boring the people who don't want to see it. And even if you don't need interactivity, proper use of it can keep the viewer feeling involved in your presentation, making it more enjoyable for him. Why, if people liked things without interactivity, then television would be popular!

You Can Click Anything!

Any object on your slide can be made interactive, so that something happens when the user clicks it. Your words, pictures, shapes, logos, and even your lines can be made clickable.

To do this, right-click the item in Slide view. It becomes selected, and a shortcut menu appears. Select **Action Settings**. The Action Settings dialog box appears. The **Mouse Click** tab of the Action Settings dialog box has what you are looking for.

Interact with this dialog box to make your interaction work.

Going to Another Slide: The Playground Hop

Most of the time, you'll probably want to create a place to click that takes you to another part of your presentation. PowerPoint calls a way to get from one slide to another slide (or to a Web page or other document) a *hyperlink*. To me, that sounds like an overactive breakfast sausage, but it's Microsoft's term, so we'll go with that.

The most common type of hyperlink you will want to make is one that takes the viewer to another part of your presentation. To do this, click the **Hyperlink to** radio button. The field below it will become active. Click the drop-down menu to see a list of the sorts of links you can create. Most of them take the viewer to another slide when the object is clicked. There are choices to let you go to the Next Slide, Previous Slide, First Slide, Last Slide, and Last Slide Viewed. One slide says just Slide… and nothing else (this lets you pick which slide to go to).

If you just want the user to step through your presentation, you will probably be using the Next Slide and Previous Slide buttons. If you are looking for real interaction, however, letting them pick their path, Slide… is the one that you will use the most.

The Hyperlink To Slide dialog box lets you create controls to skip back and forth among the slides.

Select **Slide**…, and you get a new car and a trip to Jamaica. Oh, okay, I lied. You just get a dialog box, but it's a very nice dialog box. On the left is a list of the slides in your presentation. Slides that have titles list the titles, and slides that don't have titles have the slide number listed. Click the slide that you want to link to, and an image of the slide appears in the lower right, so you can make sure that it's the slide you want. Then click the **OK** button to set the link.

140

Pop Your Peepers on Plural PowerPoint Presentations

Sometimes you want a hyperlink into *another* presentation. That way, you don't have to build everything you ever want to say into one huge presentation.

To do this, select **Hyperlink To** from the Action Settings dialog box. From the menu below it, select **Other PowerPoint Presentation**. A file browser appears. Find and double-click the file for the presentation you want. Another dialog box appears, with a list of slides in that presentation. This isn't a very good one, however, because it does not show a picture of the slide (so you just have to go by the titles and slide numbers). Double-click the title of the slide you want.

Welcome to the World Wide Web; Look Out for the World Wide Spider

You can create a link from your presentation to a page on the World Wide Web. This makes a lot of sense if you are publishing your presentation on the Web. (I show you how to do that in Chapter 21, "Putting It on the Web.") It lets the user go from the information in your presentation to relevant stuff on another Web site.

Tight Links

When you create a hyperlink to a specific slide, the link stays to that slide even if that slide is moved and changes slide number.

It can also work when someone is seeing your presentation directly from the hard disk, rather than over the Web. When you do it this way, it isn't nearly so elegant. The system that the presentation is running on needs to have a copy of Microsoft Internet Explorer (a Web browser), and it needs a connection to the Internet. When the user clicks the hyperlink to the Web, Internet Explorer starts up. If the Internet connection is a dial-up, the user may have to tell the Internet Dialer to make the connection. Then the linked-to Web site appears on the Internet Explorer screen, but the viewer may not know Internet Explorer and may not be comfortable with it. All in all, linking a non-Web presentation to the Web is probably a bad idea.

To create the link, select **Hyperlink To** on the Action Settings dialog box, pull down the menu below that, and select **URL**. Now, *URL* here does not refer to the Dook Of Url of song fame. Instead, it means *Uniform Resource Locator*, which makes it sounds like a catalog telling you where to find cub scout pants, doctors' jackets, and police hats. What it really means here is the Web page address, that big long string that starts with an *http:* and tells people where to find your Web page. (For example, http://ourworld.compuserve.com/homepages/nat/ is the URL for my Web page.) When you select URL from the menu, a dialog box appears asking you for the URL. Type it into the space provided and press **Enter**. The hyperlink will now point to that Web page.

Having a Web browser suddenly appear can be confusing to someone who is not on the Web or who may not be used to the Web.

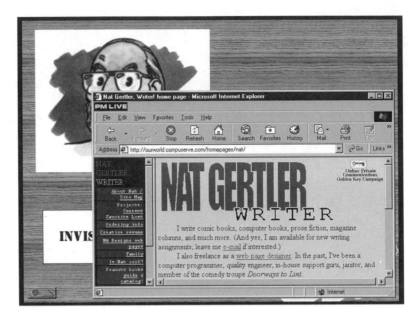

Starting a Program

You can create a link that starts another program on your computer. This can be useful if your presentation is about the program, or if you want to give people an easy way to start Solitaire while the boss isn't looking.

To make this choice, instead of picking Hyperlink To from the Action Settings dialog box, select **Run Program**, and then click the **Browse** button that's under it. A file navigator opens. Click the drop-down button at the end of the Look In field and select the hard disk with the program from the menu that appears. A list of folders on the hard disk appears below. Double-click the folder the program is in. (If it's a folder within a folder within a folder, you will have to do this several times to get to where the program is.) When you find the program file, click it. Then click the **OK** button. Voilà! You have now got a program linked in.

When the user clicks this hyperlink, a dialog box appears warning that some files can contain viruses. The user has to click **Yes** before the program will actually start.

Putting a Sound with the Click

You can make it so that when you click something, it makes a noise. It can make that noise along with linking to another slide or program, or it can just make that noise. This way, you could have them click a picture of a car to hear it go vrooom, or a picture of a duck to hear it go quack, or a picture of Leonardo Da Vinci to hear him go quack.

For the sound to work, the presentation will have to be viewed on a computer that has a sound card and speakers. Most computers sold these days have these things, but some don't—mostly ones bought by companies. A lot of companies think that sound systems have no business application (wrong), and that having them only encourages people to spend their time blowing up aliens when the boss isn't looking (less wrong). So if you are creating a presentation for people to view on their own machines, you may not want to rely on sound.

To add a sound, on the Action Settings dialog box, click the **Play Sound** check box. Click the drop-down button under it to see a list of standard available sounds, and then select the one you want. If you don't want one of the prepackaged sounds, you can select **Other Sound** to get to the Add Sound dialog box, which contains a list of sound files you can use—but you probably won't find anything *interesting* there unless you have put it there yourself. (I tell you about making your own sounds in Chapter 17, "Sound Advice on Sound.")

Flash That Thing!

Under the Play Sound check box is another check box. Check off this **Highlight Click** check box, and your object will flash when someone clicks it, which helps users know that they have clicked the right thing.

More Than One Thing at a Time

The **Play Sound** and **Highlight Click** options can be used in combination with each other, as well as in combination with the **Hyperlink To** or **Run Programs** options, to cause more than one reaction to a click. It's like teaching your computer to walk and chew gum at the same time!

Done with the Dialog Box

After you have set what the link goes to and chosen the sound if you want one, click the **OK** button at the bottom of the Action Settings dialog box. To test out your new hyperlink, you can click the **Slide Show** button to see the slide in action, click the hyperlink to see it work, and then right-click and select **End Show** to return to your work. Look out, however—you will now be at the slide you linked to rather than the one that you linked from, and you will have to find your own way back!

Clickless Actions

If you scan the other tab on the Action Settings dialog box, you will find it has the same contents as the Mouse Click tab. The difference is hidden in the *name* of this other tab, which is Mouse Over. The action you select on this tab is what happens when the pointer passes over the object. Why would you want to have an interaction without clicking? Three good reasons come to mind:

➤ You are making an interactive presentation for little kids. Pointing without clicking is both simpler to understand and easier to do, because most mouse devices aren't designed for kids' little paws.

➤ You are making a *kiosk*, an information center like you might see in the middle of your local shopping mall. If you don't need a click, you can create a presentation that can be entirely controlled by a trackball without any buttons, which is easy for shoppers to figure out and leaves fewer parts to worry about breaking.

➤ You want to have a sound or have the object flash when the pointer passes over it, and then take another action when you click it. When the pointer passes over the picture of a flying sheep, the user could suddenly hear "Click here to learn more about flying sheep!" Then when the sheep is clicked, a slide about famous flying sheep in history displays.

As the third reason suggests, you can set separate actions for passing over the object and clicking it. Just set one action on the Mouse Click tab and one on the Mouse Over tab. Make sure the action on the Mouse Over tab isn't a hyperlink, however, because if a new slide appears when the pointer is on the picture, the user will never have a chance to click it!

Missing Link: Getting Rid of an Interaction

To get rid of hyperlink, just right-click the object, select **Action Settings**, and then select **None** from whichever tab you set the link on. This clears the hyperlink. To get rid of a sound action, just click the **Play Sound** check box so that the check mark goes away, and your presentation will be that much quieter!

Click Pick: Shaping Your Clickable Area

The clickable area for a shape is that shape. For example, if you make a circle and link it to a sound, the user can click anywhere on the circle to hear the sound. (This is true even if the circle has no fill. Although you can see through the center, if you click there, PowerPoint knows that you are clicking the circle.) The corner areas outside the circle, but inside the circle's box, are not clickable.

The clickable area for most other objects is rectangular. If you have a picture on your slide, for example, and you give it an interactive action of some sort, the user can click anywhere on the picture. This is true even if the picture has an invisible edge color—users can click the invisible edge and it still works the same as if they had clicked on the visible part of the picture.

How It Stacks Up

If someone clicks somewhere where you have several objects stacked up, what happens? The answer is that whatever's on top where the user clicks controls what happens. If it's an object with some interaction, that action takes place. If it's an object with no interaction, PowerPoint acts the same as if the click was on the background, even if the clicked object is on top of an object that has an interaction. As with many things in life, whoever's on top gets control. See Chapter 6, "Layout: Not Just Something You Do in the Sun", to learn how to rearrange where objects are in the pile.

If you have an unfilled shape with an action on it, and someone clicks the unfilled interior, the action does take place. This is a handy feature, useful in one of my favorite tricks:

Nat's Nifty, Patented, Pick-Parts-of-a-Picture PowerPoint Trick

Let's say that you have a picture of you and your dog, standing side by side. (No, you don't have to say it out loud!) And you want to make it so that when users clicks on you, they hear the sound of a laser, and when they click a your dog Squishie, they hear a whoosh. Now, it's one picture, so it's one object, so you can only have one click action on it, right? Right.

But let's say you use the circle tool to draw a circle over your dog. You don't want to hide Squishie at all, so you select **No Fill** for the circle's fill, and **No Line** for the outline. Now we have a completely invisible circle. Nobody even knows it's there!

Right-click the invisible circle, select **Action Settings**, and set the sound played when the circle is clicked on to **Laser**. Make another shape to cover you, and set the sound for that picture to **Whoosh**. Voilà! The user *thinks* he is clicking on you, but the clicking is really on the invisible shapes. (You can use any AutoShape this way. A circle or rectangle easily covers most picture items. If you need something that carefully follows the outline of an item, however, pick one of the freeform drawing tools in the AutoShapes Lines menu.)

145

Setting the Shape

Placing an invisible shape is hard, because you can't see where the edges are. Instead, when you draw it, you should use a thin, visible outline. That way, you can see where you are putting it. After you have it in place and set your Action Settings, you click the drop-down button next to the Line Color button and select **No Line**.

Links Within Text

A text box links the same way as any other object. Just select the text box, right-click it, select **Action Settings**, and so on.

You can also make individual parts of the text have their own links, however. To do this, first select the text box, and then select the text in the box that you want to link. Right-click the selected text to get the pop-up menu. Then set that action just like you would set any other. Text with an action setting will show up in a different color and with an underline, so you can tell it has an action setting.

These Buttons Were Made for Action

There's a nice set of pre-made button shapes designed just for interactivity, lurking there under the **AutoShapes** button. When you click that button, select the **Action Buttons** command, and you will get a menu full of buttons. Put these buttons on your slide like you would any other AutoShape—just drag to draw on the slide where you want the button. You can make them any size. After you place an action button, the Action Settings dialog box will automatically open up. Some of the Action Buttons are specially designed for going to the next slide, previous slide, first slide, or last slide, with pictures on them that look like the controls on a VCR or a CD player. When you place one of these, the right hyperlink is already set for you in the Action Settings dialog box. Just click **OK** to accept the hyperlink.

The action buttons look a little different from most AutoShapes, because they have a built-in, sticking-out button appearance. An action button, by default, appears in the color you have set for fill color, but you can change its color like any other drawn object (see Chapter 7, "WordArt: Your Low-Calorie Logo-Making Friend"). Whatever color you select for the object, the edges will look shaded to create that effect. Because of this effect, action buttons look best without an outline.

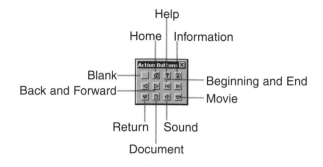

Action Buttons are designed for special commands, like "next slide" or "first slide" or "get donuts." Well, except for the "get donuts" one, alas.

Action Master: Interactivity on Your Slide Master

By putting interactive elements on your Slide Master, you can easily have them on every slide of your presentation. This is a good place for Action Buttons such as the VCR-style buttons and the Help button.

If you don't want one of the buttons on an individual slide, just cover it up with some other object!

The Least You Need to Know

➤ Interactivity lets you make it so that some action occurs when you point to or click certain objects.

➤ To give an object an action, right-click that object in Slide view, and select **Action Settings** from the shortcut menu.

➤ Selecting **Hyperlink To** in the Action Settings dialog box lets you select what is linked to from the menu below.

➤ Clicking **Play Sound** in the Action Settings dialog box lets you pick a sound to play from the menu below. You can play the sound whether you're performing another action or not.

➤ The Action Buttons on the AutoShapes menu are designed specially for interaction.

Look Up in the Sky!: Flying Text and Pictures

In This Chapter

➤ Add animation to your presentation

➤ Make words and pictures appear and disappear when you want

Motion is the greatest invention of all time. Before motion, life was pretty dull. Nothing happened. Everything stayed as it was. All you could do was sit there and watch TV all day, and you couldn't even change the channel.

Now that motion exists, life has improved a lot, because now we can change channels. You can bring that same sort of motion excitement to your onscreen presentations, with text, pictures, and shapes moving all over the place! Used well, it's a real eye-catcher for your key points.

A Presentation with Animation Is Your Destination

The animation capabilities of PowerPoint control how an object is brought onto a slide. Instead of appearing immediately when the slide appears, the object that you animate comes in afterward, appearing in some special fashion. You can have the object appear automatically, or wait until the user clicks a button before appearing. If you have more than one animated object on a slide, you can control the order that they appear in. The object always ends up wherever you have placed it.

The Quick Way: Animation for Lazy Folks

You can animate any object quickly, if you are willing to settle for one of a number of basic, useful animations. To do this, get into Slide view, and select the object that you want to animate. On the **Slide Show** menu, select **Preset Animation**, and a sub-menu will appear with a list of different animations that can be performed on this object.

Certain animation styles work only with text; others work with pictures and shapes only—so you won't ever see all of the styles on the submenu at once. Each style automatically includes an appropriate sound that goes with the animation, such as a *whoosh* sound when you bring an object flying onto the screen. The animation styles include the following (some of which you may need to click the down arrow at the end of the menu to see):

➤ **Off** Removes any animation from the object.

➤ **Drive-In** Makes the object move into place from the right side of the screen.

➤ **Flying** Makes the object move in from the left side of the screen.

➤ **Camera** Makes the center of the object appear first, and then it grows in a circle until it reaches the edges.

➤ **Flash Once** Makes the object appear, disappear for a moment, and then reappear.

➤ **Laser Text** Makes the letters in a text box appear one at a time, flying in from the upper-right corner of the screen.

➤ **Typewriter** Makes the letters in a text box appear one at a time, in place.

➤ **Reverse Order** Makes the bottom item on a list appear, and then the item above it, and so on up to the top of the list. (This is good for Top Ten lists, where you can count down to the top.)

➤ **Drop In** Makes text appear one word at a time, coming down from the top.

➤ **Fly from Top** Brings the object down from the top of the screen.

➤ **Animate Chart** Displays numerical charts one piece of data at a time.

➤ **Wipe Right** Makes the object appear, in place, from left to right, as if a piece of paper that had been covering it up is pulled to the right.

➤ **Dissolve** Treats the object as a bunch of little squares, making the squares appear one at a time until the object is complete.

➤ **Split Vertical Out** Shows the center, fully top-to-bottom, of each word first, and then spreads that out to the edges, one word at a time.

➤ **Appear** Makes the object just appear.

All these animations require clicking the mouse button (or pressing the space bar) to start them. This is very good for showing the presentation to someone, enabling you to control when each new item appears. It's not so good if the viewer is in control, because it encourages the user to just keep clicking the button—next thing you know, users are skipping over slides altogether!

Big, Slow, and Clunky

It takes a lot of computing power to animate a large object, particularly if the object is moving (Fly or Crawl) rather than just appearing in place (Wipe, Dissolve, and so on). Because of this, large objects will move jerkily on slower computers. If you have a Pentium running at 150 megahertz or more, with a good graphics card, you shouldn't worry about it. If your presentation is going to be seen on slower machines, don't move the big stuff.

Animation Demonstration Station

There are two ways to check your animation. One is to go into Slide Show mode, and actually see your show at work. For those looking for the quick and lazy way to do it, however, pull down the **Slide Show** menu and select **Animation Preview**. A small color window will appear over the Slide view, showing the animation (without waiting for your click to start each bit of animation). If you want to see the animation again, just click the window.

Animating for Control Freaks

If you want to have more control over your animations, you can use a lot more animation effects, pick the sound that goes with each animation, pick the order that animations take place in, and set the amount of time to wait between animations. It takes a little more work (Ugh! Work!), but it can give you so much more than the quick method.

To start, pull down the **Slide Show** menu and select **Custom Animation**. A dialog box appears, with a list of all the animated objects on the slide, and four tabs of animation-related settings.

The Custom Animation dialog box is your one-stop, 24-hour animation station!

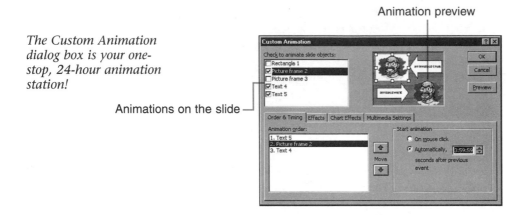

Animation preview

Animations on the slide

Animati-On and Animati-Off

The upper-left corner of the dialog box has a list of all the objects on the current slide. They are named pretty simply, so just by looking at the list, there is no easy way to tell two text boxes apart—they are both called *text*, followed by a number. This is about as handy as naming all your kids *Charlie*. If you click an item in the list, however, the object will appear selected in the preview box at right, so you will be able to tell which one it is.

Next to each name is a check box. If there's a check in the check box, it means that this object is animated. If there is no check, it's not animated. To turn the animation for that object on or off, just click the check box.

Putting the Order in Order

Click the **Order & Timing** tab to see a list of the animated objects on the slide. PowerPoint animates only one thing at a time, and the list shows you the order that animation takes place.

To rearrange the order of these events, select an item whose order you want to change. Click the up-arrow button to move it earlier in the list, or the down-arrow button to move it later on the list.

When?

The Order & Timing tab also lets you select whether animation should happen automatically, or wait for a button push. If you select **On Mouse Click**, it will wait for the push; if you select **Automatically**, that animation will take place immediately after the preceding one finishes. You can choose how long to wait by typing a length of time into the field next to Automatically. This time can be entered as a number of seconds (for example, 317) or as a number of hours, minutes, and seconds, with the numbers separated by colons (1:17:39). You can set the wait for as long as one second short of twenty-four hours. (And you can imagine how relieved people will be

152

when the next object animates after twenty-three hours, fifty-nine minutes, fifty-nine seconds. "Thank goodness!" they will say, "I thought I was going to have to wait a full day for that next animation!")

What?

Choosing an object and turning animation on is like telling a child to "Go do something!" You haven't told it what to do, and it probably won't think of something by itself. (And if it did, you probably wouldn't like it.)

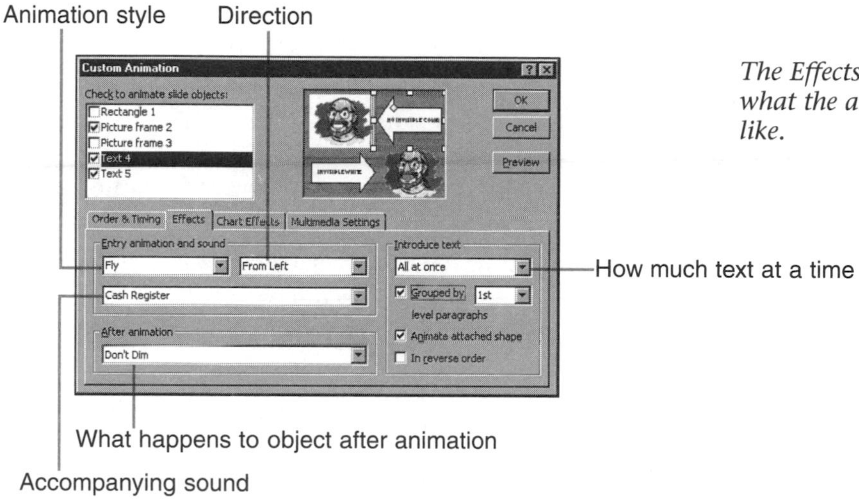

Animation style   Direction

The Effects tab controls what the animation looks like.

How much text at a time

What happens to object after animation

Accompanying sound

The **Effects** tab has all the settings you need. The Entry Animation and Sound area contains three drop-down lists. The top one has the style of movement. Click the drop-down button for it, and you will see a long list. The types of movement are as follows:

➤ **Appear** Makes the object just appear in place.

➤ **Fly** Makes the object move into place quickly.

➤ **Blinds** Reveal the object as if you were opening venetian blinds in front of it.

➤ **Box** Shows the object from the edges to the center (*in*) or from the center to the edges (*out*).

➤ **Checkerboard** Treats the object as a bunch of little squares and wipes each square into place.

➤ **Crawl** Is the same as Fly, only slower.

➤ **Dissolve** Treats the object as small squares, which appear in random order.

➤ **Flash Once** Makes the object appear, disappear, and reappear in the same spot.

➤ **Peek** Moves the object in from the edge of the object's box.

153

➤ **Random Bars**   Puts up lines from the object until it is whole. (Strange. Most people I know who go to random bars tell the bartender to line them up until they go to pieces—but I suppose that's the difference between lush animation and animated lushes.)

➤ **Spiral**   Brings the object moving onto the screen along a spiral path, getting larger as it does.

➤ **Split**   Starts showing the object in its horizontal or vertical center, and then spreads out to the edges.

➤ **Stretch**   Starts with the object squished small and grows it until it's full size.

➤ **Strips**   Reveals the object starting from one corner and heading to its opposite corner.

➤ **Swivel**   Causes the object to repeatedly grow and shrink from side to side, making it look as though it is a flat item suspended by a string.

➤ **Wipe**   Starts revealing the object from one edge and spreads to the opposite edge.

➤ **Zoom**   Makes the object grow (*in*) or shrink (*out*) into place, making it look like it's moving toward or away from the viewer.

This menu contains two other choices. Choosing **No Effect** means that no animation takes place, and choosing **Random Effects** means that the computer gets to pick which effect is done, and may choose differently each time the slide is shown.

After you select the type of movement, check the direction drop list. For some types of movement, this option is unavailable and the box will be grayed out. For others, you can use it to choose a movement direction, such as picking whether something flies in from the left, right, top, or bottom.

Action Words

Folks in the presentation business refer to animations where the object is moving as *moves* and animation where the object appears in place as *reveals*.

What Does a Spiral Sound Like, Anyway?

The field below the Effect field lets you pick the sound that goes along with the animation. If you want it to be silent, pick **[No Sound]**. Otherwise, you can pick one of the sounds listed, or you can pick **Other Sound** (the last option on the list), which will display a list of sound files for you to select from. Unless you have created your own sound file, however, there won't be anything interesting for you to pick. (I tell you about creating your own sounds in Chapter 17, "Sound Advice on Sound.")

After the Thrill Is Gone

Eventually, the animation is over, and the object is where it's supposed to be. Now, you can just leave it lying there, you can make it disappear, or you can change its color. The After Animation field on the **Effects** tab lets you pick what happens.

To just leave the object lying there, like wrapping paper on Christmas, click the drop-down menu and select **Don't Dim**. To make it disappear immediately, select **Hide After Animation**. To have it wait until the next mouse click and then disappear, select **Hide On Next Mouse Click**.

Also on the menu are a bunch of colors, and a choice to let you pick even **More Colors**. Choosing these will make your object change color after the animation.

Changing the object's color sounds like a pretty weird thing to do, and in many cases, it is. If you choose a color, the whole object changes to that color. If you do this to a picture, you end up with just a rectangle of color—unless the picture has an invisible color, which will stay invisible, so you are left with a picture-shaped blob.

But changing the color of text after it appears can be pretty cool. If you are animating a list (and I will get to how to animate text in a second), this lets you bring up one point, show it, and then make it dim while the next point comes up. This way, the current point is always brightest on the screen, while the previous points are still visible!

Nifty Disappearing Tricks

If you want the disappearance of an object to be an event, don't make it disappear at all! Instead, cover the object with a rectangle the same color as the background. Animate this rectangle into place just after you animate the object into place. For example, if you Dissolve the rectangle, it looks like the object is dissolving away!

By changing black text to gray after animation, the most recently animated text stands out.

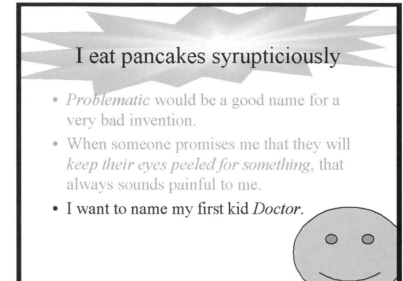

Moving Words: Words of Motion (Not Emotion)

A number of special settings apply only to objects with text, whether they are titles, text boxes, or text that is connected to a shape or picture. These are available in the Introduce text area of the Effects tab on the Custom Animation dialog box.

The Introduce Text list revealed!

The first field here is a drop-down menu that lets you select how much text is introduced at a time. Your choices are as follows:

➤ **By Letter** Animates on the first letter, then the second letter, then the third, and so on.

➤ **By Word** Brings on the whole first word in one animated step, then the second, and so on.

➤ **All at Once** This sounds like it should bring the text all at once, right? Well, that's true if your text is only one paragraph. It really should be called *By Paragraph*, because it brings on the first paragraph, then the second, and so on.

If you check the **In Reverse Order** check box, the final letter, word, or paragraph will appear first, and then each preceding one until it reaches the first. If you have people in your company who think backward—Admit it! You do!—this is good for giving presentations to them.

Check the **Animate Attached Shape** check box if the text is on a shape object, and you want the object zoomed in just as the text is. Otherwise, the shape will be on the slide from the very beginning, waiting for the text to appear.

Moving up the Chart: Chart Effects

In the world of PowerPoint objects, charts are the privileged class with their own tab on the Custom Animation dialog box. This is for graph-type charts; lowly organizational charts need not apply.

Select the **Chart Effects** tab to decide which parts of the charts get animated. If you check the **Animate Grid and Legend** check box, the grid and legend appear as the first step of the animation. If you don't check either, those things are onscreen from when the slide first appears.

The things that really get animated on your graph are the bars, points, lines, or however you present your data. The drop-down **Introduce Chart Elements** list enables you to pick what order the data appears in. The choices are as follows:

➤ **All at Once** Animates them all at once.

➤ **By Series** Animates all the same colored data at once.

➤ **By Category** Animates the data from left to right, a group at a time.

➤ **By Element in Series** Animates each of the first color, from left to right, and then goes on to the next color, and so on.

➤ **By Element in Category** Animates each piece of data, from left to right, one at a time.

The other settings on the Chart Effects tab are the same as settings on the Effects tab, letting you pick the animation style, direction, sound, and what happens to the data after being animated.

157

Chart Choices

Bar-style charts look good using a Wipe in the direction that the bar is going (right for bar charts, up for column charts). It makes it look like the bar is growing to the data point. Similarly, line charts look best with a Wipe Right, making it look like the line is being drawn.

This chart is being animated by series, with a Wipe Up. The East series has already appeared, the West series is shown growing to its points, and the North series will begin when the West series has completed.

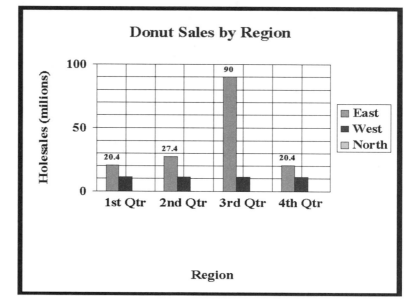

Checking the Animation

To test your animation while still using the Custom Animation dialog box, just click the **Preview** button. The preview box will show all the animation for the slide, straight through, without waiting for any mouse clicks.

When you are happy with what you have got, click the **OK** button to make the changes official, and then go into the Slide Show view to see it at work full size.

Hey! What About the Other Tab?

The Multimedia Settings tab on the Custom Animation dialog box is used when displaying video (movies) in your presentation. As such, the information on that is just down the block a few pages, in Chapter 16, "Movies in PowerPoint: Like TV, Only Smaller."

The Least You Need to Know

➤ To quickly animate an object, select it in Slide view, pull down the **Slide Show** menu, and select one of the animation styles listed in the **Preset Animation** submenu.

➤ The **Slide Show**, **Animation Preview** command opens up a small window on your screen. Click this window to see the slide's animation.

➤ PowerPoint can animate only one object at a time.

➤ To get more control over animation effects, select **Custom Animation** from the **Slide Show** menu to get the Custom Animation dialog box.

➤ To select what object's animation you are working on, click the object name on the Check To Animate Slide Objects list.

➤ When displaying your presentation, you may have to click the mouse button after an object is animated to start the next object. The lower right of the Order & Timing tab is used to set if the slideshow waits for a mouse click before animating, or if it waits a fixed period of time.

➤ The left side of the Effects tab lets you select the animation style, the accompanying sound, and what happens to the object after it is animated. The right side has special controls for text animation and lets you pick the order in which the text appears.

RIGHT ON TIME, LITTLE DUDE...

Chapter 15

Tricky Transitions and Terrific Timing

In This Chapter

➤ Pick how one slide disappears and the next one appears

➤ Set a sound to go with the slide change

➤ Set the slides to change automatically after a fixed amount of time, thus saving much wear and tear on the mouse button

➤ Twiddle your thumbs like a professional

You see transitions all the time on televisions, it's how they get from one scene to another. Sometimes you just see one shot, and then the next shot. That's a transition, although a boring one. When the commercial ends, and the screen is black for a moment before the Enterprise fades into view, that's a transition. When a checkerboard pattern comes over Ralph Malph's face and when the pattern goes back, we're at Pinky Tuscadero's Demolition Derby; that's a transition. When Tom Hanks puts on a dress to masquerade as "Buffy," that's ... well, actually, that's transvestitism, which is different.

Transitions: What They Are, Why You Want Them, and How You Get Them

Each slide on a presentation has a transition associated with it, which tells PowerPoint how to change the display *from* the preceding slide *to* this slide. If you want to set the transition *from* this slide *to* the next slide, do it on the next slide!

When it comes time to work out your transitions, use the Slide Sorter view. This way, you can see the slide you're working on as well as the next slide, and you can easily hop from slide to slide to set the transitions.

From Slide Sorter view, right-click the slide whose transition you want to set, and select the **Slide Transition** command on the shortcut menu. A Slide Transition dialog box appears, full of all sorts of meaningful things, plus a dog (or, at least, a picture of one).

The Slide Transition dialog box. The dog, like most dogs, doesn't mean anything.

Transition Decision

The menu to select the type of transition that you want is directly under the dog, which may not be the cleanest of places to be. Click the arrow, and you find a list of different transition styles, many of which have a choice of direction (such as Cover Up and Cover Right, which are the same style with two different directions). Some of these styles are similar to animation styles. The following styles are available:

➤ **No Transition** Means that the slide just appears in place, with no special effects.

➤ **Blinds** Replaces the slide as if the new slide was on opening venetian blinds behind the old one.

➤ **Box** Replaces the old slide from the edges to the center (*in*) or from the center to the edges (*out*).

➤ **Checkerboard** Treats the slide as a bunch of little squares and wipes each square into place.

➤ **Cover** Makes it look like this slide is being slid across in front of the old one.

➤ **Cut** Is the same as No Transition.

➤ **Cut through Black** Replaces the old slide with a black slide for an instant, and then puts up the new slide. The black isn't really visible, but this may look a little better than just Cut on projection screens.

➤ **Dissolve** Treats the new slide as a lot of little squares that it displays one at a time.

➤ **Fade through Black** Makes the old slide fade away until it's completely black, then the black fades into the new slide. (This is a good way to mark the end of one topic and the start of another one.)

➤ **Random Bars** Puts up short lines from the slide until it is whole.

➤ **Split** Treats the new slide as two halves, wiping in opposite directions.

➤ **Strips** Is a diagonal wipe.

➤ **Uncover** Makes it look like the old slide is being pulled away to reveal the new one.

➤ **Wipe** Replaces the slide a bit at a time, moving from one side to the other.

➤ **Random Transition** Randomly picks a style and direction each time the transition takes place.

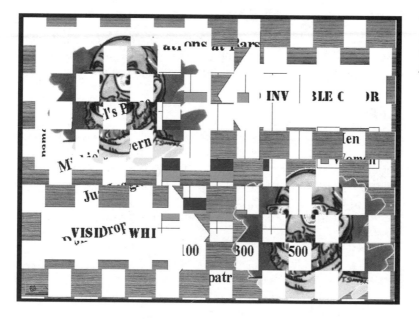

The Checkerboard Across transition is starting to reveal a slide with a graph.

When you select the transition you want, the picture of the dog turns into a picture of a key, enabling you to preview the type of transition that you selected. Exactly what this presentation is that involves a dog and a key, I cannot tell you. Select another transition, and the dog replaces the key.

163

Handy Transition List

The Slide Sorter toolbar has a handy drop-down list of the transition types, letting you pick the style of transition for a slide quickly. If you don't see this toolbar, pull down the **View** menu; and from the **Toolbars** menu, select **Slide Sorter**

Slow Change or Fast Change

Below the transition style field is a set of radio buttons, which let you choose between **Slow**, **Medium**, and **Fast**. This sets how quickly the transition takes place. When you select one of these, the dog/key transition takes place again at that speed.

Something Not to Use

Below the transition Effect area is a set of check boxes that let you set whether the program waits for the user to click before showing this slide, or whether it just waits until a selectable number of seconds after the last slide is done. You can set these things here if you want—but you shouldn't want to. Leave it set to waiting for the mouse click. I show you a better trick for setting the waiting time later in the chapter. (I'm teaching you all the powerful tricks. Remember to use them for good, not for evil.)

Listen to the Transition

Using the Sound area of the dialog box, you can pick a sound to accompany the transition. Click the drop-down arrow and select a sound from the ones listed, or select **Other Sound** to bring up a file explorer that will let you find the sound file you want. (For information on creating your own sound files, see Chapter 17, "Sound Advice on Sound.")

After you have selected a sound, the Loop Until Next Sound check box becomes clickable. If you click it, the sound will repeat like a kid wanting to know whether he can get an ice cream cone, please please please please please please? It will stop when another sound appears. (If you don't select this box, the sound just plays one time.)

Sound Ceaser

All the sound selectors include a choice called **Stop Previous Sound**. This lets you stop a repeating transition sound without starting a new one!

(Dialog) Box Out

After you finish picking your transition settings, you can click the **Apply** button to use them on the selected slide, or you can pick **Apply to All** to use them on all the slides. Using the same settings on all the slides is not that bad an idea. Watching one different transition after another can get tiresome after a while and even distracts from the point you are presenting.

When you do this, the transition will quickly be displayed on the selected slide in the Slide Sorter view.

This symbol means this slide has a transition set.

Transition being demonstrated after closing dialog box.

The Slide Sorter view gives you handy transition information at a glance.

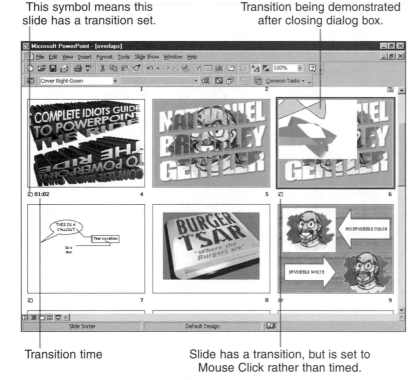

Transition time

Slide has a transition, but is set to Mouse Click rather than timed.

Time for Timing!

Estimating time is not a human being's greatest ability. How often has someone said to you, "I'll be with you in a minute," only to take a vast number of minutes, combined into a large block of time? How many times were you supposed to get a date home by 11, but when you checked your watch, it had suddenly become next Tuesday? How many times have you opened the door just as someone was about to knock? That has nothing to do with the topic at hand, but man, is that spooky!

Trying to estimate how long it will take you to present a slide, or how long you need between animations on a single slide, is tricky when you're just staring at some dialog box. That's the main reason for the *Rehearse Timings* feature. (That, and the fact that they wanted a feature name that's an anagram for *Her Steaming Sire*, which is what you often have to face if you don't bring your young date home next Tuesday rather than at 11.)

Running the Timer

To start setting your timings, pull down the **Slide Show** menu, and select **Rehearse Timings**. The slideshow will start from the beginning. After the first slide is up, however, you will see one difference from a normal slide show: a Rehearsal control panel that appears onscreen.

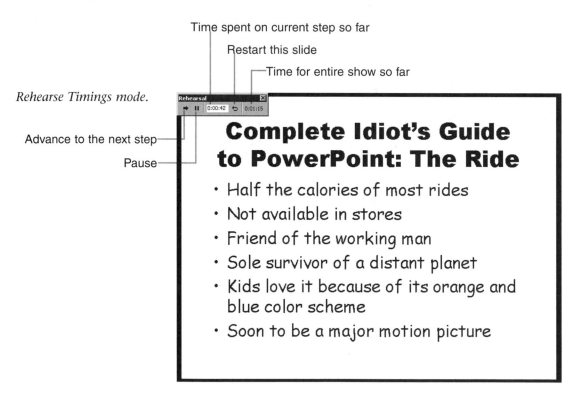

Time spent on current step so far

Restart this slide

Time for entire show so far

Rehearse Timings mode.

Advance to the next step

Pause

Complete Idiot's Guide to PowerPoint: The Ride

- Half the calories of most rides
- Not available in stores
- Friend of the working man
- Sole survivor of a distant planet
- Kids love it because of its orange and blue color scheme
- Soon to be a major motion picture

When your slide comes up, stare at it for as long as you want it to appear in your show, and then click the **Advance** button. If you are planning to talk while you show your presentation to people, give your talk while doing this—that will let you know how long to wait. If you are counting on someone else seeing the presentation and reading the content to themselves, try reading it yourself, out loud, slowly, and use that to determine when it's time to move on.

Make a Whoopsy?

If you mess up while giving your speech, reading it out loud, or you want to restart the slide for some other reason, just click the **Repeat** button. The timing will start over from the beginning of the slide, so you can keep doing it until you get it right.

When Your Good Time Is Over

After you have run through the entire presentation, the Rehearsal control pad goes away. If your last slide is still showing, click it once. A dialog box appears, telling you how long your whole presentation was, and asking Do you want to record the new slide timings and use them when you view the slide show? Click **Yes**, and all the transition and animation timings will be set!

Mixing Untimed in with Timed

If you want most of your presentation to be timed, but a few things to wait for a mouse click, go ahead and use the Rehearse Timings feature, and then go back and use the Slide Transition dialog box to set the slides you want to pause to wait for the mouse click.

The Least You Need to Know

➤ A transition is the method used to move from one slide to another. Transition settings include the way the replacement is animated, the sound that accompanies it, and whether it takes a mouse click or waiting a period of time to trigger it.

➤ To set the transition settings for a slide, go into Slide Sorter view, right-click the slide, and select **Slide Transition**.

➤ Pull down the drop-down menu under the dog to select a transition style. The transition style will be displayed using the dog picture and a key picture. Under the transition style, you can select the speed of the transition.

➤ It's best to leave the **On Mouse Click** check box checked, and set the screen timings using the Rehearse Timings feature.

➤ To set the time lags on all your slides, as well as on the animations, select the **Slide Show**, **Rehearse Timing** command.

➤ Step through your slideshow using the **Advance** arrow button on the Rehearse control panel. However long you wait before advancing, that's how long the wait will be when the slideshow is playing. (If you mess up your timing on a slide, click the **Repeat** button and try again.) Be sure to consider how long you will be talking about the item displayed and how long it will take people to read the text shown.

Movies in PowerPoint: Like TV, Only Smaller

Movies are very useful. These onscreen bits (often referred to as *video*) are great for showing things that move, like trains or chimps. Or, if the camera making the movie moves, you can use it to show all the sides of something that doesn't move, like mountains or Uncle Oswald. You could hold the camera still and shoot video of something that doesn't move, but then you would probably be better off just using a normal photograph or, in the case of Uncle Oswald, not using anything at all.

Some Warnings About Movies

Before you start gearing up to fill your presentation with movies, you have to be aware of the problems with it. These won't be big problems if you are doing this on your own computer, but they will be big problems if you want to use this presentation on someone else's.

Problem One: Moving Movies

Even though the movies in presentations seem small, only taking up a part of the screen and a few seconds of time, they are very big on your disk. One 10-second clip can sometimes fill up a floppy disk. Five minutes of video that only take up a tenth of the screen will take someone using a modem more than an hour to download. The files are big. This can be a problem even if you aren't trying to move it to someone else's machine, because your hard disk only has so much space on it.

Problem Two: Projector Problems

In the same way that Beta tape won't fit in a VHS player, or a 35 millimeter film won't fit in a 16 millimeter projector, or a new trick won't fit an old dog, your movie may not be able to play on someone else's machine. This is because the other person

Different Formats

The different video file formats use different **codecs**. A codec (short for **compression/decompression**) is the method used to store video in the least necessary disk space.

doesn't have the computer equivalent of the "right projector," which would be the right *driver*. A driver is a program that tells the computer how to deal with a certain device or a certain type of file. In this case, the driver tells the computer how to understand the movie file. Because there are many different movie file formats, there are many different drivers, and most computers won't have them all installed. If you use the Video For Windows format, most PCs that are set up for multimedia will be able to understand it. (You can recognize a Video For Windows file because of the .avi at the end of the filename.) If your file uses one of the other formats, however, the odds are good that someone else's PC won't have a driver for it.

Problem Three: Slow-Go Is a No-No

Computers with slow processors or without high-quality video cards can process video very slowly. This can mean either a movie that looks like it's in slow-motion or a movie that looks very jerky because a lot of the individual pictures that make up the movie (the *frames*) are being skipped over. If you have such a machine, you will see the problem quickly. If you have a good machine but share your presentation with people who have bad machines, then they will see the problem.

Mommy, Where Do Movies Come From?

The stork doesn't bring movie files, unfortunately. Even if he did, they would probably just be movies about things that interest storks, such as migrating, eating fish, or the New York Stork Exchange. If you want people-interesting movies, you have basically three choices: buying them, getting them for free, or making them yourself.

Buying Movies for Less Fun and Less Profit

Just as there are clip-art disks full of pictures, there are also disks full of movies (and ones with some movies, some pictures, some sounds—a multimedia smorgasbord). There aren't as many of these out there, however, and they are of limited usefulness. Check out the contents of any such disk before you buy it to make sure that it has what you need on it. Because movies take up so much room, they can't put something-for-all-occasions on it the way they *try* to do with some of the picture disks.

At best, however, this can only get you a fairly generic shot. You may be able to get a short clip of planes flying, or a flower growing, or an animation of the earth rotating; but if you want a specific plane, or a specific flower, or a specific earth, your odds of finding it are slim.

Free Movies: Two of My Favorite Words, Together

Movies are digital files, and you would figure that any worth having would be out on the Internet. You would be right, but there aren't nearly so many movies as you might expect. People aren't using a lot of movies in their Web pages, because they are so slow to transfer. Only two sorts of movies are really plentiful out there, and you can't really use either of them. The first type is, umm, "adult" movies; and while those do get attention, they are generally not appropriate in presentations. The other is clips from TV shows, movies, and music videos; most of these are made by people who have the equipment to make them, but not the legal right to do so. Don't use these—your *presen*tation might turn into a *prison*tation!

Microsoft offers some useful clip-art movies that you can get over the Web. Pull down the **Insert** menu, and from the **Movies and Sounds** submenu, select **Movie from Gallery**. The Clip Gallery dialog box opens, with only the Motion Clips tab displayed for you. Click the **Clips Online** button. (If a message appears letting you know that you are going to be using the Internet, click **OK** to answer it.) Your Web browser opens bringing up Clip Gallery Live, a site for free pictures, sounds, and videos. This site contains its own instructions for downloading clips, including a link there offering first-time users help. Click this link, and you are guided through finding and getting what you want based on the type of media you want (video, of course) and the category.

You can see only smaller, simplified versions of the videos before downloading them. The Microsoft videos are mostly short cartoons, good for humorous highlights that you can use with business topics.

After you have downloaded the clip, it will be added to your Clip Art Gallery on the Motion Clips tab, handy for not only PowerPoint but also other Microsoft applications.

Click here if you want to get clips from the Web.

The Motion Clips tab of the Clip Art Gallery displays the first frame of each movie in the gallery.

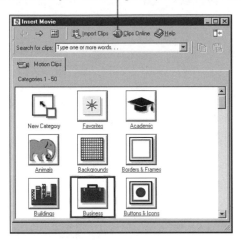

Movie Making: You Can Become You-Nited Artists!

If you have a camcorder, you can shoot whatever movie you need. So you have got the perfect movie that you want, but it's on video tape, not in the computer. How do you get it in there? Well, you could tear the tape out of the cartridge and stuff it into your floppy drive slot—but all you would end up with is a stuffed-up floppy drive.

What you really need is a *video capture card*, a device you install in your computer that you can connect to your VCR. The card takes the signal coming from the VCR and converts it into a movie file. Video capture cards cost anywhere from a couple hundred dollars up into the thousands. The cheaper ones can only make smaller movies that use up a small part of the screen, but that may be all you want anyway!

If you just want to make movies of things around your desk, particularly if you want to show yourself talking to the presentation viewers, you can get by with a simple digital video camera. Starting at prices under $100, you can get a digital desktop video camera that lets you create small movies. These little cameras are a lot of fun, particularly if you like watching yourself on the screen while you work! (They are also really handy for video teleconferencing.)

Compu-Toons

You can also create your own computer-animated movies! Most of the time people talk about computer animation, they are talking about things like *A Bug's Life*, where entire 3D worlds are designed on a computer, and then the computer generates films of things moving in that world. This sort of animation is called *modeling*, and to do it you will need some modeling software with animation capabilities (such as *TrueSpace* or *Ray Dream Studio*). Don't expect to do anything as complicated as *A Bug's Life* unless you have a lot of computers, a lot of friends, a lot of time, and a lot of talent, but there are plenty of examples of nice short pieces done by one person with some spare time.

Self-portrait: a QuickCam digital desktop video camera films itself in a mirror.

Another type of computer animation is *morphing*, which involves changing the shape of things on a picture or turning one object into another. If you have seen one of those ads where a cow turns into a glass of milk, or an unshaved man turns into a shaggy dog, or a car turns into an alley, you have seen morphing at work. It's not that hard to learn to use a morphing program well enough to take a photo of yourself and give yourself pointy Spock ears; it's only a little harder to use it to make a movie of your ears growing the points on them.

Finally, a number of programs let you use the computer to create more traditional animation, combining a series of individual drawings into a movie.

Adding a Movie

To insert a movie onto your slide, go into Slide view and view the slide where you want the movie to start. (As you will see soon, you can have a movie run over several slides.) Pull down the **Insert** menu and select the **Movies and Sounds** submenu. There, you will see two commands that let you insert movies. **Movie from Gallery** opens up the Clip Art Gallery to the Motion Clips tab, where you can select any movie that's already on the Videos tab by right-clicking it and selecting **Insert**. **Movie from File** opens up a file browser, enabling you to pick any video file from any of the disks in your system. Double-click the filename to add it to your slide.

When you do this, PowerPoint asks you `Do you want your movie to play automat-ically in the slide show?` Click **Yes** to have the movie run when the slide first appears, or **No** to have the movie play only when you click it.

The first frame of your movie appears on your slide. As with any box, you can click it to see the sizing handles or to drag it.

173

Resizing Your Movie

Don't.

As with a picture, the movie appears at its *natural size*. Making a movie larger won't make it any more detailed, it will just look grainy and may display more slowly. Making a movie smaller will lose detail and won't speed it up at all.

Having said that, you can resize it if you really want to. Just use the sizing handles.

Roll the Picture: Interactive Activation

A movie can start playing in three ways. You can have it start playing when the viewer clicks it, when the mouse passes over it, or automatically. ("Mouse passes over" should not be confused with "mouse's Passover", which is a holiday for Jewish mice.)

To have a click or a mouse pass-over start it, right-click the movie and select the **Action Settings** command. The Action Settings dialog box appears, with separate tabs for Mouse Click and Mouse Over settings. Select **Object Action** on the appropriate tab. The drop-down menu under that option will now be usable. Because **Play** is the only choice on that menu, however, it will already be selected for you.

Most of the action settings are designed for other types of objects. Your choices for movies are to either play or not play.

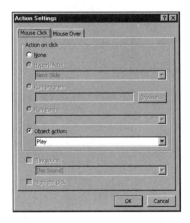

Go to the other tab and make sure that **None** is selected, so that you don't have conflicting settings.

Roll the Picture: Activation Automation

As if the overworked Custom Animation dialog box didn't already have enough to do, it's stuck with the automatic control of movies. To bring up the dialog box, right-click the movie and select **Custom Animation**. The dialog box opens, with the Multimedia Settings tab selected for you.

Use the Order & Timing tab to set when the animation starts, and the Multimedia Settings tab to set when it stops.

Click the **Play Using Animation Order** check box to show that you want the animation controls to start the movie. Click the **Order & Timing** tab, and you can select **On Mouse Click** (which starts the movie on the next mouse click after the previous object was animated), or **Automatically**, which starts the movie a fixed number of seconds after the last object was animated. To see more about how these work, check out Chapter 14, "Look up in the Sky: Flying Text and Pictures." (That chapter also tells you how to arrange the animation order, which it affects when your movie starts if you also have animated objects on the page. It also has moving prose, scintillating illustrations, and a lot of punctuation!)

Check This Out

Animating Movies Works... Sort Of

You can use the Effects tab to set how the movie appears on your slide. However, only the first frame gets animated. After the animation is done, the movie starts playing.

When Will It Ever End?!

Clicking back on the **Multimedia Settings** tab lets you set how long the movie keeps playing. If you select **Pause Slide Show**, the next slide won't show up until this movie is done. (Animations can still continue while this goes on. If you want, you can animate pieces of popcorn flying at the screen while the movie is showing, just like a real movie! However, anything you animate will pass *behind* the movie area, never *in front* of it.)

Choosing **Continue Slide Show** lets you pick one of two Stop Playing choices. Choosing **After Current Slide** means that the movie is stopped when it's time for the next slide. If the movie isn't over, tough luck for it! Choosing **After (number field) Slides** will wait until not only the end of this slide, but for however many more slides you enter into the number field. That's right, the slides will go away, but the movie will just keep being seen, like some demented dinner guest who decides to stay for the week whether you like it or not!

After the Movie Is Over

The Multimedia Settings tab has a **Hide While Not Playing** check box that will make the movie appear only when it starts playing, rather than having the opening frame displayed while waiting for it to play.

There's also a button marked **More Options**, which is about as uninformative as a button name can possibly be. Click it, and the **Movie Options** dialog box appears.

If the real world had a Movie Options dialog box, you could turn on **Free popcorn** *and turn off* **Crying babies in the audience!**

Movie Options Shortcut

To get to the Movie Options quickly at any time, right-click the movie in Slide view and select **Edit Movie Object**.

This dialog box has two check boxes. Check on **Loop until stopped**, and the movie will repeat over and over until something stops it (such as moving to the next slide). This is handy if you have a movie that's designed to repeat, like a cartoon of someone juggling where repeating it makes it looks like he keeps juggling. It's also good for driving the viewer nuts, if you have a movie that is annoying or distracting.

The **Rewind movie when done playing** check box has a goofy name. After all, the movie is a file, so what is there to rewind? Is it going to make your hard disk spin backward? No, actually if you check this, the first frame of the movie will be shown after the movie is over. If you don't check it, the last frame shows.

Movie by Design: Slides with Built-In Movie Space

A couple of AutoLayout slide designs include a place for a movie. You will find these designs by clicking the **New Slide** button and scrolling toward the bottom of the AutoLayout display. These layouts have a picture of a movie *clapper*—that hinged board that someone claps in front of the camera before they shoot each scene of a movie. (The purpose of this is to scare the bejeebers out of anyone on the set who isn't paying attention.)

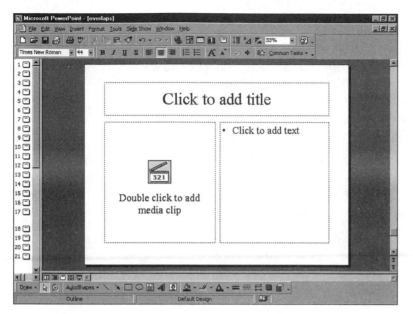

This slide suggests you double-click to insert a media clip, but it really means "movie".

If you double-click the media clip area of the slide, PowerPoint opens up the Clip Gallery, and when you select your movie, it will appear in the Media Clip space.

The Least You Need to Know

➤ Movie files take up a lot of space and showing them takes a lot of computing power. Keep your movies small and short, particularly if you are distributing them to others. PowerPoint can play movie files of a number of different formats, but if you want your presentation to run on other machines, you are best off with the Video For Windows format (.avi files).

➤ There are a lot of existing movies in formats that PowerPoint can read. You can also transfer movies from video tape using a *video capture card*, or record movies directly on to your hard disk using a *digital video camera*. There is also software that lets you make computer-animated movies.

➤ To insert a movie file onto your slide, use the **Insert, Movies and Sounds, Movie from File** command. To use a movie file from the Clip Art Gallery, use the **Insert, Movies and Sounds, Movie from Gallery** command. Clicking the **Clips Online** on the Clip Art Gallery lets you copy free movies from Microsoft's Web site into the gallery.

➤ To have a mouse click start the movie, right-click the movie in Slide view, select **Action Settings**, pick the **Mouse Click** tab on the dialog box that appears, and select **Object Action**. To have the movie start playing automatically, right-click the movie and select the **Custom Animation** command.

➤ In the Custom Animation dialog box, select the **Order & Timing** tab to select when the movie starts and the **Multimedia Settings** tab to set when the movie ends.

➤ On the Multimedia Settings tab, choosing **Pause Slide Show** means that the slide won't be over until the movie ends. Choosing **Continue Slide Show** lets you pick between stopping the movie when the slide ends or continuing the movie on to other slides.

 # Sound Advice on Sound

In This Chapter

➤ Record your own sounds

➤ Add sound effects to your animations, transitions, and button presses, until your presentation is cacophonous!

➤ Record a narration to accompany your presentation

➤ Play sounds right off of a CD to accompany your presentation

Sound can take many forms, and serve many purposes. There's music, whose charms have been noted for their savage breast-soothing properties. There is the spoken word, which is so powerful that it can cause a war, or stop one. There are the sounds of nature, like the whipping of the wind, the crackling of the fire, and the chirp of the cricket, all of which reminds us of the beauty and wonder around us. And there is the din of the loose computer fan that has been rattling for 16 chapters now and it won't go away, no, won't go away until it's driven me mad! But I won't let it, for my invisible friend Jojo and I have crafted a plan.

Things to Spend Money On: Your PC Sound System

To use sound in your presentations, you need a computer that can play sound. Otherwise, all your hear is the unending torture of the rattling computer fan that we can prove, yes prove, is under the command of the CIA!

These days, most PCs are sold as being *multimedia ready*, which means that the sound system is already built in. If you are not so lucky, you can add one. What you need is a *sound card*, which the computer uses to create and shape the sound, and some computer speakers (or, if you don't want everyone to hear, a pair of headphones will do fine). You can get these things as a kit for less than $100, and then all you need is a few spare hours to install the card and its software, much of which time will be spent cursing because although it's supposed to be easy to do, it rarely works out that way.

If you are recording your own sounds, you will also need a microphone. There's a microphone connector in the back of your sound card. There's also a *line in* connector, which you can connect to your stereo if you want to record something from there.

If you are going to be playing CD audio, you will need a CD-ROM drive, and it will have to be properly connected to your sound card—which it probably is if you bought a multimedia system. (If you install your own sound card, you will just have finished putting your whole system back together when you first notice the cable that's supposed to connect the CD-ROM drive to the sound card.)

Recording: Yes, You Really Do Sound Like That

To record your own sound, whether it be a short speech extolling your product or capturing the sound of a whirring fan to use as evidence of a CIA plot, you have to tell PowerPoint that you are inserting the sound onto a slide. This might be a lie; you might be using the sound as part of an animation or transition, which is different from making it part of the slide itself. However, PowerPoint doesn't get mad if you lie to it.

To start off, pull down the **Insert** menu, and from the **Movies and Sounds** submenu, select **Record Sound**. The Record Sound dialog box appears, with a simple set of recording controls.

The recording buttons have a triangle, a square, and a circle—simple, yet meaningless symbols.

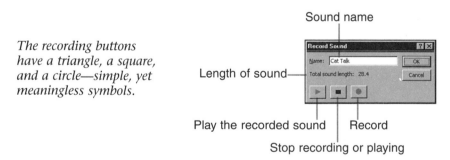

Sound name

Length of sound

Play the recorded sound

Record

Stop recording or playing

Get your microphone in position and click **Record** to start the recording. When you're done, click the **Stop** button, and then on the **Play** button to check your sound. If you don't like it, click **Cancel** and start over (but you never will sound as good as you do in your own head). If you do like it, type a name for your sound into the name field, and then click the **OK** button.

A sound icon, a little picture of a speaker, will appear on the slide. If you keep this picture in your presentation, when the user clicks it, he will hear the recording. (In fact, if you double-click it in Slide view, you will hear the sound.) There are other ways you can start the sound playing in the slideshow, which I show you soon. And you can hear the sound while you are in Slide view just by double-clicking this!

Sound Sound Bad?

Adjust how loud and how good your recordings will be by clicking the **Start** button and selecting **Control Panel** from the **Settings** submenu. Double-click the **Multimedia** icon in the window that appears. The lower half of the **Audio** tab controls recording; the exact controls depends on your audio setup and which version of Windows you are using. Realize that the higher the audio quality you use, the more disk space your audio takes up.

Slammin' Down That Slide Sound

There are a number of ways for you to trigger the sound you have recorded. You can have it so that the user clicks a sound icon to hear it, or the user clicks something else to hear it, or it plays automatically during the transition, animation, or some other point during the display of the slide. You can also make it play in all of those situations, causing an awful and annoying din!

Click the Speaker Picture

To have the user click the picture of the speaker to hear the sound, you really don't have to do anything except move the picture where you want it to be. It's already set up to wait for the mouse click.

You can do anything to that speaker picture that you can do to a normal picture, including resize it.

Sound Tricks You have Already Learned

If you have read earlier chapters of this book, you have already seen a drop-down list of sound effects that you can select sounds from. The sound you have just recorded is automatically added to that list, so you can select it when choosing your sound. You can use the sound in the following circumstances:

➤ Having the sound go off when a certain object is clicked, or having it go off when the mouse passes over that object. To see how to do this, read Chapter 13, "Click Here for Interactivity."

➤ A sound effect accompanying an animation. This information is in Chapter 14, "Look up in the Sky: Flying Text and Pictures."

➤ A transition sound effect. Check out Chapter 15, "Tricky Transitions and Terrific Timing."

If you are using the sound for any one of these, you aren't going to need the speaker picture. Click it and press the **Delete** key to get rid of it!

Playing the Sound Automatically

You can use the animation features to trigger the sound automatically, as part of the slide's sequence. To do this, you need to still have the speaker picture—but dagnabbit, you really don't want the speaker showing up on your slide! Is there some bizarre incantation or arcane ritual that will rid you of it?

No need to switch to some antiquated religion! Just drag the speaker off the slide, and leave it either to the right or the left of the slide. You will still see it in slide view, but it won't show up on the Slide Show view!

To set when the sound will appear, right-click the speaker picture and select **Custom Animation**. That's right, this all-purpose command can trigger your sound as well!

The Custom Animation dialog box displays the Multimedia Settings tab. Click the **Play using animation order** check box, and the options below it will become selectable. This lets you set when the sound ends. The sound will end automatically when the sound is over, of course, but you can tell the sound to shut up before that! Choosing **Pause Slide Show** means that the next slide will not automatically appear until after the sound is over. Choosing **Continue Slide Show** lets you choose between **After Current Slide** (which means that when this slide is over, the sound will stop) or **After (number field) Slides**, which means that the sound can keep going for the number of slides that you enter into the number field and will then stop.

If you want the sound to keep repeating, click the **More Options** button on the Multimedia Settings tab, click the **Loop Until Stopped** button, and then the **OK** button.

Use the **Order & Timing** tab of the Custom Animation dialog box to choose when the sound starts in relation to the animated objects on the slide. (For more on the Order & Timing tab, see Chapter 14, "Look up in the Sky: Flying Text and Pictures.")

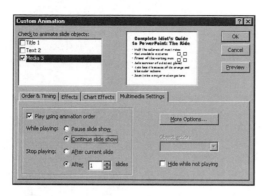

The Multimedia Settings tab lets you select when the sound ends.

Using a Stored Sound

Sounds abound in this world, and you can't record them all yourself. Luckily, you can use any sound file on your system, or even one from your Clip Gallery, as an automatic sound, giving you access to many more sounds.

To use a sound from a file, select **Insert**, **Movies and Sounds**, **Sound from File**, and then select the sound file using the file browser. To select a sound from the Clip Gallery, select **Insert**, **Movies and Sounds**, **Sound from Gallery**, and then right-click the sound you want and choose **Insert**. (And yes, you can click the **Clips Online** button to download sounds from Microsoft's Web site into the gallery! You can get free boings, free clicks, free music ... everything but free speech! It works much the same as downloading video clips, as described in Chapter 16, "Movies in PowerPoint: Like TV, Only Smaller.")

Click to get sounds from Microsoft Web site.

All sounds look alike. Luckily, they have their names under them, so we can tell them apart.

CD: OK 4 U!

Your CD-ROM drive can be used as more than just a retractable donut caddy. It can also be used to play audio CDs, and PowerPoint takes advantage of that. You can play audio tracks in your presentations.

Mostly, you will use this to add music to presentations. The CD-ROM drive may be quick, but it's a little too slow for use with things like sound effects. Although many good sound effects CDs are available, the lag between the effect-triggering event and when the effect actually starts is just too long.

To add CD playing to a slide, first put the CD in your drive. Make sure that it's the CD you are going to have when you do the actual presentation; if you meant to have Wagner's "Flight of the Valkyrie" and instead use Grungemunch's new hit, "I Fell Off of The Complete Idiot's Guide to PowerPoint the Ride and Fell in Love," it's not only going to confuse your audience, it can also confuse your computer.

No "Chipmunking" Your Music

Your CD-ROM drive may be double speed, quadruple speed, even 32-times speed, but audio CDs will still play at the normal speed (doggone it!).

It will also confuse your computer if the CD is playing while you are trying to set this up. If you have your system set to automatically start playing CDs when they are inserted, just hold down the **Shift** key while inserting it; this keeps the CD from playing automatically.

After your CD is safely inside the CD-ROM drive, yank down the ever-popular **Insert** menu and, from the **Movies and Sounds** submenu, select the **Play CD Audio Track** command. The Movie And Sound Options dialog box will appear. When we have seen this box before, most of it has been grayed out, but that won't be the case now.

The CD controls in the Movie and Sound Options dialog box are usable when you want to control a CD. Of course.

You get to pick where on the CD to start playing, and where to stop. Every CD is broken down into numbered tracks, usually one track for each song. The fields here let you pick which number track to start on, where on that track to start (in minutes and seconds), which track number to end on, and where to end it. You can type in these numbers, or you can use the up and down arrow buttons at the end of each field to adjust them.

Always set the track number before you set the time, because whenever you change the track number, the time is reset, either to the beginning of the track (for the start time) or the end of the track (for the end time). Set the time in minutes and seconds, with a colon in between (such as 2:35). If you want to play a complete single track, just enter that track number as both the starting track and ending track.

You can have the selection repeat by clicking **Loop until stopped**. After you finish setting things up, click the **OK** button, then answer the dialog box that asks if you want the sound to start automatically, and you will see a CD picture on your slide. If you want to change the settings (if, for example, you set a time incorrectly), right-click this picture and select **Edit Sound Object** to bring back the dialog box. (If you set *both* times incorrectly, that makes you a no-good two-timer!)

Starting the CD

You can set the CD to be started by clicking an object, passing the mouse over an object, or automatically. These things are done using the same instructions as you use when using a sound (including having the option of dragging the CD icon off of the slide).

Remember, you can only run one sound at a time off of a CD. You *can* play a CD track and a sound file at the same time. And, of course, the sound of a rattling, Illuminati-controlled fan can accompany any other sound, and haunt you no matter how far you get from the computer.

Narration: Sharing Your Snide Comments with the World

You can record a narration to go along with your presentation. This would be good if you designed your presentation so that you deliver it while talking live to the audience, but then realize you need to send a copy of your presentation to some people who aren't there. This way, they can get the advantages of your comments, your insights, and your ill-concealed belches.

There is a down side to using narration, however. Because PowerPoint can only handle one non-CD sound at a time, you shouldn't use both narration and other recorded sound clips on the same presentation. One sound or the other will be heard, but not both.

To record a narration, pull down the **Slide Show** menu and select **Record Narration**. This pops open a Record Narration dialog box that warns you about how much space you have left on your hard disk and how much narration that allows.

The Record Narration dialog box tells you how long a narration you can fit on your hard disk, so you know whether you have to talkrealfast.

Now, your narration may not take up a lot of time, but it could eat up your disk space very quickly. There are two ways to deal with this: changing the quality of your recording, or storing your narration on a separate disk.

Degrade Yourself: Lowering the Audio Quality

To change the narration quality, click the **Change Quality** button. This brings up the Sound Selection dialog box, opened to the Audio tab. Open the **Name** drop-down list box and select one of the following options: **CD Quality**, **Radio Quality**, or **Telephone Quality**.

Now, CD Quality sounds like it's a good choice, but it takes up a lot of disk space. It really doesn't sound that much better than Radio Quality for voice recordings, and it takes up *12 times* as much disk space. Half an hour of Radio Quality recording takes up less space than three minutes of CD Quality. Practically, it's not worth it.

Radio Quality is good, and probably the best choice if people are listening on the same computer as you are recording it on. If you are hoping to send this presentation out on floppy disks, however, you will want to use Telephone Quality—or be prepared to use a lot of floppy disks. Although Radio Quality is noticeably better than Telephone, it takes up twice as much disk space.

Disk-o Dancing

PowerPoint tends to put everything into one big presentation file, which is really handy when it comes to moving the presentation from one system to another, but not really handy when it comes to making the most efficient use of a multidisk system.

If you click the Record Narration dialog box's **Link Narrations In** check box, PowerPoint stores your narration in separate files, one file for each slide. Click the **Browse** button, and you will see a standard file browser where you can select the disk drive and folder for the narration to be stored in. The identity of this location will be stored in the presentation file, so PowerPoint will know where to find it. (The filenames will start with the presentation name, have additional info, and then end with a .WAV extension.)

Recording the Narration

After you have settled on your settings, click the button marked **OK** (which, as we all know, is short of Oklahoma, where narration has been honed to an art form). If you are not on the first slide, PowerPoint will ask you whether you want to start with the first or current slide. Then the slideshow starts.

Plenty of Disk Space? Link Anyway!

Your narration will be read more smoothly if it's stored in a separate file.

Record your narration by speaking into the microphone, clicking to advance the presentation as appropriate. Keep going through the entire presentation. Remember to breathe occasionally.

You may want to practice your narration a few times before recording, because if you mess up, you have to start all over again. However, you can pause the recording by right-clicking and selecting **Pause Narration**. Grab your lunch (or whatever you are pausing for), and then right-click again and select **Resume Narration**.

After you have gone through the entire presentation, a dialog box appears, letting you know that the narration has been saved, and asking whether you want to save the timings also. This is a great way of setting the timings for your slides so that they go along well with the narration. Click the **Yes** button if you want to save them and the **No** button if you don't. Choosing Yes or No is up to you. You have free will. After all, the aliens aren't brainwashing *you* using subliminal messages hidden in the rattling of your computer fan.

Skip the Talk

If you want to show your slideshow without the narration that you recorded for it, select the **Slide Show**, **Setup Show** command and select the **Show without Narration** option.

The Least You Need to Know

➤ To play sounds with a presentation, you need speakers and a sound card. To record sounds, you also need a microphone.

➤ To record a sound, use the **Insert, Movies and Sounds, Record Sound** command. Press the **Record** button, record your sound, and then press **Stop**. Type in a name for the sound, and then click the **OK** button. The sound will be added to the list of sound effects, and a speaker picture appears on your slide.

➤ To use a pre-made sound from the Clip Gallery, use the **Insert, Movies and Sounds, Sound from Gallery** command, right-click a sound in the gallery, and choose **Insert**. The speaker picture appears on the slide.

➤ To use a pre-made sound file that's on your disk, use the **Insert, Movies and Sounds, Sound from File** command. Select a file using the file browser, and the speaker picture will appear on the slide. When the user clicks this picture, the sound will play.

➤ You can use sound on a standard CD by putting the CD in your CD-ROM drive and giving the **Insert, Movies and Sounds, Play CD Audio Track** command. In the dialog box, select which track to start playing, where in that track to begin, which track to finish with, and how far into that track to go, and then click **OK**. A picture of a CD appears on the slide. The user can click this picture to hear the CD.

➤ To have the sound play automatically as part of the slide, drag the picture off the side of the slide, right-click it, and select **Custom Animation**. Click the **Play Using Animation Order** check box. Use the **Order & Timing** tab of the Custom Animation dialog box to set when the sound begins, and the **Multimedia Settings** tab to set when it ends.

➤ To record a narration to go with your presentation, use the **Slide Show, Record Narration** command. A Record Narration dialog box appears. Click the **OK** button when you are ready to start your narration. Speak into the microphone while clicking the mouse to advance forward through your presentation.

Part 4

Sharing the Presentation with Others

A presentation is like Kissing Disease—it's not much fun until you share it with someone.

In this part, you learn to prepare your presentation for display, whether it's in print form, for computer display, for a real slideshow, or even to put out on the Web. And once you start showing it to others, you'll learn a lot, like how quickly other people can spot mistakes you miss.

Chapter 18

The Scene Is Seen on Your Screen

In This Chapter

➤ Display the presentation on the computer that you set it up on

➤ Mark up the slides as you present

➤ Show the slideshow in a window

➤ Idiot-proof your presentation so that you can leave it running as a kiosk without people messing up your computer

You have already designed the presentation. That's the fun part. You don't actually have to show it to anyone. You can take pride in your own work instead of seeking outside confirmation.

But then again, if you don't show it to anyone, your boss doesn't pay you, or your customer doesn't buy your product, or The Complete Idiot's Guide Ride never gets built and you never make royalties off of it. Let's face it, pride is nice to have, but so is money. It's hard to walk into a donut shop and say, "I have a lot of pride, so give me a dozen glazed."

Speaker Mode: Full-Screen Show-Off

It's your presentation, you are showing it to people, and dadgummit, you want to have full control over it. This is the time to show it in Speaker mode.

To tell PowerPoint you want this presentation to appear in Speaker mode, yank down that **Slide Show** menu and select **Set Up Show**. The Set Up Show dialog box appears. Stare intently at it. You are going to get to know this dialog box quite well over the course of this chapter. Someday it may save your life. But probably not.

Your control over how the slideshow runs starts here, at the Set Up Show dialog box. All those animations, narrations, and timings you spent time setting up, you can disable here!

The very top selection in the dialog box is **Presented By a Speaker (full screen)**, and that's the one that you want to pick. Odds are that it is already selected, because that's what PowerPoint defaults to if you haven't selected anything else.

At the bottom of the dialog box under Advance Slides is a choice between advancing to the next slide Manually or Using Timings, If Present. When you are giving a presentation, odds are that you will want to choose **Manually** (which means waiting for a mouse click), because you are there talking to people about each slide.

Click the **OK** button, and then pull down the **Slide Show** menu again and select **View Show** (or just press **F5**) to get the show rolling!

The (Poorly) Hidden Menu

While the slide show is showing, the slides all look perfect and pristine, just the way you designed them—until you move the mouse. Then, not only does the pointer appear, but also a little arrow design appears in the lower left of the screen. This is the hiding spot for the hidden menu. Click it, and the menu appears. (You can also bring up the menu just by right-clicking anywhere on the screen.)

The hidden shortcut menu has a wealth of tools for the presenting speaker.

Slipping Slideways: Moving to Another Slide

You don't need the menu to move you to the next slide; just click anywhere that doesn't have anything designed to be clicked, and you will move to the next slide.

To back up one slide, select **Previous** from the hidden menu. To go ahead to any other slide, select **Go** and, from the submenu, select **By Title**. Another cascading menu appears, listing the titles of your slides, and you can select the slide that you want there.

Doodle Diagramming: Writing on Slides

Sometimes, it is handy to be able to mark up your slides while you are showing them. You may want to circle something to highlight what you are talking about, or draw lines showing how one item is connected to another item, or scribble over the name of the person who just stormed out of the room on the corporate organization chart.

PowerPoint lets you do this, but don't expect it to look great. A mouse is not the world's greatest drawing tool, and trackballs are even worse. The capability is there if you want it.

To start, just select **Pointer Options**, **Pen** from the hidden menu. Your arrow pointer will turn into a pen, and when you drag the pointer, it will draw a line.

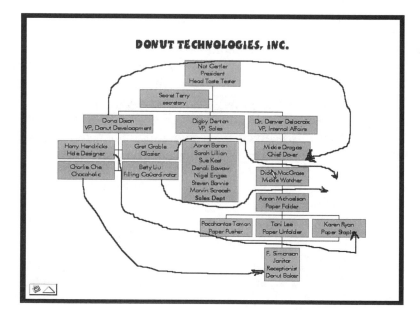

The markups show the development department's planned blitz against the administrative branch, aiming to tackle their quarterback and steal their coffee mugs.

Avoiding Invisible Ink

You can set a default pen color on the Set Up Show dialog box. Pick a color that shows up against the background you are using.

You can change the pen's color by selecting **Pointer Options**, **Pen Color** and selecting a pen color from the list. You can erase everything you drew by selecting **Screen**, **Erase Pen** or type the letter e— but you don't have to worry about erasing the slide when you are ready to move on. The pen is automatically erased when you move on to the next slide; if you come back to this slide, it won't be there.

But what if you want to draw a full diagram, without all the stuff on the slide getting in the way? Well, you could take a pen and slowly and carefully cover up everything on the slide with one color, much like the way you once sat there and scraped all the silver stuff off of your Etch-a-Sketch so that you could see the inside. Or you could do it the easy way: Select **Screen**, **Black Screen**. The whole slide will go black, and you can select **Pen** and start drawing on it. After you finish, select **Screen**, **Unblack Screen** and you will be back to working with your slide.

You can return to using the arrow pointer at any time just by selecting **Pointer Options**, **Automatic**.

A Slide up Your Sleeve

What if there's a slide you are not sure you want to show? Perhaps it has the answers to a question that you think someone is going to ask at a certain point, but you don't want to show it unless they ask. The answer is easy: Hide the slide!

In Slide Sorter view, select the slide that you want to hide, and then pull down the **Slide Show** menu and select **Hide Slide**. (You can tell this works, because the slide number will now be crossed out.) Then, when you are showing the slide before the hidden one, and you suddenly want to show the hidden one, just press **h**. The hidden slide will be displayed. If you don't purposefully go to the hidden slide, the slide will be skipped right over in order. You can have as many hidden slides as you want in your presentation, as long as you don't hide them all!

Show's Over!

To quit the show at any time, just select **End Show** from the hidden menu or press the **Esc** key. Otherwise, the show will end when you try to advance past the last slide.

A Sly Innuendo... Er, a Slide in a Window

You can show your slideshow in a resizable window on your screen, which is really handy if you are trying to play Space Bunnies of Death in another window. To do this, pull down the **Slide Show** menu and select **Set Up Show**. Then, in the dialog box, click the **Browsed by an Individual (Window)**. Click the **OK** button, and then issue the **Slide Show, View Show** command. The window will open up, and the show starts.

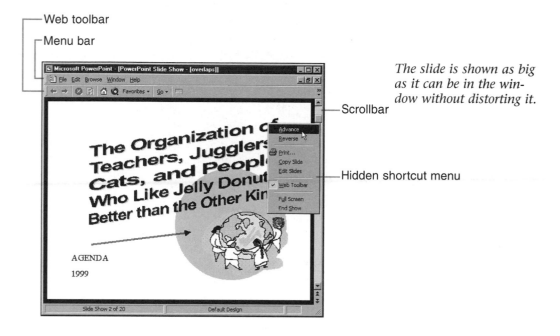

Web toolbar

Menu bar

The slide is shown as big as it can be in the window without distorting it.

Scrollbar

Hidden shortcut menu

Menus: Hidden No More!

Windows have menus. It's as sure a thing as dogs having fleas, or computer manuals having obfuscating terminology. As such, the slideshow doesn't need a hidden menu in this mode. It still has one, but everything on there is also on the standard menus.

And while they are there, you might as well use them. Your window may well have a Web-related toolbar showing, and if your presentation doesn't link to the Web, there's no need for it. It's just additional screen clutter. To get rid of it, pull down the **Window** menu and select **Web Toolbar**.

Sliding Ahead

As usual, if you are using the timing feature, the slides will advance automatically, and if you aren't, you can move quickly through the presentation by using the scrollbar at the right of the window. And if you want to see the names of the slides so that you can pick which one to leap to, pull down the **Browse** menu and, from the **By Title** submenu, select the slide you want to go to.

Finishing Up

After you finish with the slideshow, just choose **File, End Show**, and away it goes!

Kiosk: Accident-Proof, Idiot-Proof, Safety in a Can!

Letting people use your computer to view a presentation is just asking for trouble. The next thing you know, they have stopped the slideshow, and in an attempt to restart it have somehow managed to reformat your hard drive, and you smell the faint but telltale scent that lets you know that someone has stuck a slice of individually wrapped, processed American cheese food into your CD-ROM drive.

This is not good. This is something to be avoided, unless you have your computer heavily insured and want to collect. However, if you start the presentation running in Kiosk mode, you can avoid worrying about this. Why? Because you can hide away your computer and the keyboard somewhere where cables can reach but prying hands cannot. All the users need is the mouse and the monitor, and they can't stop the presentation using the mouse. All they can do is use a hyperlink or wait for the timings to advance to the next frame. If they hit the end of the presentation, it starts all over again.

It's referred to as *Kiosk mode* because it can be used to set up a *kiosk*, a standalone unit like you might see in the mall—a big wooden box with a monitor showing and a trackball sticking up through a hole. The computer is all locked inside, away from prying hands (unless the prying hands have a crowbar).

Attractive Trackball

If you are trying to quickly throw together a kiosk-like setup that younger kids or the elderly may be using, considering getting Microsoft's EasyBall trackball. It has an oversized ball that's better for those who are not so nimble, and it only has one button, which reduces confusion.

Setting Up a Kiosk Show

Pull down the **Slide Show** menu and select **Set Up Show** to bring up everyone's favorite dialog box (well, it's probably someone's favorite, at least). Click **Browsed at a Kiosk (full screen)** option and then the **OK** button to set Kiosk mode. Finally, pull the menu down again and select **View Show** to get it rolling.

Viewing Slides

You can't back up, you can't select a slide to go to, and you can't pull off any of those nifty tricks. There is no hidden menu to help you. You can just wait for the timing feature to take you forward, or follow a hyperlink built in to the presentation. Idiot-proof and powerful do not mix.

There are no menus, hidden or otherwise, in Kiosk mode, as this Ride Guide slide shows.

COMING SOON FROM QUE BOOKS
COMPLETE IDIOT'S RIDE: THE GUIDE!

➤ Everything you've ever wanted to know about the world's most popular theme park attraction.

➤ See how 107 tons of steel, 15 miles of cables, and 30,000 Pixie Stix were used to build this thrill-ride.

➤ Tricks and Tips to getting the most out of your Complete Idiot's experience.

You can't even click to go forward, unless there is a hyperlink to the next slide. This would be a good place to include a hyperlink to the next slide on the Slide Master, because if you are not doing a time-based presentation, you are going to need to give the user some way to move ahead.

Check This Out

Kiosk Planning

It's a good idea to have all but the transition from the first to second slides timed. That way, if someone walks away from the kiosk, the show will keep showing until it reaches the first slide, and then it will stop, waiting for someone to click a hyperlink to continue the presentation. On long presentations, you should also have a hyperlink to restart the show, for people who come across the kiosk in mid-presentation.

Finishing the Show

After the show is over and the viewer has viewed the last slide, the show automatically starts all over again, ready for the next person! Then how do you stop the show when you want your computer back? Just press the **Esc** key!

Simple Show–Starting

You can save a copy of your presentation that automatically starts showing when you double-click an icon on your desktop. This can save time for you, and make things a lot easier for anyone who wants to look at it without having to learn about PowerPoint.

To do this, pull down the **File** menu and select **Save As**. A file navigator appears. Click the drop-down button for the **Save in** drop down menu, and select **Desktop**. This tells PowerPoint that you want an icon for the file on the desktop. Then, pull down the **Save as Type** drop-down menu at the bottom of the navigator, and select **PowerPoint Show (*.pps)**. This tells PowerPoint that you are saving it as an automatically starting show.

A PowerPoint Show icon.

Click the **OK** button, and the icon for this presentation will appear on your desktop!

The Least You Need to Know

➤ Pulling down the **Slide Show** menu and selecting **Set Up Show** gives you the Set Up Show dialog box, which has many functions for controlling how your show appears.

➤ Selecting **Presented by a Speaker** gives you the most control over the presentation when you present it. When running a slideshow in Speaker mode, there's a hidden menu that can be brought up by pointing at the arrow symbol that appears in the lower left of the slide, or by right-clicking. The Speaker mode show ends when you reach the end of the presentation or when you select **End Show** from the hidden menu.

➤ In Speaker mode, select **Previous** from the hidden menu to back up one slide, or select **Go**, **By Title** to go to any slide of your choice. If you have created a hidden slide (by using **Slide Show**, **Hide Slide** in any slide editing mode), you can go to it from the preceding slide by selecting **Go**, **Hidden Slide**.

➤ In Speaker mode, you can draw on a slide by selecting **Pointer Options**, **Pen**, change the pen color by selecting **Pointer Options**, **Pen Color**, and erase your drawing by selecting **Screen**, **Erase Pen**.

➤ If you select **Browsed by an Individual** on the Set Up Show dialog box, your presentation will be shown in a resizable window with visible menus (Window mode). In Window mode, you can see whichever slide you want by choosing **Browse**, **By Title**. Finish a Window mode slideshow by reaching the end or by hitting the Esc key.

➤ To view the slideshow in Kiosk mode, select **Browsed at a Kiosk** on the Set Up Show dialog box. In Kiosk mode, the slideshow constantly repeats, and you cannot click to advance to the next slide. You can only advance through hyperlinks or through timing. To end the show in Kiosk mode, press the **Esc** key.

Chapter 19

Sending the Presentation to Others

In This Chapter

➤ Make a presentation that is easy to send to others

➤ Send your presentation through email

➤ Put your presentation on a floppy disk and send it through real mail

---

You have created your presentation, and there are people all over the country, all over the world even, who you want to have see it.

You could send them all plane tickets and fly them in to see the presentation on your computer. Or, you could pack up your computer and fly it to every place that they are, dedicating the next few years of your life to spreading your presentation.

Unfortunately for the airlines, there is another option, one which doesn't involve you giving them a lick of money. You can just send the presentation, either via email or on floppy disks through the regular mail. And, unfortunately for Microsoft (and they have no one to blame but themselves), you don't even have to give everyone personal copies of PowerPoint, because you will also be sending them a program that lets them view the presentation.

Preparing Postal-Possible Presentations

So you have created this great presentation, filled with lights and sounds and video clips of the entire run of the *Mr. Peepers* TV show. And you start to put it on a floppy disk. And another floppy. And another. Seventeen thousand five hundred and thirty-six floppy disks later, you have your presentation stored and ready to ship. Where are you going to find a box big enough?

But hey, it would be worth it. Just imagine the look on the recipients' face when it arrives! And the days of installation fun these lucky souls will have installing it on their own PCs to view it!

Obviously, this is something you want to avoid. If your goal is to send your presentations to others, you want to try to keep it lean, make sure it isn't too big. That doesn't mean, however, that you can't have a lot of slides. A slide with just text on it takes up very little space, and you could fit dozens of them on a single floppy disk. No, the culprit in creating a bloated presentation is more likely to be all those nice little multimedia touches.

That video presentation of you reading the Declaration Of Interactivity is a prime culprit. Video eats up disk space really fast. A minute video, even in a small window, can easily take up 10 megabytes, which would add seven floppy disks to your presentation. That same 10 megabytes could take an hour to transfer to someone's computer via email, if that person has a dial-up connection to the Internet.

After video, the next big culprit is audio. Small sound effects here and there don't eat up that much, but if you are using narration, you will fill disks quickly. You can cut down how much space the narration takes by reducing the audio quality of your recording (as discussed in Chapter 17, "Sound Advice on Sound").

Finally, pictures can take up a lot of space too. Highly detailed, high-resolution photographs eat up disk space very quickly. Try to keep your original pictures small and to a minimum. (Don't do it by just resizing the photo once you bring it into PowerPoint; that doesn't reduce the amount of disk space it takes up.)

Phiercely Phorcing Photos

To use photos while keeping file size to a minimum, store your photos in JPEG format. Your photo software should offer that as an option and give you the choice between a range of qualities of JPEG storage (the lower the quality, the less room it takes). Then, when you use the **Insert, Picture, From File** command to add the photo to your presentation, the Insert Picture dialog box appears. Select your file, and then click the down arrow next to the Insert button and select **Link To File**.

Pack It Up

You have your presentation all shipshape and ready to pack up for its trip. If you are putting it on a floppy disk, you will want to run a special program called the Pack and Go Wizard, which will lead you through the steps of this process. You also want to use this wizard if you are going to email the presentation.

To get the process rolling, open the presentation in PowerPoint, and then pull down the **File** menu and select **Pack and Go**. If this is the first time you've used the Pack And Go feature, your computer may prompt you to insert the Office CD-ROM, so that it can install the feature.

The Pack and Go Wizard appears, listing the four steps you need to go through. Click the **Next** button to get to the first step.

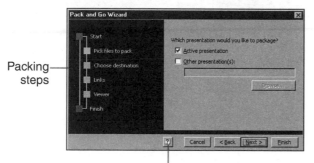

Packing steps

Click here for help

The Pack and Go Wizard: Not just a fly-by-night magician!

Step One: Pick to Pack

The first step asks you to pick the presentation that you want to pack. By default, Active Presentation is already checked off. Because that's the one you want, just click **Next** to move on to the next step!

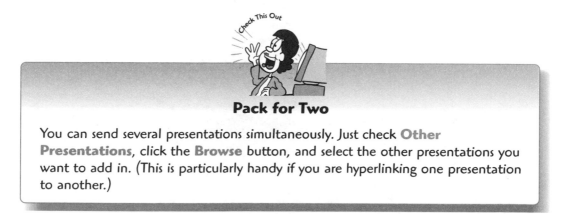

Pack for Two

You can send several presentations simultaneously. Just check **Other Presentations**, click the **Browse** button, and select the other presentations you want to add in. (This is particularly handy if you are hyperlinking one presentation to another.)

Step Two: Stick This on Your Disk

The next step that appears is to choose which disk drive the presentation is going to be stored on. Option buttons list all the floppy drives on your system, and one option button is marked Choose Destination. If you are putting the presentation on a floppy disk, click the option button for the right floppy drive. Stick a formatted floppy disk into the drive.

Opt for a floppy disk, or find a folder.

If you are preparing this to be emailed, you will want to store it on your hard disk. Click the **Choose Destination** button and then the **Browse** button. A file browser will appear. Select the disk drive and folder where you want the presentation stored, and then click the **Select** button to show you have made your selection.

After selecting your disk drive, click the **Next** button.

Step Three: Include Linked Files

The dialog box now asks whether you want to include your linked files. Of course you do! Linked files are pictures, video, and sound files used in your presentation, but not built in to the main presentation file. It's a silly question to ask! Check off the check box for this.

Don't create the missing link! Include everything!

A check box also asks whether you want to include your font files. Check this one as well. Otherwise, all those fonts that you carefully picked because they looked just right may be replaced by other fonts on other people's PCs.

After putting a check in all the check boxes here, click the **Next** button to move on to the next step.

Step Four: Pick to Pack a Player

The final step of the wizard is choosing whether you want to include the Viewer program with your presentation. This program will play the presentation for users who don't have PowerPoint. If you are not sure whether the person has PowerPoint (or if their version of PowerPoint may be earlier than PowerPoint 97), include it. Even a person who doesn't have PowerPoint will need a system that's running Windows 98, Windows 95, or Windows NT in order to watch your presentation. These days, that includes most of the people you are likely to send the presentation to.

A PowerPoint Player permits PowerPointless people to properly peruse PowerPoint presentations.

After making your choice, instead of clicking the **Next** button, just click the **Finish** button. The packing process will start.

The Computer Packs Like a Thing That Packs Very Well

The computer will start packing the files away, while showing you a status dialog box that lets you know what is happening. The first file that it creates is *pngsetup.exe*, which is the program that people who get the presentation will run to unpack it on to their machines. This only takes up less than one tenth of the space on a standard floppy disk.

Next it creates pres0.ppz, which has the presentation information in it. If you are writing to a floppy disk and this file fills up the disk, PowerPoint will ask you for another floppy disk. It will then create a file on this one, with more of the presentation in it. If this one fills up, it will ask for another one, and so on. Make sure that you number the floppy disks in the order that you put them in! Otherwise, the user will have to keep guessing which one is which, and will probably throw a large weasel at you the next time the two of you meet.

After the packing is complete, PowerPoint proudly shows you a dialog box, letting you know that the job has been completed successfully.

Make sure you tell the recipient to unpack the presentation by running the pngsetup.exe program, which can be done by clicking the **Start** button, selecting **Run**, and then clicking the **Browse** button and finding where the file is (either on the floppy disk or wherever email gets stored). If you are sending it via email, remember to send both files! (Also remember that if you make changes to the presentation, you will have to repack it.)

CD-ROMming Your Presentation

If you do have a large presentation full of sound and video to share, you may want to consider making your own CD-ROMs. CD-R recorders, which can make CD-ROMs, have dropped to a few hundred dollars, and individual blank disks can be had for as little as $1 each.

If you do put your presentation on a CD-ROM, don't use Pack and Go to put it on there. Packing it just means that the recipient will have to unpack it on to his hard disk, and you will take up a lot of unneeded room there. Instead, don't use any linked pictures or linked narrations (ones included in the presentation file are fine), and use only standard Windows fonts. Copy the presentation file and the Viewer program (a file named Ppview32.exe found on the Office CD-ROM in the Pfiles\MSOffice\Office\Xlators directory) onto the root directory of your CD-R disc. (This is done differently than copying to floppy disk. Check your CD-R manual for details.) This way, the recipient can view the presentation directly from the CD-ROM.

Shoo! Send It Away Quickly

If you have Microsoft Outlook set up to handle email and you just quickly want to send off the presentation without packing it (which is fine if you are sending it to someone who already has a player or has PowerPoint 97 or 2000), you can do it really quickly.

Open the presentation you wish to mail, pull down the **File** menu, and from the **Send To** submenu select **Mail Recipient (as Attachment)**. Your email program will appear to find out whom you want to send it off to. Tell it that information (this is no time to keep secrets from your computer), and it will ship the file right off. If you want everyone in your organization to be able to get it, use the **File**, **Send to**, **Exchange Folder** command, and select a public folder to put it in.

The Least You Need to Know

➤ To keep your presentations small enough to be easily sent on floppy disk or via email, avoid using video and high-quality audio in them.

➤ If you want to send your presentation, use the Pack and Go Wizard. Pull down the **File** menu and select **Pack and Go** to get it started. On the Pack and Go Wizard dialog box, click the **Next** button to get it started, fill in each piece of information each screen asks for, and click **Next** to move to the next one. After doing this, click **Finished**, and the packing will take place.

➤ If the Pack And Go feature has not been used on your computer before, you may need the CD-ROM that PowerPoint came on.

➤ As your presentation gets packed, PowerPoint will tell you when you need to stick another floppy disk in the drive. Make sure to number them all.

➤ If you are emailing the presentation, you will need to send two files: pngsetup.exe and pres0.ppz. Be sure to tell the person receiving the file to run pngsetup.exe to unpack the presentation so that it can be run.

➤ To use Microsoft Exchange to send your presentation file to another PowerPoint user, just use the **File**, **Send To**, **Mail Recipient** command.

Chapter 20

Reaching a Crowd: Slides, Overheads, Projection Screens, and Network Presentations

In This Chapter

➤ Make slide-projector slides of your computer slides

➤ Create overheads

➤ Use computer screens projectors to make your image huge

➤ Convince your boss that you need two monitors: one to run the show, and the other to show the show

➤ Run your presentation over a network, at a safe distance from your audience

With your typical computer setup, you can show your presentation to up to 273,000 people. Of course, you can only show it to about three of them at a time—but hey, you've got nothing better to do, right?

By projecting your presentation onto The Big Screen (even if it's not a very big Big Screen), you can show it to lots of people at once. Maybe not 273,000 of them (unless you project it on the scoreboard during the Super Bowl), but certainly more than three.

You can use any of four different forms of projection. You can use a slide projector, actually making slides out of your slides. You can put them onto clear sheets and project them with an overhead projector. You can use one of several methods of projecting your computer display directly. Or, you can send it out over a network, so that your audience members are at their desks, looking at their own PCs.

Slides on Slides

Using a slide projector to show your presentation places some strong limitations on what you can do. A slide can't show animation, or play sound, or be interactive. All it can do is project an image, which reduces PowerPoint to a drawing program.

It does have some useful advantages that should not be overlooked, however. A slide projector is very easy to carry around, and you can ship slides off to most corporations and schools and feel confident that they have the equipment to not only see what you have sent, but to show it to a large group. And, if enemy agents have you cornered, slides are easier to swallow than floppy disks.

Slide-Maker, Slide-Maker, Make Me a Slide!

If you want to make your own slides, you could try just photographing your screen and telling the Fotofolk that you need them developed as slides. They will look horrible, but you will have done it on the cheap!

The proper equipment to use is a *film recorder*. This is a device that you attach to your computer using a card and a cable. The computer treats the film recorder the same way as it does a printer, sending the image to the recorder when you tell it to print. You can get film recorders that can turn out a slide in a minute and a half. You just step through your presentation on the computer, and tell it to take a picture when each slide shows up.

The bad news, however, is the cost. It's quite likely that you will spend more on the film recorder than on the computer that you attach it to. Generally speaking, this is not a device that you get when you want to throw together a quick presentation. This is something that you get for the graphics department of your company, when they need it for this and a number of other things.

Let Someone Else Pay for the Big Stuff

Luckily, you can hire someone else to make your slides. *Computer imaging service bureaus* specialize in dealing with computer graphics, and they can make the slides for you. You can look them up in the Yellow Pages, or you can ask whoever does your company's computer graphics.

You will need to find out from the service bureau what media they take. They can certainly handle floppy disk. If your file is too big for that, they might be able to take it on tape, on CD-R, on a removable hard disk, in compressed format on a ZIP disk, or any of a number of other possibilities. This will probably cost you about $10 per slide, which can quickly add up to hundreds of dollars. Most of these places are using very good quality equipment, however, so your slides will come out looking sharp.

Service Bureau via Modem

Microsoft made a deal with a company called Genigraphics for them to accept PowerPoint presentations by modem, email, or physically mailed disks, and have the slides (or full-color overheads, or posters) delivered to you by overnight delivery. The cost ranges from $4.50 to $13.50 per slide, depending on how quickly you need it done. Volume discounts are available.

To send the file to Geningraphics, pull down the **File** menu and select **Send To**, **Genigraphics**. From there, a wizard takes you through the process. (If this is the first time that you've used the Genigraphics feature, PowerPoint may ask you to insert the Office CD-ROM so it can install this feature.)

Preplanning the Presentation

If you are preparing a presentation for slides, it's best to plan ahead. (It's best to plan ahead even if you are not doing that, but then the plans that you make are different!) When you first open up your presentation, but before you put anything on it, pull down the **File** menu and select **Page Setup**. A dialog box appears which controls the ratio of the page width to the height.

Using the Page Setup dialog box, you can set the height and width separately.

Click the drop-down button on the **Slides sized for** field, select **35mm Slides**, and then click the **OK** button. This makes the slides a little shorter than they were, which is the right ratio of height-to-width for slides. (If you view this show on your screen, there will be black bands at the top and bottom to make it fit your screen, like a letterboxed movie on TV.)

Changing an Existing Presentation

Using Page Setup to change the size of existing slides will squish or stretch the graphic elements. The text won't stretch, but it may get rearranged on the page; so check all your slides to make sure they still look okay.

Preparing the Files for a Service Bureau

The service bureau doesn't want to handle your PowerPoint presentation. What they want is a file all ready for their printer. To get this, call them and ask them what *printer driver* they want you to use. (You may have to install this driver from the Windows installation disk, if you don't already have it installed.) Then pull down the **File** menu and select the **Print** command.

Use the Print dialog box to create a file that your service bureau can use to make slides.

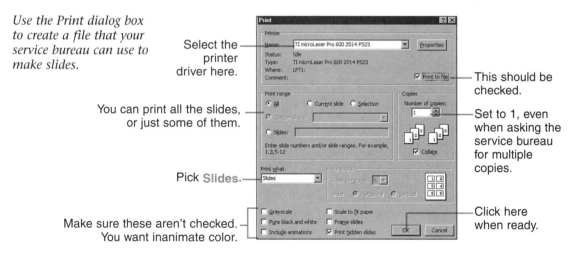

Select the printer driver here.

This should be checked.

You can print all the slides, or just some of them.

Set to 1, even when asking the service bureau for multiple copies.

Pick **Slides**.

Make sure these aren't checked. You want inanimate color.

Click here when ready.

Select the printer driver that the service bureau requested in the **Name** field, put a check mark in the **Print to File** check box, select **Slides** in the Print what field. Make sure none of the Grayscale, Pure Black and White, and Include Animations options are checked off, and then click the **OK** button. A file browser will pop up, wanting you to name the file and pick a disk and a folder to put it in. You might as well put it directly on the disk you will be sending to the service bureau. After selecting where it goes, click the **OK** button, and the file will be created. (Make a copy of the disk to keep for yourself, so if something goes wrong at the service bureau, you have a copy.)

Fitting onto Floppies

If you're using standard floppy disks, you probably won't be able to fit your entire presentation onto one disk. Instead, you should try putting just four slides on each floppy. To do this, in the print dialog box, click the **Slides** option button in the Print Range area. In the field next to that, type the number of the first slide you want on this disk, then a dash, then the number of the last slide (such as 1-4 or 13-16), then click **OK** and finish the procedure. Repeat this with a fresh floppy for each group of four slides on your presentation.

I Own a Film Recorder, and Want to Use It!

To send the image to your own film recorder, take the same steps described earlier for sending it to the service bureau, only select your film recorder in the Print dialog box's **Name** field and *don't* put a check in the **Print to File** field. Click the **OK** button, and all the necessary information will be sent to the film recorder.

Overheads Over Easy

Overheads (sometimes called *transparencies*), clear sheets that you use with an overhead projector, are kind of keen. Not only are they big, translucent versions of your slides, but if you take a blank overhead sheet and use it to block the cat's favorite path, the cat will try to walk right through it.

Transparencies are a handy way to show your presentation because you can make them yourself without a vast expense, and most places you are likely to want to show your show will probably have an overhead projector (and if they don't, you can get one for $200-$300). If everyone involved is too cheap to buy a projector, you can just show the sheets to people. (You can try that with slides, but people will end up squinting a lot!)

To make your own transparencies, you need a printer (either a laser printer or an ink-jet printer) and you need some transparency sheets. Make sure that you get sheets specifically designed for whichever sort of printer you have. (If you take a laser printer transparency sheet and run it through a color inkjet printer, the ink won't stick to the page and you will end up projecting psychedelic puddles that used to be your information. This may look cool to people on acid, but if most of your audience is on acid, it's probably time to find a new line of work! On the other hand, if you run an ink jet sheet through your laser printer, the sheet could melt and turn your laser printer into a high-tech lump.)

Blank overhead sheets cost between 50 cents and a dollar apiece, and you buy them in packs of 20 or more. You should get some cardboard frames for them, if you are going to be using them repeatedly and want to keep them in good shape. You can also keep them in a three-ring binder by using clear binder sheet protectors, which is handy because you don't have to take the overheads out of the protectors to project them.

Overhead Set Up (and Then Follow Through with a Backhand?)

Setting up for overheads is much the same as setting up for slides, only you select **Overheads** on the Page Setup dialog box rather than 35mm Slides. However, you have one other choice to make: **Portrait** or **Landscape**. Now, Microsoft throws these two art terms at you just to confuse those of us who work in words rather than in art, but they are really quite simple. *Portrait* means that the page is turned so that it's tall and narrow. *Landscape* means that it's turned so that it's short and wide. (If you are changing the setup on an already-designed presentation, check your slides afterwards, as this will tend to stretch your graphics and rearrange your words to fit the new dimensions.)

Landscape transparencies are wider. Portrait transparencies are taller.

Portrait mode is really nice if you are doing lots of text and long lists of things. Landscape has the big advantage of being the same relative dimensions as the computer screen, however, so you can show your show on the screen or on the overhead projector, and it will look the same.

Clear Thoughts on Transparent Printing

If you are making your slideshow for overheads, there are a few things you should remember. Write them on your hand, if you have to (but be prepared to swallow your hand if captured by the enemy).

The first thing to remember is that if your printer is black-and-white, your transparencies will be black-and-white (well, black-and-clear). All your fancy colors will be for naught, and if you put one color on top of another, it may be hard to tell them apart. To plan for this, while designing your slides, click the **Grayscale Preview** button on the Standard toolbar. PowerPoint will now show your slides in black and white, so you know what to expect. (In Slide View mode, it will also show you a color version in a small window.) The black-and-white version may look very different from what you expect; for tips on telling PowerPoint to make black-and-white presentations as you want them, check out Chapter 22, "Printing Printouts and Handling Handouts."

If you are using a color printer, you may still want to avoid overlapping colors and using backgrounds. Ink-jet inks often smear a bit, and this can cause an ugly, muddy effect if you have large areas of color connecting. Even single colors can come out muddy, because the printer has to mix several colors to make the color you want. Much of this depends on the quality of your color printer and how well it works with the overhead sheets you have. If you want to try color backgrounds anyway, test it out on one overhead first and see how it comes out, before committing to doing a whole bunch that way.

Color Overheads with Lower Overhead

If you don't have a color printer and want color overheads, or if you want to make sure that the overheads you use are of the highest quality, you can use a service bureau to print them. You do this by printing them to a file (as shown in the slide section) and taking the file to the service bureau, where they will have high-end color printers to print them on.

This, however, is not cheap. You can expect to pay somewhere around $15 apiece for color overheads. If you are just looking for color, it

Ink-Jet Smear Fear

Make sure you let each ink-jet–printed sheet dry thoroughly before stacking them! Otherwise, you will end up with overheads with smudgy printing on both, not good for anything but harassing the cat.

may be cheaper to buy a color printer. Cheap color printers cost about as much as you would pay for 10 to 15 service bureau overheads.

Two Screens, or Not Two Screens

Slides and overheads are nice, but they can't show all that beautiful animation and those movies that you built in to your presentation. Wouldn't it be the nicest thing if you could take what's on your computer monitor and project it on to a large screen?

No, it wouldn't; the nicest thing would be if eating ice cream made us svelte and healthy. The projection thing is nice too, and there are several ways to do it. You could get a card that converts your computer video into video that TVs can handle, and hook your screen up to a projection television system. The image may be blurred a little, but if you use large fonts, that shouldn't be a problem.

Another way to do it is to use a device designed to project computer information. An *LCD projector* is like a television projector, only it's designed for sharp computer graphics. An *LCD panel* is like the screen of a color laptop computer, only it doesn't have a back, so light can shine right through. If you put the LCD panel on an overhead projector, light shines through the display and projects the color image on the screen!

LCD: Little Color Dots

LCD stands for *liquid crystal display*. Such a display is made up of little segments that are normally clear, but become visible when a small amount of electricity is applied to them. Digital watches have LCDs, with eight segments being used to make up the numbers.

If you are using this display, you really don't want to be looking up at the big screen, and you probably don't want to be showing everyone the hidden menus and other things you are doing with the system. A good presentation should look like magic. Wouldn't it be the nicest thing if you could have one display that you are looking at, doing all the work, while the users just see the projection of the slides that you want them to see? No, the nicest thing is the ice cream, remember? But this thing is not only nice, it's possible!

It Ain't Cheap, but Here's How

First, you need a PC running Windows 98 or Windows NT 5.0; earlier versions of Windows won't let you do this. Next, you need to set up this PC to handle two monitors. You do this by turning off your computer, installing a second video card, attaching your LCD projector, and then turning on your PC again. Windows will detect the second video display and will attempt to configure it. (Have your Windows CD handy; it may be needed.)

After your dual-monitor PC is set up, load your PowerPoint presentation. Choose **Slide Show**, **Set Up Show**, and the Set Up Show dialog box appears. On the **Show On** menu, select the monitor you want your audience to watch. Click **OK**. Now, when you run your presentation, it will appear on both monitors, but the one that the audience sees will not show all the menus and controls that you are working with.

Network Presentations: Avoiding Your Audience

Having the PCs at work linked together with an intranet so that each member of the audience is at their own desk, on their own PC, can be handy because it's less disruptive of the work day. It's also really useful if you are delivering bad news or bad puns, because you will be out of the audience's donut-throwing range. In some cases, you can even do the broadcast over the Internet, which means you can be far away in a remote mountain cabin when word of your nefarious scheme goes out.

Intranew

This method of sending the presentation to people's Web browsers is new with PowerPoint 2000. Earlier versions of PowerPoint had a more cumbersome, more costly, and much more limited way to handle presentations over an intranet.

The person presenting the presentation (you) needs to have a copy of PowerPoint 2000. Each PC used to view the show needs to have a copy of Microsoft's Web browser: Internet Explorer, with a revision number of 4.0 or higher. This keeps Microsoft happy.

Additionally, if the presentation will be viewed on more than 15 PCs, or if you want to include video in your presentation, you need a local NetShow server. If you want to broadcast this presentation over the Internet to people in other locations, you need to lease a NetShow server.

Set Up and Pay Attention

Before you can do an online presentation, you need to tell your PC what you are going to do. No keeping secrets from your PC! To do this, save your presentation. Next, pull down the **Slide Show** menu and from the **Online Broadcast** submenu select **Set Up and Schedule**. (If this is the first time you have used this feature, PowerPoint may ask for the Office CD-ROM so it can install it.) A **Broadcast Schedule** dialog box appears. Make sure the **Set up and schedule a new broadcast** option button is selected, and then click **OK**.

The Description tab of the Schedule A New Broadcast dialog box helps you warn your poor helpless audience of what to expect.

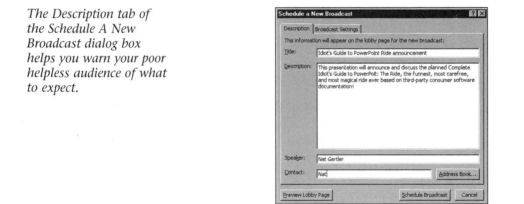

A Good Description Is the Prescription for Viewer Subscription!

The Description tab of the dialog box that appears is used to create information that the audience will see when they sign on for the presentation. Use the **Title**, **Description**, **Sender**, and **Contact** fields to let your audience know what the presentation is about and who is giving it. If you click the **Preview Lobby Page** button, you will see a sample of the Web page that the users will see when they log on for the presentation.

Getting Service from the Servers

Next, click the **Broadcast Settings** tab and view the options that you have there. Put a check in the **Send Audio** check box, and anything you say into your PC's microphone will be heard during the presentation, as long as the viewers have remembered to turn their speakers on. Of course, you could just tell everyone to turn their speakers on when you begin your talk... no, wait, that won't work.

The Broadcast Settings tab is where you let your PC and the network know what to expect.

If you are using one of those desktop digital video cameras and your network has a NetShow server, you can check the **Send video** check box. That way, the viewers will see your lips moving and say to themselves "Aha! He's saying something! My speakers must be off!"

If this is your first presentation, click the **Server Options** button. The Server Options dialog box (surprise, surprise) opens up. Click the **Browse** button and use the file navigator to select a directory on the intranet that your presentation will be broadcast from. Be sure to pick a directory that the other users will have access to. On the bottom half of the Server Options dialog box, select between not using the NetShow server (in which case, you can't use video and must limit your audience to 15) or using a NetShow server—in which case, you will have to enter the server name and a location for the files. Your system administrator should be able to help you. Click **OK** to return to the Schedule A New Broadcast dialog box.

You only have to set up the Server Options the first time that you broadcast a presentation, unless your LAN setup changes.

Just Say When!

Finally click the **Schedule Broadcast** button. If your office uses Microsoft Outlook, this will let you add your presentation to not only your schedule, but the schedules of the audience as well. If you don't have Microsoft Outlook on your system, then PowerPoint will just start up your email program with a preformatted email that you can use to announce the presentation, including information on the intranet location for viewers to see the presentation.

Starting the Presentation

When the time comes to begin the broadcast, load up the presentation and use the command **Slide Show, Online Broadcast, Begin Broadcast**. Everyone who has their Internet Explorers open to the location you sent them via Outlook or email will begin seeing your presentation.

A Tag-Team of Tools to Use with Two to Two Hundred Views

PowerPoint has a couple of tools that you can use whether you are running your presentation on one screen, two, or many over a network, but that you are more likely to be using when running on more than one screen. That's because they cover up part of the screen, which would ruin the effect for your audience.

The *Speakers Notes* feature gives you a text display for each slide. You can put whatever you want into these notes—a little script telling you what to discuss on the slide, a reminder that there's a hidden slide, a dirty limerick, whatever. You don't have to worry about what you put up there, because everyone else is going to be watching the main screen—unless you have one of those weirdos in the front row who tries to watch the presentation's backward reflection in your glasses.

The *Meeting Minder* is used for taking notes during your presentation, and is particularly helpful if your presentation is meant to organize the project.

Notes on Notes

You can create Speakers Notes either in Normal view, Outline view, or Notes Page view. Outline view is best for working on this because it gives you a larger area for the notes (unlike Normal view) and shows them at a reasonable text size (unlike Notes view).

The Speakers Notes field is in the lower right of the PowerPoint window. Enter your notes by clicking inside the field and typing.

For Speakers Notes, the Outline
view is surely the right one for you…

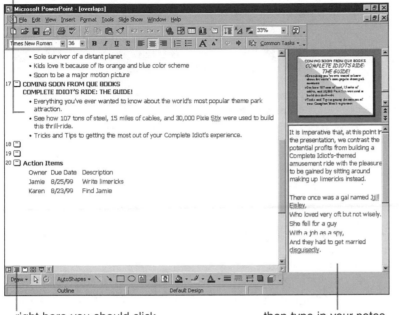

*There is no rule that says
you have to put limericks
in your Speaker Notes,
but why not?*

…right here you should click,
and it shows up quick…

…then type in your notes
'til you're through!

After you have your notes in place, you can start the slideshow. You have to do the
slideshow in Speaker mode for this to work. Right-click any slide and select **Speaker
Notes**, and a Speaker Notes dialog box will appear. You can even edit the notes during the show. As you advance to each new slide, the dialog box will show the notes
for that slide.

Use the Meeting Minder, or
Never Mind Your Meeting!

There's another notepad you can use during
your presentation, the Meeting Minder. This is
really designed for tracking feedback and planning during the presentation, but it can also
be used for limericks and perhaps for other
things.

To pull up the Meeting Minder while showing
a presentation in Speaker mode, just right-click
and select **Meeting Minder**. A dialog box
opens, with two tabs. The Meeting Minutes tab

**Speaker Notes for Non–Two
Screeners**

You can print out your Speaker
Notes to use as cheat sheets or
handouts. Just select **File**, **Print**
and choose **Notes Pages** in the
Print What field.

221

is used for general notes, and the Action Items tab is used to create a schedule listing things that need to be done and who needs to do them.

The Action Items tab lets you schedule items for other people to do. With a little planning, you can avoid doing them yourself.

Click to enter notes.

Click to record to-do items.

> **Meeting Minder**
>
> Meeting Minutes | Action Items
>
> Description: Find Jamie
>
> Assigned To: Karen   Due Date: 8/23/99
>
> | Jamie | 8/25/99 | Write limericks |
>
> Add
> Edit
> Delete
>
> OK   Cancel   Schedule...   Export...

Select the Meeting Minutes tab, and you see it's just one big field. Type whatever you want in there.

Click the **Action Items** tab, and you see fields to enter work assignments, including a description of the work to be done, the name of the person to do it, and the date due. Enter this information and click the **Add** button, and this info gets added to the list below it. (You can change things on the list by selecting them and clicking **Edit**, or remove them entirely by selecting them and clicking **Delete**. These are both handy for making sure that anything assigned to you gets reassigned from you to someone else!) When you hit the end of your presentation, you discover that PowerPoint has made a new slide, listing the action items!

Minding Your Meetings at Other Times

You can pull up the Meeting Minder while editing your presentation. Just pull down the **Tools** menu and select **Meeting Minder**.

If you have installed Microsoft Office 2000 (not just the standalone PowerPoint product), clicking the **Schedule** button opens the Microsoft Outlook Appointment Calendar/Meeting Planner program—which is another complete program of its own. You can have PowerPoint send email to Outlook on every action item you recorded so that it appears on the appropriate person's schedule and to-do list. Clicking **Export** lets you export all the Meeting Minder information to Microsoft Word, the word processor part of Microsoft Office. There's not room here to tell you how to use either of these products, but feel free to spend your hard-earned shekels on *The Complete Idiot's Guide to Microsoft Office 2000* and *The Complete Idiot's Guide to Microsoft Word 2000.*

The Least You Need to Know

➤ To set up your presentation with the right dimensions for slide-projector slides, use the **File**, **Page Setup** command and select **35mm Slides** on the **Slides sized for** list. To send the images to a film recorder, use the **File**, **Print** command and select your film recorder on the **Name** list.

➤ You can print overheads (transparencies) on a laser printer or an ink-jet printer, if you have the appropriate blank sheets. To set up your presentation with the right dimensions for transparencies, use the **File**, **Page Setup** command and select **Overhead** on the **Slides sized for** list. If you select the **Landscape** option, the dimensions will be the same as for an onscreen slideshow.

➤ You can show a presentation on two monitors simultaneously if you have a second graphics card installed in your PC. This is particularly good if you use one of the monitors to project a large image that everyone can see. To show a show this way, select **Slide Show**, **Set Up Show**, and choose which monitor the audience will see from the **Show On** list. The other monitor will show the slides and all the control features.

➤ To show the presentation to other folks over an in-house network, everyone in your audience has to be running Internet Explorer. To see all the controls you need to set up this show, pull down the **Slide Show** menu and from the **Online Broadcast** submenu select **Set Up and Schedule**.

➤ The Speaker Notes feature lets you create a little onscreen sheet of notes to help you with each slide. Enter Speaker Notes in the lower-right pane of Outline view or Normal view. To view the notes while giving the presentation in Speaker mode, right-click and select **Speaker Notes**.

➤ The Meeting Minder lets you take notes and schedule events for Microsoft Outlook while presenting your presentation. Bring it up by right-clicking and selecting **Meeting Minder**

Chapter 21

Putting It on the Web

In This Chapter

➤ Get your presentation ready for publication on the World Wide Web

➤ Set the size and format of your presentation

➤ Pick a better tool for making Web presentations

The World Wide Web is wide indeed. The most important thing about the Web, however, is that it can reach the whole world. Odds are that most of the people you want your presentation to reach are somewhere in the world. By turning your presentation into a World Wide Web site, you make it so that anyone with a connection to the Internet can take a look at your presentation. PowerPoint includes the tools to make your presentation ready to be placed on the Web.

Why You Shouldn't Use PowerPoint to Build a Web Site

When you use PowerPoint to make a Web site (a publication on the Web), it doesn't try to make it seem like a normal Web site. Instead, it tries to make the Web act more like PowerPoint. PowerPoint is really designed to present small amounts of text at a time, leading to discussion, with a lot of fancy design possibilities. Web sites, however, are better with presenting a deeper amount of text, fully covering a topic on a single Web page, and all the ornate graphics and complex text layouts are likely to just increase the amount of time it takes for the Web viewer to get the page while making it harder for the reader to read the page. It's also designed to make the page run a lot like a PowerPoint presentation *if* the viewer is using the latest version (5.0) of Microsoft's Internet Explorer Web browser. People using earlier versions of Internet Explorer or other Web browsers entirely are likely to see the page very differently, making it tricky to anticipate exactly what the viewer is going to see.

This isn't to say that you should never use PowerPoint to create a Web site. It's very good for one thing, and that's taking a presentation that you created for some other form and making it available on the Web. If you create a presentation for your students on The Rise and Fall of the Designated Hitter, and you want them to be able to refer to it while working on their term papers, you can give them instant access to it over the Web. This way, you don't have to re-create all your work.

If you have Microsoft Office, you already have a better Web designing program, and you may already know how to use it. The word processor Microsoft Word has some very good tools for making proper, straightforward Web pages. For more information on using these features, head down to your local bookstore and grab a copy of *Complete Idiot's Guide to Microsoft Word 2000*!

Real Web Site Tools

If your goal is to create the best possible Web site, your best bet is to use a program designed just for that. Both Netscape Communicator and Internet Explorer have better Web design tools built in. Microsoft offers FrontPage, a powerful tool (included in some versions of Office!) that's a bit awkward for the individual user, but great if you have a bunch of people working together to build a site. For the maximum control over your pages, you should learn HTML, which stands for *Hypertext Markup Language*, the language used to describe Web pages so that the Web browser will know what to display. All the other tools just take what you want and translate it into HTML for you.

Presenting: Web-Presentable Presentations

If you hope to put your presentation on the Web, you should keep that fact in mind while you design it. Some things are good for Web design; other things aren't so hot. Planning ahead of time can help you avoid heartache later. (Although if you are one of those people who like heartache, not planning might be a good idea!)

Some things work well on the Web, other work less well, and some things don't work at all.

Things That Work Well

Text and pictures work well on the Web. The Web is likely to reduce their size on the screen, so you should keep them large; other than that, they should be fine.

Hyperlinks from slide to slide work well, and hyperlinks to Web sites work far better on the Web than they do in a non-Web presentation, because those sites get displayed in the same window as used by the presentation itself.

Things That Work Less Well

Animations. Transitions. Sound effects. Narrations. Video. Mustard. A viewer who is using Internet Explorer 4.0, or later, can experience all these things. Oh, except for the mustard. That just ended up on my screen because I missed the hot dog with my squirt. If the viewer is using some other browser, however, few or none of these things will work. If your presentation needs the narration to be understood, for example, someone not using the right Web browser won't be able to understand it. And at this point, *most* World Wide Web users aren't using a recent version of Internet Explorer.

Even graphics won't work on some Web browsers. Some people (particularly people working from academic environments, or people using handheld computing devices) will only be able to see the text of your presentation.

Sophisticated Webbing

The quality and flexibility of Web site creation has been vastly improved in this new version of PowerPoint. Previous versions could not support audio or video at all, among other things.

Things... That... Work... Slowly... on... the... Web

The Information Superspeedway is coming. Soon, with the mere click of a single button, you will be able to have any *Police Academy* film you want sent directly into your home in seconds, over special Internet wiring known by its simple acronym, ASDBLCNUTZYZYZYBFHIMOMGGH!

But that's the future. Today, people are using slow modems to dial in to a slow Web. Web sites should be designed to keep file sizes down to a minimum, which will keep things zooming along. The biggest culprit on most Web sites is graphics. If you are going to put your presentation on the Web, try to keep the drawings simple and the photographs small.

Audio and video do not work well for most people over the Web. Don't blame Microsoft (for this, anyway). Trying to deliver full-speed video on the Web is like trying to deliver a new car to someone by passing it piece by piece through a straw: By the time you get enough of it through to be of use, the recipient has lost interest. Even if you choose to include these things (if you count on your audience having the right browser), keep the videos small and short.

Start That Web Magic!

To convert your presentation to a form that can be used on the Web, open it up, pull down the **File** menu, and select **Save as Web Page**. The Save As file browsers opens up. Click the **Publish** button, which opens up a new dialog box where you can choose from a range of options for how your presentation will appear on the Web.

You must make a lot of decisions when webbifying your presentation, but they are all simple little ones.

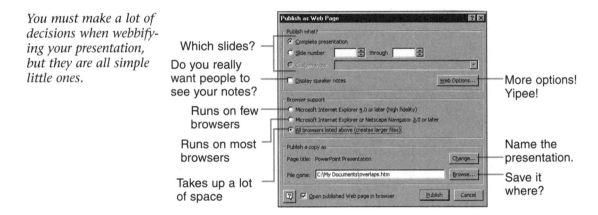

Simple Decisions for Complex Times

The top section of this dialog box lets you select whether you want to put the whole presentation on the Web, or just one group of slides. There's also an option to select whether you want your slide notes displayed. Slide notes will show up in a separate part of the screen from the slide. Again, this is part of the difference between a slide show and a Web page; on a good Web page, everything is integrated rather than broken into separate sections like that. If you don't have notes, or if the notes are meant for you rather than for the public (such as some of those racier limericks), clear the **Display speaker notes** check box.

In the Browser Support section of the dialog box, you have to decide who your viewers are. If they are all going to use the new versions of Internet Explorer, choose the first option. If they are likely to use other browsers, pick the second or third option. The second creates a version most browsers can see. The third creates two versions, one that will show on the current Internet Explorer and one for everything else. (This takes up more disk space.)

Below that, you will see the title for your Web site, which will show up on the title bar of the viewer's browser. If you created your presentation without giving it a title, this will just say PowerPoint Presentation. Click the **Change** button to replace this title with a better one.

Click the **Browse** button to get a file browser for selecting where to store the files. You can pick a spot on your hard disk, on your network, or you can even publish it directly to your World Wide Web space.

Options More! Options Galore!

That's not the end to the options. Click the **Web Options** button, and you get the joy of making a lot more decisions. Ah, sweet decisions.

The General tab controls the appearance of your Web presentation, which is important if you want your presentation to actually appear.

General Options, Commander of the Fourth Marine Option Battalion

If you put a check in the **Add slide navigation controls** check box, your Web site will have a navigation bar added to it, so the viewer can easily move to any slide. You can also choose the color scheme for this bar.

The next option lets you choose to **Show slide animation while browsing**. If you are going to have animations, you might as well show them. However, these animations will not show up on all browsers.

Finally, this tab contains an option to resize graphics to fit the size of the viewer's browser window. If maintaining the layout of your page is important to you, choose this option. Otherwise, viewers with relatively small browser windows will have the graphic fill the space, and those with large windows on high-resolution monitors will see a small graphic.

Generally, you will want all the check boxes on the File tab checked.

File Options, Such as "Should the Battalion File Out Now?"

The **File** tab has a series of options about how the files get saved and stored. The only one of these you might want to turn off is the one marked **Organize supporting files in a folder**, and you only want that one turned off if the Web service you are publishing on limits you to just one folder.

Don't check these Picture options unless you want to harass people for not having the same browser as you.

Picture Options, Such as "Should the Battalion Say 'Cheese'?"

The **Pictures** tab contains two check boxes that you shouldn't check. These serve mainly to make sure that anyone who doesn't have the latest version of Internet Explorer can't see your Web presentation.

The one option you have to worry about is the **Screen size** menu, which tells PowerPoint what size browser window the presentation should be set up for. If you selected the **Resize graphics to fit browser window** option on the General tab, you should set this to **800×600**. Otherwise, set it to **640×480**.

Atchway Ouryay Anguagelay

You need only to worry about the Encoding tab if your presentation is in a foreign language that needs its own character set, such as Cyrillic or Turkish or Martian.

After you have set all the options you care to, click the **OK** button to return to the Publish As Web Page dialog box.

Publish or Perish! (Hint: Pick "Publish")

Click the **Publish** button on the Publish As Web Page dialog box, and PowerPoint will save the presentations Web files to the location you specified. (If you are publishing directly to the Web rather than to your hard disk, PowerPoint will open up your Web connection. It may request the password for your Web connection and another password to have publishing access to your Web space.)

If you published the files to your hard disk, you will have to transfer them to your Web server. Different Web servers have different ways of accepting the files. The best way to handle this step is to ask the person in charge of the Web site how to put the pages up there. If you fumble around a little and act only semi-competent, perhaps the Web administrator will even take care of it for you and save you all the work!

What Hath Thou Wrought? Looking at Your Web Presentation

If you had the **Open published Web page in browser** option checked when you pushed the Publish button, PowerPoint will automatically open up your browser to display your Web presentation. Otherwise, start your browser and press **Ctrl+O** to start browsing so that you can find your presentation.

The names for all slides are listed. Slides without
names are numbered. Click a name to see the slide.

A presentation viewed as a Web page.

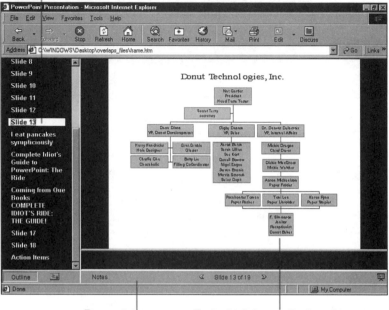

Presentation
navigation toolbar

Text which is small when the
slide is shown full-screen can be
unreadable in a reduced window.

The Least You Need to Know

➤ When you are preparing a presentation for the World Wide Web, you should avoid audio, video, complex drawings and large photos.

➤ To save your presentation in Web-ready form, use the File, Save as Web Page command.

➤ On the Save As dialog box, click the Publish button to be able to choose options about how your presentation will appear on the Web.

➤ The Microsoft Internet Explorer 4.0 Or Later option on the Browser Support list will severely limit who can view your presentation. More people will be able to view it if you pick a different option.

➤ Click the Web Options button to set additional options about how your presentation will appear.

Chapter 22

Printing Printouts and Handling Handouts

In This Chapter

➤ Print your slides and information about them onto genuine paper

➤ Specify what to print, how many copies, and how they should look

➤ Print up handouts with several slides per page

➤ Run the paper through a shredder to destroy the evidence (actually, you can figure that out for yourself!)

The advent of computers was supposed to bring us the paperless office, with everything being taken care of electronically. Alas, this has not happened. About the only part of the office that is likely to be paperless is the bathroom, and then only if the janitor has been lax about refilling the dispensers.

Instead, computers have given us the ability to create more items and many copies of those items with great efficiency. The office is now being buried under a mountain of paper—and there's no reason that PowerPoint shouldn't be in on the act!

Quick Print

If you want to quickly print out your presentation, just click the **Print** button. This will print it all out. However, the printed version may not look just like you want it to. PowerPoint has a lot of different options to set in regard to how the printed version should look. When you use the Print button, it uses whatever settings you set the last time you printed using the File menu Print commands described over the next few pages.

Printing PowerPoint Presentations Perfectly

For greater control over the printout, yank down the ol' **File** menu and select the **Print** commands. You will see that PowerPoint gives you a lot of control over how your printouts turn out. There are probably more options than you are ever going to use, but that's what a powerful program is all about. If it didn't have all that power, they would probably have to call it just Microsoft Point, which is a really dumb name for a program.

The Print dialog box sure has lots of things to click!

What printer?

Which slides?

How should it look?

How many copies?

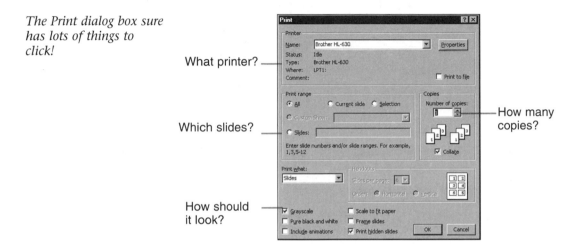

Which Printer?

Click the arrow button on the end of the **Name** field to see a drop-down list of all the printer devices on your system. Even if you only have one printer, you may have a number of devices set up. This is because Windows counts printers on the network and fax/modem systems as printers. You can even have actual printers configured that aren't attached to your computer. (This can be handy if you want to create a file that you can carry to someone else's computer and print on its printer.)

Select the printer that you want to print to. If you need to change something about how that printer is set up (such as which paper tray it should use or how dark the printout should be), click the **Properties** button.

Paperless Fax

If you have a properly configured fax modem, you can fax your presentation from PowerPoint without printing it out. Just select the fax driver from the printer list. When you click **OK**, a fax program will appear asking you for details like what number to call and what the cover sheet should be.

Which Slides?

The Print Range area of the dialog box has a number of choices that you use to control which parts of your presentation get printed. Click **All**, and all the slides are printed. Choose **Current Slide**, and just the slide you are working on gets printed. Choose **Selection**, and all the slides that are currently selected get printed. (This is usually the same as Current Slide, unless you have selected multiple slides, as described in Chapter 4, "Sliding Slides into Place".)

Pick **Slides**, and the text box next to it lights up. Type the numbers of the slides that you want printed, separated by commas. You can include *ranges* of slides, all the slides from one slide to another, by listing the first slide, then a dash, and then the last slide. For example, if you put 3-5,7,9 into this field, PowerPoint will print slides 3, 4, 5, 7, and 9.

How Should It Look?

When it comes to figuring how your printout should look, it would be nice if there were an option marked Just Right. There isn't such a thing, so you have to pick for yourself.

First, click the drop-down arrow on the **Print What** field. One option is **Slides**, which prints out one slide per page. Then there's **Handouts**, which prints out several miniature slides per page. Choosing **Notes Pages** prints one slide at the top of each page, with the Speakers Notes for that page under it. Choosing **Outline View** prints the text outline for the pages.

Underneath that is a series of check boxes. Selecting the first one, **Grayscale**, causes the printout not to include any colors. Colors will be turned into shades of gray instead. If you have a black-and-white printer, PowerPoint will automatically use this feature for you. (It would be a neat trick for PowerPoint to find a way to print in color on your black-and-white printer, wouldn't it?) Selecting **Pure black and white** means that there are no shades of gray. Your colors will turn black or white. In cases where you have a colored item on a colored background, this may be easier to read than black and white, or it may be impossible to read (if both colors turn black or both turn white).

Avoiding the Black-and-White Blues

When you print with the Grayscale or Pure black and white options, printouts may not look like you would expect. That's because PowerPoint tries to clear up items that may not look right when all the colors are converted to black, white, and gray, and some of its attempts work badly. For example, PowerPoint puts lines around otherwise lineless shapes (which can add lines you don't want), and prints all text in black (which makes it invisible when the background is also black). To avoid this, in Slide view use the **View, Black and White** command to see what your slides will look like on the printout. If something doesn't look right, right-click it, and select **Black and White** from the pop-up menu. A submenu lists different ways that PowerPoint can display this item in black and white; selecting **Grayscale** from this list will usually give you what you want.

The **Include animations** option will print a copy of how the slide looks before any animations, and for every animated object on the slide, one copy of how the slide looks after that animation. If you don't select this, only one copy of each slide is printed, showing how the slide looks after all the animations are over.

Picking **Scale to Fit Paper** will stretch the slide to fill up the page. Picking **Frame Slides** will draw a rectangle around each slide, to show where the edges of the slide are (much like the way that they appear in the Slide Sorter view).

Print Hidden Slides tells the computer to include the hidden slides in your presentation. This check box will already be selected if you have chosen a hidden slide to print; you will have to clear it if you want to keep your hidden slides, well, hidden.

How Many Copies?

If you want to print out more than one copy, enter the number of copies that you want to print into the **Number of copies** field. If you want to print out *less* than one copy, you are really wasting your time here, aren't you?

When you print out more than one copy of more than one page, collation becomes important. If you put a check into the **Collate** check box, it will print all the pages in the first copy, and then the entire second copy, and so on. If there isn't a check there, it will print all the copies of the first page, then all the copies of the second page, and on to the last page. Not using collation may get it to print faster in many cases, but then you have to waste time putting all the pages in order.

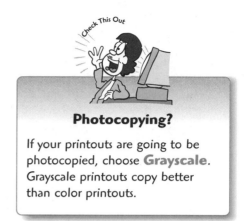

Photocopying?

If your printouts are going to be photocopied, choose **Grayscale**. Grayscale printouts copy better than color printouts.

What Are You Waiting For?

After you have everything selected, click **OK** to start printing. Okay, the printing doesn't start immediately. That doesn't mean that the computer is ignoring you. What's happening is that the computer is sending the information on what to print to the disk. Then the information will be sent from the disk to your printer. This way, you don't have to wait for your printing to be finished before you go back to working with your presentation. But you are probably sneaking away to get a sandwich anyway, aren't you?

Handouts That No Panhandler Would Want

A *handout* is a set of pages that reprint all the slides in your presentation, several slides to a page. They are called handouts because you are supposed to hand them out to your audience so that they can take your presentation with them when they go. It also helps the viewer follow the presentation.

If you select **Handouts** in the Print What field, the area of handout options becomes usable. The main option is the Slides Per Page drop-down list, which lets you choose to print two, three, four, six, or nine slides per page. If your favorite number is not on that list, you are out of luck.

If you select **2**, the slides will print out two per page, one above the other.

Select **4**, **6**, or **9**, and you get to choose whether the slides are numbered across the page (Horizontal) or down the page (Vertical). If you are printing four slides per page and choose **Horizontal**, the first slide on the first page will be number 1, and to the right of that will be slide 2, and then below those will be a row with slides 3 and 4. If, on the other hand, you choose **Vertical**, slide 1 will still be in the upper-left corner, but slide 2 will be below it. To the right of slide 1 starts the second column, with slides 3 and 4. Usually, you will want to use Horizontal, unless you want to confuse your audience (which can be fun).

If you choose **3**, you get something a little different. Instead of just printed slides, you get three slides on the left side of the page each accompanied by a row of lines on the right. These lines can be used for making notes about the slide, which makes this form of handout great for handing out *before* your presentation.

A three-slides-per-page handout.

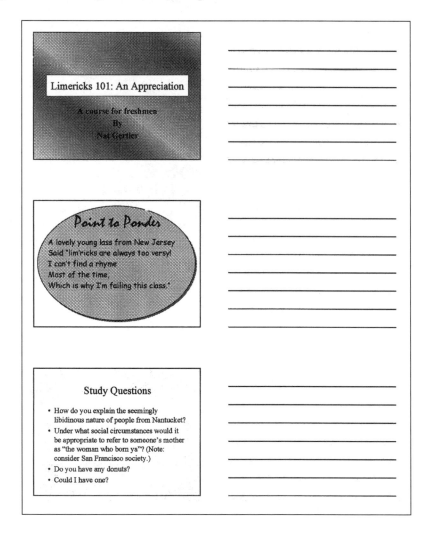

The Least You Need to Know

➤ To print out all or part of your presentation, use the **File, Print** command.

➤ On the Print dialog box, first select the printer that you want to use from the list in the Name field.

➤ You can select **All** to print out all the slides, **Selection** to print just the selected slides, or **Slides** to type in a list of the slides that you want to print.

➤ In the Print What field, selecting **Slides** will print one slide per page, **Handouts** will print 2, 3, 4, 6, or 9 slides per page depending on the option you pick, **Notes** will print one slide per page with your Speaker Notes, and **Outline** will print the text outline of your presentation.

➤ Put the number of copies you want printed in the **Number of copies** field. If it's more than one, make sure that **Collation** is checked; otherwise, you will have to arrange the sets yourself.

➤ Selecting the **Grayscale** option will print it in black, white, and shades of gray; **Pure black and white** won't use gray.

➤ If you want to print the hidden slides as well as the non-hidden ones, select **Hidden slides**.

➤ When you are ready to print, click the OK button.

Part 5

Getting the Most out of PowerPoint

If you like giving presentations, you'll want to get the most out of PowerPoint. If you don't like giving presentations, you'll want to get out of PowerPoint altogether. But by this point in the book, it's too late! You're now the expert!

In this part lie the secrets to making a good presentation, one that communicates clearly and directly, one that people want to pay attention to and can understand. And you'll learn to take things from (and pass them back to) other programs to save yourself effort.

Chapter 23

Office Gossip: Swapping Info with Other Office Products

In This Chapter

➤ Copy words and pictures from any word processor or painting program into your presentation

➤ Turn a Word document into a presentation (Kazam!)

➤ Turn a presentation into a Word document (Unkazam!)

➤ Copy numbers and charts from Microsoft Excel into your presentation

---

You are probably using your computer for more than just PowerPoint. There's Tetris, there's Tomb Raider, there's Solitaire... and oh yes, there are all those word processors and spreadsheets and other silly things you have to use to get your work done.

Because you have a copy of PowerPoint, odds are that you have all of Microsoft Office installed on your machine, including the Microsoft Word word processor and Microsoft Excel spreadsheet. Sometimes, you will have information you created in one of those programs that you want to use in PowerPoint.

Stealing Bits from Anywhere

Windows has a built-in set of copying and pasting tools that make it easy to yank words out of a document, no matter what program you created them in, and slam them into your presentation. To do this, select the text in the document. Press **Ctrl+C**, which is the standard copy command. The text will be stored in an area of memory called the Clipboard. Then, go to your presentation, open up a text box for it (or select a spot in existing text), and press **Ctrl+V** or the **Paste** button for the Paste command. This will take the text from the Clipboard and slam it into the text box.

Working with pictures is much the same. In whatever picture program you are using, select the area of the picture that you want to copy. Press **Ctrl+C**. Go to your presentation, and in Slide Show mode, press **Ctrl+V**. The copied material will appear on the page.

Documents That Are Out of this Word!

Microsoft Word is a very good outline editor. It's so full of rich features and tools that I really can't describe how to use it here. So it's certainly reasonable that you would want to make the outline for your presentation in Word, or take an outline that you already made there and make a presentation out of it.

How a Word outline becomes a presentation.

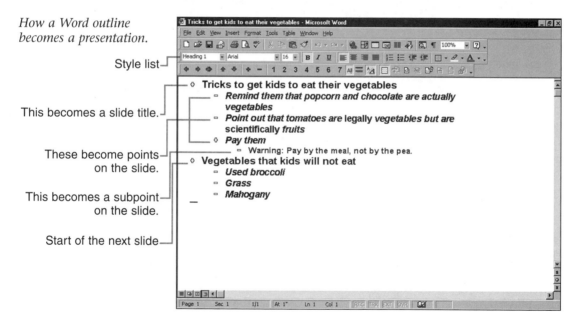

Doing this is as easy as pie (one of those easy sorts of pie, not one of those tricky lattice pies). Open the document in Word, pull down Word's **File** menu and, from the **Send To** submenu, select **Microsoft PowerPoint**. Word will start up PowerPoint (unless it's already running, in which case it doesn't have to), and the outline will appear as a new presentation. Each main point will be the title at the top of a new slide, and the items under that will appear as the text on the slide.

Even if you are not comfortable with Outline mode, you can still turn your Word document into a presentation. For each slide, you will want one paragraph to be the title, and one or more paragraphs of text for the slide. After you have that all set up, press **Ctrl+A** to select all the text in your document. Then click the **Style** drop-down menu and select **Heading 2** as the style. Then, for each of the title paragraphs, click the paragraph, pull down the **Style** list, and select **Heading 1**. Finally, use the **File, Send To, Microsoft PowerPoint** command to turn it into a presentation.

Word-ward Ho!

You can turn your presentation into one of several sorts of Word documents. You can create a Word document with pictures of the slides accompanied by your notes. You can make one with pictures of your slides accompanied by underlines. Or, you can just make one with all the text from your slide. It's up to you. I really don't care which you choose. I have a problem with apathy.

Doing any of these is as easy as a very-slightly-more-difficult pie. With your presentation loaded in PowerPoint, pull down the **File** menu, find the **Send To** submenu, and select the **Microsoft Word** command that you find there. A Write Up dialog box will appear, wanting to know what sort of document you want to make out of it.

Pick from a range of formats for the Word document.

Select the style of Word document you want by clicking the radio button next to that style, and then click the **OK** button. The new document will appear in Word.

Bouncing Back and Forth

You can take an outline that you have been working on in PowerPoint, send it to Word, make some changes there, and then send it back to PowerPoint. When you do this, you will lose all your graphics, and your bullet formatting may change; so only do this if you haven't put much work into those things yet, or had so much fun doing the graphics the first time that you want to do it all over again!

Excel-erating Your Presentation

If you want to do pie, well, that's about as easy as copying a spreadsheet from Excel into PowerPoint. However, I won't teach you to do pie here. (Write in and insist that they have me write *The Complete Idiot's Guide to Pie!*) In Excel, select the cells that you want to copy over, and then press the **Copy** button or press **Ctrl+C** to copy it. Then head over to PowerPoint, pull down the **Edit** menu, and select **Paste Special**. Why Paste Special rather than paste normally? Because this will allow us some special tricks.

This is a special paste, even better than library paste!

When you select Paste Special, a dialog box comes up. At the center of this dialog box is a list of styles that it can paste this as. Pick **Microsoft Excel Worksheet Object**.

Over at the left is a pair of option buttons. If you select the one marked **Paste**, this will be pasted as its own little worksheet in PowerPoint. If you choose **Paste Link**, you get a nifty side benefit: Whenever someone changes the original spreadsheet, the change is automatically made in your presentation! This is because PowerPoint doesn't actually store the spreadsheet. Instead, it stores it as "Here we will display cells A3 through J27 from the Profits 99 spreadsheet." Whenever PowerPoint loads up the presentation, it checks the spreadsheet again for what is currently there.

You may not want to use Paste Link, however. For one thing, you might want your presentation to reflect the spreadsheet as it currently is rather than change with the time. For another thing, if someone moves, deletes, or rearranges that spreadsheet, it can mess up your presentation.

After you have that selection settled, click **OK**. The spreadsheet section appears on your slide (although you may have to resize it using its sizing handles to get a clear look at it).

Moving a Chart

Copying a chart from Excel is as easy as pie chart! In fact, it's almost the same as copying a spreadsheet. In Excel, select the chart by clicking it near the edge. (Make sure you are not clicking part of the chart or its markings.) Click the **Copy** button to copy it to the Clipboard. In PowerPoint, pull down the **Edit** menu and select

246

Paste Special. This time, the type you select is **Microsoft Excel Chart Object**. Once again, you can choose between Paste and Paste Link, for the same reasons. Click **OK**, and the chart appears on the slide!

It's a Complete Copy

When you use Paste Special to paste in a spreadsheet or chart, PowerPoint actually gets the whole spreadsheet, not just the part you copied. It only shows the part you copied; if you double-click it, however, you get the Excel menus and toolbars and can work with all the data of the spreadsheet.

The Least You Need to Know

➤ To copy text or pictures from any editing program, select them, press **Ctrl+C** to copy, and then go to PowerPoint and click the **Paste** button to paste them in.

➤ To use a Word outline as the basis for a new presentation, load up the outline in Word and use the **File**, **Send To**, **Microsoft PowerPoint** command.

➤ To copy all the text from your presentation to a new Word document, use PowerPoint's **File**, **Send To**, **Microsoft Word** command.

➤ To copy an Excel chart or section of a spreadsheet to your slide, first select it in Excel, and then click Excel's **Copy** button. Then, in PowerPoint, use the **Edit**, **Paste Special** command, select the appropriate type of **Microsoft Excel** object from the Paste Special dialog box, and click **OK**.

➤ The Paste Link option in the Paste special dialog box tells Power Point to recheck the source document every time the presentation is loaded and to update the copied part to match any changes.

Chapter 24

Making Your Presentation a Doozy! (Not a Don'tzy!)

In This Chapter

➤ Make a slideshow that people can see

➤ Make a slideshow that people want to see

➤ Put control links on your slide that people can use

➤ Keep your slideshow on the topic and interesting

➤ Avoid getting carried away

So far, the book has told you how to put together a presentation. That's like a book on painting teaching you how to dip the brush into the paint and then to drag the brush across the canvas. You now have all the tools to make a really good presentation, or a tremendously awful one. This chapter has a few hints that should let you know just which you are doing.

Can You See the Forest Through the Polychromatic Hyperlinked Trees?

PowerPoint is a powerful tool, full of features and tricks that you can use to make an amazing slam-bam presentation. With all the things you can do with your presentation, it's easy to forget that you don't really want a presentation. Having a presentation is not your ultimate goal.

Unless you are just sitting around using PowerPoint for the fun of it (and if that's how you have fun, there's nothing wrong with that), your ultimate goal is to give information to people (and even that may well be a step toward something else, such as getting people to buy your new all-plastic reusable donuts). Your presentation is just a tool to inform people. PowerPoint is a tool-making tool.

Keeping the Point in PowerPoint

The first step to making a good presentation is to have something worth telling people about. Before you put in the big effort, think about what you are doing. Do you have information that people will want to know? Do you have all the information they want, or are you going to leave them with more questions than answers? You should know the information that you are going to tell them before you put the very first word on a slide.

It isn't hard to find out if what you have will interest people. All you have to do is find people, tell them what you know, and see whether it interests them. (This may sound tricky because there is no entry for *people* in the Yellow Pages, but if you check the White Pages, you will find some there. Odds are, someone you know may already be a people!) Get someone who would be a member of your audience, and then just talk about the topic at hand. Don't mention you are planning a presentation, just talk a bit and see if you are able to spark any interest. If so, you have something. If not, it may be time to rethink. And if you are asked any questions about it, pay attention to those questions, and consider putting the answers in your presentation.

Cool-Looking Augmented Obfuscation

The tools in PowerPoint have a lot of options. You can spend hours trying different metallic background fills on your logo, using different gradients, different directions, and so on. You probably *will* spend hours doing this, because it is easy to get caught up in this manipulation. You can get so entranced in rotating it to just the right angle, adjusting the shadow, and tweaking the spacing between letters, that you don't notice that the words in the logo say *How To Talk Goodly*.

Having a clear and understandable presentation is a lot more important than having a keen-looking one. Sure, you should take care that it looks good, but adding in all the flashes and gimmicks, the multimedia bells and hyperlink whistles, should be the last thing on the list, not the first.

It's more important that the information be in a reasonable order, so that you don't need something that comes later in order to understand something that comes earlier, than it is to have your logo in 3D on each slide. If you spend some time planning the presentation before you even start PowerPoint, you save a lot of time that you would have wasted rearranging things later.

If you find yourself spending more time in PowerPoint than you did putting together the information for the presentation in the first place, you have probably turned into a PowerPoint addict, and should try to do a little less.

Watch Your Language

A picture is said to be worth a thousand words, and that's before inflation. However, a few words, well chosen, can communicate an awful lot. A few words, badly chosen, can quickly confuse your entire audience.

Check your spelling. The built in Spell Checker is really handy, underlining words that it doesn't recognize. It is not smart enough, however, to recognize a typo that turns one word into another. If you are trying to type Shakespeare's phrase Now is the winter of our discontent, and accidentally press the Spacebar rather than the *n*, PowerPoint will have absolutely no complaint about Now is the winter of our disco tent.

One good tool to catch your typing mistakes is the AutoCorrect feature. This keeps an eye on your typing, finding the most common mistakes and correcting them automatically, without even bothering to ask. To take advantage of this helper, pull down the **Tools** menu and select **AutoCorrect**. An AutoCorrect dialog box listing all the kinds of things that AutoCorrect can catch appears, with check boxes for each type. Make sure all of your favorite mistakes are checked, and take particular care that the **Replace Text as you Type** box is checked, or else AutoCorrect won't correct at all.

Exceptional Exceptions

If you use an abbreviation that ends in a period (such as abbr. for abbreviations), click the **Exceptions** button and add the abbreviation to the list on the **First Letter** tab so that AutoCorrect won't assume it is the end of a sentence and capitalize the next letter. Similarly if you use words that have more than one capital letter in a row but aren't all capitals (such as TVaholic), add them to the list on the **INitial CAps** tab.

I keep trying to type a list of mistakes that AutoCorrect corrects, but the same feature in my word processor keeps correcting them!

AutoIncorrect

AutoCorrect automatically replaces (c) with the copyright symbol, which can be a problem if you are trying to display lettered points. You may want to delete this one.

You can even add the typos that you make most often so that AutoCorrect will always fix them for you. Just type the typo into the **Replace** field, and the correct version into the **With** field, and then click the **Add** button. It will be added to the list of common mistakes at the bottom of the dialog box. To remove one from the list, just click it, and then click the **Delete** button.

Some of the corrections on the list aren't even errors. For example, if you type (tm), AutoCorrect will turn that into a little trademark symbol at the end of the word.

Grammar is something that you will have to catch yourself, unless you are wily enough to rope someone else into checking it for you (which isn't a bad idea, because your own mistakes are the hardest to catch. I have a whole team of editors working on this book, so my grammar be perfect). Pay attention to this; a blatant grammar mistake can make you look less intelligent and more careless.

The grammar mistake that seems to get people's attention most quickly is the misused apostrophe. Apostrophes are easy to mess up, because although there are only a few exceptions to each apostrophe rule, those exceptions appear often. Don't use an apostrophe to make a word plural (*The monkey's got their report cards* is wrong) unless what you are pluralizing is a single letter (*The monkey got all A's on his report card* is right.) Do use the apostrophe when adding an *s* to make something possessive (*The monkey's report card was delicious* is right, because it's the report card belonging to the monkey), except when you are adding it to a pronoun, as with its, ours, hers, and yours. (*The monkey ate its report card*, not *it's report card*.) Always use an apostrophe when contracting two words into one. (*It's a bad idea to make edible report cards* is right, because *it's* is short for *it is*.) Don't confuse the contractions *you're, they're,* and *we're* with the similar-looking *your, their,* and *were*.

Watch Someone Else's Language

When it comes to technical terms, be aware of who your audience is. Are they going to know the terms you use? If you are not sure, you have two choices. You can either avoid using the term altogether, or you can define it for them. A definition doesn't have to be a big, meticulous thing that interrupts the flow of what you are saying. You can use quick *sidebar definitions* (short definitions in parentheses after you use the term) without jarring much. There, I just used one! That was pretty painless, wasn't it?

In some applications, you have to worry about the entire language. This is particularly true of consumer applications like kiosks. In large parts of the United States and Canada, a significant number of people have something besides English as their first language. You will usually run into French (Canada) or Spanish (United States), but in specific areas there are other languages as well. Bringing your message to people in a tongue they are comfortable with is not only good business, it may be legally required in certain situations.

There are several ways of dealing with the multilingual problem. One is to avoid language altogether, which you may be able to pull off in a store window display with nothing but pictures and prices, but cases where you can get away with this easily are more the exception than the rule. You can also put multiple languages on the screen simultaneously. If you do this, you should be consistent from slide to slide about exactly where each version is placed. You also have to be sure that you are not using recorded dialog . Finally, you can have a hyperlink on your first slide that is marked with the name of the language, taking the viewer to a version of the slide show in that language.

Make the area's dominant language easier to notice so that most people gravitate to the correct text. Smaller type is useful for languages with long or many words.

The discovery of the donut goes back to primitive times. Early donuts were made of stone, and were considered to be quite a delicacy among those with the strength to chew them.

Modern donuts are made from a broad range of materials, including something called "pumpernickel." Those seeking authentic early donut taste need only keep their donuts for a few days.

Ehtay iscoverday ofay ethay onutday oesgay ackbay ootay imitivepray imestay. Earlyay onutsday ereway ademay outay offay onestay, anday ereway onsideredcay ootay ebay itequay ayay elicacyday ongamay osethay ithway ethay engthstray ootay ewchay emthay.

Odernmay onutsday aray ademay omfray ayay oddbray angeray offay aterialsmay, includingay omethingsay alledcay "umpernickelpay." Osethay eekingsay authenticay earlyay onutday astetay eednay onlyay eepkay eirthay onutsday orfay ayay ewfay daysay.

Make sure you get a good translation. Translations which have on them much badnesses are hard read and you be to avoiding them like the turtle that snaps!

That Isn't Wrong, It's Foreign

When you include foreign-language text, select it and use the **Tools, Language** command. This way, the automatic Spell Checker knows not to check it, and the spell checking part of the Style Checker knows to check a foreign dictionary for it.

The Awful Eyeful: Slides That Are Hard to Look At

Making a truly ugly slide is like making a truly ugly house—it usually happens not from trying to do too little, but from trying to do too much, all at once, throwing in so many different styles and clashing colors. Trying to do less will often let your slide have more effect.

Look Here! No, There! No, Wait, Over Here!

A slideshow shouldn't be like three-ring circus, with a bunch of things calling for the viewer's attention all at the same time. This isn't to say that you can't have a reasonable amount of things on a slide, but there should only be one thing that says "look at me first", and should lead to looking at all the other important things.

There are several ways of deciding what gets seen first. Bigger items tend to get seen before smaller items. (That's why people read headlines first and then the articles: The text is bigger.) Colors that stand out against the background are more visible than colors that are similar to the background. The eye picks up on simpler designs (like a cartoon drawing) quicker than on more detailed things (like a photograph). Things at the top of the slide are read before things lower on the slide. Things that are animated call attention to themselves before things that are standing still.

All of this isn't to say that you can't put a number of things on a slide, but if you do, many of them should seem more a part of a background design rather than individual eye-grabbers. If you want to put your logo on every slide, just make it a key element on the first slide, and put it in a subtle color on all the rest. If you want control buttons that appear on every slide, put them at the bottom of the slide. People will be able to find them if they look for them.

When Colors Collide!

Color is tricky.

When you want something to be easily visible, the natural reaction is to just use a different color than the background. Put a red object on a green background, and it should be easy to look at, right? Not necessarily.

What really makes things easy or hard to look at doesn't have much to do with what color they are. Instead, it has to do with how bright or dark they are. If you put light-blue text on a dark-blue background, it will be easy to read. If you put bright-red text on a bright-green background, it will be hard to read. Black will stand out on any light background, and white will stand out on any dark one.

There's a neat trick for checking the readability of the colors you have chosen, and that's to forget the colors altogether! Click the **Black and White** button on the Standard toolbar, then right-click the items you are worried about, and choose **Black and White**, **Grayscale** from the pop-up menu. The black and white display doesn't show the colors (obviously), but merely the darkness level, turning bright colors into light grays and dark ones into dark grays. If it is hard to see in this mode, it will be a strain on people's eyes in Color modes. If you are planning to print this presentation on a black-and-white printer, you may want to right-click the items again and choose **Black and White**, **Automatic**, which will make your non-black text print in black, rather than gray.

Similarly, things that are supposed to be part of the background design of the page shouldn't stand out. This doesn't mean that they have to be the same color, just the same brightness. Using the contrast and brightness controls on the picture toolbar, you can make washed-out versions of pictures, which will be just fine for use in the background.

Be aware of the moods color creates. Red is often associated with danger, warning, and financial losses; it shouldn't be used to convey good news or positive financial results. Green is often associated with moving ahead, and is good for messages of encouragement. Blue has a calming effect, and purple suggests strangeness. Don't overload your presentation with colors; if you use more than three or four basic colors for text, chart colors, and backgrounds in your presentation, you are probably overdoing it.

Color Concern

Checking the Black and White view also ensures that color-blind people will be able to see objects on your slide. Color-blindness hits about 1 person in 25.

Too Textravagant

There are already far too many ugly words in this world, such as *famine, hatred,* and *disease*. The text on your slides shouldn't add their own form of ugliness. There are a lot of ways you can go wrong with the look of your text.

Having text that's too small to read easily is an obvious problem. How small is too small is a tough decision, but keep in mind that just because it looks fine on a computer display doesn't mean it will be fine on a projected display. In projection environments, not only are people trying to read it from clear across the room, but you also have the problem of focusing. Unless you focus exactly right, the text will be blurry.

Having too many bulleted points on a slide is also a problem. A bullet should call attention to a point. Too many bullets and they stop calling attention to anything.

By now, we have all seen forms of font abuse. One common form of this is taking a font with complex capital letters and using them for all-capitals, so that every letter is calling out for attention. This is usually pretty blatant. A subtler problem, easier to fall into, is using too many different fonts. Every time you use a new font family, the reader has to adjust somewhat. This isn't too bad if there are two or even three fonts in a presentation, used for different things. When you get above three, you are looking for trouble. You are usually better off going for variations in the same font (using bold or italic or a different size) than going with a completely different font.

Fonts often get divided into two categories, called serif and san-serif. *Serif* fonts have little detail lines (called *serifs*) on the end of many letters. These little lines help the eye recognize the letters; so serif fonts are good if you have a lot of text (for example, this paragraph is in a serif font). *San-serif* fonts don't have these little lines, which make them simpler and therefore more eye-catching for headlines and short amounts of text. That's why all the section names in this book are in san-serif fonts.

To save the eyes of the world, PowerPoint includes a feature called Style Checker. Pull down the **Tools** menu and select **Options**. On the Option dialog box, click the **Spelling and Style** tab. Check to make sure the **Check style** check box has a check in it (checkity check check check), and then click the **Style options** button.

The **Visual Clarity** tab lets you choose to check all the different forms of text atrocities already listed, except for ugly usage of all-capitals. For that, you will just have to develop some taste… or steer clear of all-capitals altogether. You can also choose your own limits to things, in case you think that more than three fonts is fine, but more than 53 should be a no-no.

Keep your fonts big enough to read.

Use the Visual Clarity tab to set up the Style Checker to keep from making your fonts hard to read.

Don't put too much on a slide.

The **Case and End Punctuation** tab sounds like it will make a case for bringing an end to punctuation as we know it. Actually, it will help you make sure that you are using capital letters and punctuation consistently. In the case section, you have separate drop menus for the slide titles and the points on your slide (the *body text*) to enable you to choose whether you want *Sentence case* (only the first letter of every sentence capitalized), *Title Case* (The First Letter Of Every Word Capitalized Like This), *lowercase* (no capitals) or *UPPERCASE* (ALL CAPITALS)... or you can clear the check boxes. Similarly, in the End Punctuation section, you can choose separately whether the titles and the points on your slides should have punctuation at the end.

Title Case: Capitalize Every Word.

Sentence case: Capitalize the first word.

The Case And End Punctuation tab lets the Style Checker see that you are properly, ummm, casual and punctual... no, wait, that's not right.

To punctuate, or not to punctuate?

Slow Down for that Yellow Light

The Style Checker automatically checks your text for all the elements listed on the two Style Option tabs. When it sees you type something that doesn't match the listed style, it will display a light bulb.

If you see a yellow light bulb, click it. The Office Assistant will let you know what your stylistic *faux pas* (French for *fake dads*) is, and will offer you a correction for it. Click the correction to have it change your text to match your style guidelines, or click **Ignore** to just make the light bulb go away without changing anything.

Controls: Don't Reinvent the Steering Wheel

If you are building an interactive presentation, you have to let the user know how to use it. Otherwise, the user will just stare at it for a while, and then go away.

The first trick is to make it clear that it is interactive. Don't just put a couple of pictures up and expect that someone will know to click one of them. You should also avoid trying to come up with some new way of communicating what to click. There are several good existing ways of doing this.

One way is just to tell it straight out. If you put the words `Click here to learn more about ironing soup`, people will know that they can click there to learn more about ironing soup (unless they don't know enough to understand that sentence, in which case they are probably not smart enough to iron soup).

Another way is to take advantage of the 3D buttons in AutoShape. Put a word on a button, and suddenly the idea of clicking there becomes very clear.

You should be careful, however, about using the buttons with the pictures on them. You may know what a triangle pointing toward a straight line is, perhaps because you have something similar on your VCR. A lot of people out there don't have a VCR, however, and many others who have one can't use it. The international symbol for information may be the best way to address an international audience, but if your presentation is in English, you should count on your audience using English.

Use words! Put the word `Information` on a button, and people will have a clue of what it's for. Put the phrase `Click here for information` on it, and it may take up more space but it will be hard to not understand. Putting the word on an arrow shape (pointing left to go back a slide or right to move to the next slide) may help folks find the right thing to click, but the word makes it clear what it's for.

Are Your Controls out of Control?

If you have too many controls, your presentation will be difficult to use. Imagine trying to use a mouse with 37 buttons on it, each of which does a different thing, and you will get the sense of what I mean.

If you want your user to be able to do a lot of things, don't do it with a lot of controls on the same page with your information. Keep it down to four or five controls on each page, and have one of them hyperlinked to a slide with the full set of controls on it. That way, only the person who is looking to do something tricky needs to face the controls, which aren't otherwise cluttering up the rest of your presentation.

People shouldn't have to go hunting for the controls on each slide. Keep your controls in a standard spot on each slide instead of moving them from slide to slide. Don't change what the controls look like, either.

Yelp for Help!

There was a home computer put out in the 1980s that had a lot of innovative features, but perhaps the best and the simplest was that it had a big button on the keypad marked Help. You were supposed to press that button if you needed information on how to do what you wanted to do. Unfortunately, most of the programs didn't take advantage of the button. You would call for help, but none would be coming.

If you have a complex interactive presentation, you may want to consider having an onscreen button marked Help. It's very comforting for the user to have it there, even if it never gets used. But if it is pressed, the user better be taken to a slide full of useful information!

Keep Your Content Interesting

Sometimes people have to pay attention. If you are the boss, and it's your meeting, they have to pay attention. Even if they are forced to pay attention, they will get much more out of it if they are interested. If they are not interested and they don't have to pay attention, they will just walk away.

The first step is to make sure you are giving them the right amount of information. You have to keep your eye on three levels of information:

➤ The *least* you should tell them is what they need to know.

➤ The *best* you should tell them is what they want to know. This doesn't mean that you want to tell them everything that any of them might want to know; if your presentation is trying to sell a car to everyone, you can't put in all the information that a big car-aholic will want, because you will bore everyone else. Which brings up the third amount.

➤ The *most* you should tell them is the most they want to know. What you are talking about may have a big history, and you may have spent the past decade of your life investigating it. Unless that history is either extremely fascinating or very important to them, however, skip it.

The Topic: The Topic

You should always be clear on what the topic of the presentation is, and what the ultimate goal is. Every single slide in your presentation should be about that topic and head toward that goal in some way. This doesn't mean that you can't include side comments, but you should be aware that they are side comments and not devote an entire slide (or more) to them.

Part of the trick is to define your topic very precisely. A title can be a good place for this description of your topic, so long as it's not too long. If your presentation's title is *How to Iron Soup*, you know that you don't need those three slides on the history of ironing soup, because this isn't a history lesson, it's a how to lesson.

Pictures Tell a Story

School teaches us to be word people. We are always told to write essays, never to draw them. That's a shame, because pictures are both incredibly interesting and incredibly informative.

You can write 15 paragraphs about how the new NG-57 automobile has a transwhoopdidoo suspension system that gives it a turning radius of 3.79 inches, and people will sit there and try to parse what all the technology is about. But if you show them a film clip of the car taking a tight corner, not only will they understand it all better, they will also believe it.

A drawing may not carry the sense of reality of a photograph, but it can highlight what you want to show very effectively. Of course, to get a drawing of something original, you either have to learn to draw or find someone else who can. Even a simple diagram, however, can go far.

Graphs turn numbers (which are hard to understand) into pictures (which are easy to understand). This is a good thing.

If You Can't Please One Person, How Can You Please Them All?

I know this suggestion has popped up in various specific forms, but here is the general version: The best way to make sure you have a good presentation is to have someone try it out for you. Pick one or two friends who don't already know the information that the presentation has to offer. Let them tell you what's wrong with it. They will find the missing things, the unnecessary things, and the confusing things. Listen to them, and don't put down what they say. Then fix those things, and find someone new to test it next time.

The Least You Need to Know

➤ Have something to say. Spend your time on content that communicates instead of on making your presentation as pretty as possible.

➤ Grammar and spelling count. The **Tools, AutoCorrect** command can keep an eye on your work as you type and protect you from hundreds of common errors.

➤ There should be one main thing on each slide, calling your attention to look at it first.

➤ If objects aren't easy to see in the **View, Black and White** mode, they won't be easy to read in full color.

➤ Make it clear what the user can click, either by making it into a 3D button or by having something that says "Click here to" whatever. Don't use too many control buttons on a page. A button marked Help can be extremely useful on a complex slide, if it goes to a useful slide of helpful information.

➤ Don't tell people more than they want to know, unless they need to know it.

➤ Pictures often communicate more effectively than text.

Chapter 25

Express to Impress: Delivering Good Oral Presentations

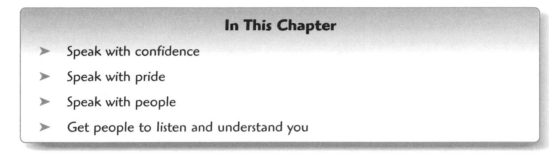

In This Chapter

➤ Speak with confidence

➤ Speak with pride

➤ Speak with people

➤ Get people to listen and understand you

When people know something that we want to know, when they get good at something we need to understand, we want them to tell us about it. The problem is that most of the time, what people are good at isn't talking to other people and explaining things. Do one thing well, and you are expected to do something else well as well. Luckily, it isn't a hard thing to learn.

Actually, you have already learned most of it. You have already learned the mechanics of it. You can open your mouth and make noises come out, and not just belches, either. You can make sounds that mean something to other people (such as, "Excuse me for belching!"). That's the hardest part, and it took a lot of work way back when. Now all you have got to do is learn the art of delivering the presentation, and luckily, there are a handful of things that, if you keep them in mind, can move you quickly in that direction. Delivery is important. Great delivery won't make a lousy presentation great (although it will improve it), but lousy delivery can slaughter a great presentation.

Rule 1: Don't Picture Your Audience Naked

Picturing your entire audience naked is an old piece of advice, and it's a really bad one. Unless you are working in the nudist colony business, standing in front of a roomful of naked people is apt to make you nervous or revolted or excited or just plain giggly. At the very least, you are going to feel overdressed for the occasion (and delivering your presentation naked to avoid that problem is not a good idea either).

Rule 2: Rehearse

Some people in this world can "wing it." They can go out, unprepared, and just talk about whatever needs to be talked about. If you are one of those people, you probably already know that you are. Otherwise, it pays to practice. This doesn't mean memorizing exactly what you plan to say, because you shouldn't lock yourself in that tightly. But if you try to wing it to yourself, you can find out what you are comfortable talking about, what you need to make notes on, and probably anticipate where you are likely to get questions. (Close your office door when you do this, if possible, or people will think you have gone crazy and are sitting there talking to your computer.) This is also a good way to catch mistakes on your slides, as well as places where you can arrange things better.

You can also rehearse in front of another person, who may have suggestions. If you don't trust other people (it's not the "people" that worries me so much as the "other"), video tape yourself rehearsing, and then watch the tape. You will notice things about your body language you might otherwise miss.

Rule 3: Use Notes, but Don't Use a Script

Make up some notes for your presentation. These can include a list of points you want to cover, specific phrases that you want to use (particularly if they explain something clearly, pithily, and memorably), quotes, and other details. If you are using a two-screen presentation, use the Speaker Notes feature to bring them up onscreen. Otherwise, you can use the printed version of Speaker Notes, or even just write it on a sheet of paper or on some index cards. There is no "right" or "official" way to organize your notes; you are the one who has to understand them. If anyone else tries to look at your notes, roll them up and bop that person on the nose. (This is particularly difficult, but effective, if you are using onscreen Speaker Notes.)

You should not write out everything you are going to say, however. First of all, you don't need that. If you are smart enough to write it out, you are smart enough to say it. Secondly, a script can't adapt to the situation; if you discover your audience knows different things than you thought they knew, a script can't adapt. Finally, if you have a script, or even very long notes, you end up staring at the paper, talking to the paper, and focusing on reading rather than what you are saying. This is a good way to become both boring and unintelligible.

Rule 4: Talk to Someone

If your response to that is, "Of course I'm talking to someone! I'm talking to a *whole room* of someones!" that's exactly the problem. You are trying to talk with a room, but it's not the room that's listening to you. You have to feel like you are dealing with people. If you aren't dealing with people, it will show in the way that you speak. You are going to sound distanced and boring.

Instead, as you say each thing, look at someone specific in the audience and talk to that person. When you are looking at one person, you are subconsciously shaping what you say to make sure it's understood, and you pick up reactions (including body language) to see that it's understood. This will make your presentation better and keep it sounding human.

Rule 5: Don't Always Talk to the Same Someone

If you constantly direct what you are saying to the same person, it will look like a one-on-one conversation to people, and they will start mentally tuning you out. Their thoughts will drift, and they will start thinking about donuts. Donuts are a good thing to think about. Did you know that donuts can provide all four major food groups: chewy stuff, squishy stuff, powder, and chocolate? Mmm, yes, donuts.

Oh, wait, now *I* have drifted off. If you address one point to one person and then address the next to someone on the other side of the room, suddenly everyone feels included, even if you never get to speak directly to them. This doesn't mean that you can't go back to the same person fairly regularly. If you have a friendly face in the audience, take advantage of it and return to that person frequently. By going to different people, however, you also see how others are reacting to what you are saying, and that will help shape your talk. You may also wake up a few people who have drifted off.

Stand-up Comedians Are Good Examples

Good stand-up comedians will look at different members of the audience as they deliver each line. Many of them find a friendly face in the audience, someone who laughs well and easily, and will deliver some quick laugh-getters to that person... but then talk to other people.

Rule 6: Look at Each New Slide

Whenever you put a new slide up, pause and look at it for a few seconds, reading it over. This isn't just to remind you of what's on the slide (although that never hurts). It also gives your audience a few seconds to read the slide, to assimilate the information that's there. By turning away from your audience and looking at the slide, you take the attention off yourself and put it on the slide, making sure people read it.

Rule 7: Don't Talk to the Slide

When you face the screen, people will have trouble hearing you. If they can't see your face, they are less likely to pay attention to you.

Rule 8: Stop for Questions

A lot of speakers will take questions during a short presentation, but for long presentations will ask you to save your questions for the end so that they can get through everything. The aim of a presentation is not to *get through* everything, however, but to have people *understand* as much as possible. If you confuse people on your first slide by using the word *squidfiddlology*, and wait until after slide 3,327 to answer questions about what it means, there are 3,326 other slides that your audience probably didn't understand, because they were all on how to get work as a squidfiddlologist.

This doesn't mean that you have to stop for questions every time someone has one. If your presentation is well organized, odds are that you will build up questions in people's minds with one slide, and then answer it with the next one. However, you should find good stopping spots in your presentation. For example, when you have just completed a single subtopic, you can ask whether anyone has any questions so far. (You may even want to add a slide marked "Questions?" at this point, which will not only remind you that it's time for questions, but will encourage the audience to feel that asking questions is actually part of the process.) Keep your answers straightforward, and if the answer is "I'm getting to that," just say so!

Rule 9: It Can Be Very Easy to Use a Lot of Words...

...when, in fact, you could have said the same thing in many fewer words, and saying it in fewer words is both easier on you and on the audience, because brevity (which is a fancy word for shortness) can augment clarity (which is to say understandability), and clarity (understandability) is a thing of value in public speaking, which is presumably what you are doing.

Keep it simple.

Rule 10: Know How Sophisticated Your Audience Is

I don't mean check to see whether they own their own tuxedoes. If you are giving a presentation on a technical topic, you want to know how much the audience knows about the topic. If you are discussing a new telephone with a bunch of telephony engineers, they are going to want to know what the FCC ringer equivalency of the phone is. If you use the term *ringer equivalency* with a less-technical audience, they are going to think that the phone doesn't really ring, it just does the equivalent of ringing, whatever that might be.

The truth is, however, that you are likely to face an audience with a wide range of sophistication. It's better to explain a few things that some of your audience already knows rather than make a lot of people feel that what you are talking about is over their heads. (Particularly if you are talking about anvils. No one wants anvils over their heads.)

Rule 11: Use Examples

Abstract concepts become easier to understand with a concrete example. For example, the first sentence of this paragraph is an abstract concept. If reading it made you think 'Well, when does something need an example?,' it's clear that this discussion is one that needed an example. And here it is! Examples can be words (this paragraph is an example of an example being words), pictures (such as the examples of slides in this book), video, sound, or even a physical object you can pass around the room. (Warning: If the physical object is an example of a donut, don't expect it to make it all away around the room.)

Rule 12: Humor Can Be Amusing!

Throw in little humorous moments. This not only keeps your audience's attention, but also gets them on your side. People like being amused. Go figure.

You shouldn't try to turn your presentation into a stand-up routine, because that would lose the point of what you are doing, but even a few bad puns or silly names can give the presentation a positive energy.

Theoretical examples are a great time to be a little silly. Look through this book, and you should see plenty of cases of that. I could just as easily have used boring slide text from some actual presentation on the physical maturation of the fruit fly, but using the silly example didn't make the example less clear. Why use Patient A, John Doe, and Smith Manufacturing, Inc. as your examples when you could use Samantha De Hoya Von O'Goldberg, Myron McGillicuddly, and International Wonder-Widget And Coffee Recycling, Inc.? Just make sure your humor doesn't obscure your point and that it doesn't offend your audience.

Rule 13: Check Your Equipment Before the Presentation

This is particularly important when you use someone else's slide projector or computer. If you are doing a computer presentation, you really should go through the whole thing once on this other person's machine to make sure there's no weird happenings; Just because everything is supposed to work the same doesn't mean that it does.

Slide projectors are notorious. They blow out, they disappear, or your slide carousel doesn't quite fit. Even when everything is in place and working correctly, you should still become comfortable with the remote control. Having trouble going forward and backward is one of the most common things that keeps a presentation from getting rolling early on.

Make sure you have all the cables you need, extra bulbs for the projector, and even an extra extension cord. Turn off the slide or overhead projector when you are not using them, to reduce both noise and heat. (You don't have to turn off your LCD panel if you are using one, because it makes very little heat and no noise.)

Rule 14: Check Out the Room Ahead of Time

You want to know where everything important is. You want to make sure you can stand by the screen and still be able to control the projector. You want to know where the light switch is, and whether you can bring the lights down part way. (If possible, you don't want to bring the lights down all the way. You still want to be able to see your audience and have the audience see you. Still, you need it to be dark enough for the projected image to be clear.) Pull down the window shades to keep the glare out. Position your projector so that your image is easy for all to see. (The farther from the screen you put it, the bigger a picture you will get, but it will look dimmer and fuzzier.)

Check out where people will be sitting. You don't want anyone blocking the projector. You want your audience to have comfortable seats, so their minds are on your presentation rather than their own discomfort. (Lighting and comfort have a lot of effect on people's frame of mind, and you want them in a positive mood.)

If you have a huge room (and a sizable budget), you may want to have multiple projectors projecting to multiple screens, so that everyone can see.

Rule 15: Introduce Yourself to Your Audience

This should be the first thing, to let your audience know who you are. Even if you are dealing with your own co-workers, they may not know what your exact job is or what it has to do with the matter at hand.

If you have a small audience, and they aren't all people you know, get them to introduce themselves to you. Get not only their names, but what they do at the company or the club. This will help you not only aim the entire presentation properly, but also to understand why they are asking the questions that they are.

Even if you can't get them to introduce themselves to you, beware of making assumptions about who they are. In bygone days, you might have been able to count on the quiet, sharply dressed young woman in the corner being a secretary, and the dignified older gent in the front being the president. These days, however, that young woman may be Head of Programming, and the president might be the unshaven gent with a Hard Rock Cafe: Alcatraz t-shirt.

Rule 16: Don't Just Read What's On the Slide

Your talk should build on what's there. Presumably, your audience can read the slide for themselves. You can read a line of what's there, but only if you are going to expand on it.

Rule 17: Tell Them Where You are Going

Your presentation isn't a mystery story (unless, of course, it is). If you let them know in advance that the aim of the presentation is to show them the advantage of squirting the jelly into donuts after they are cooked, they will understand why you are spending all this time explaining all the tedious work that goes into wrapping dough around the existing lump of jelly.

This doesn't mean that you have to tell everything about your conclusions. The details of the conclusion are for the end. But they should have the gist of where you are going—unless you are building up to news so bad that no one would pay attention ("As I intend to show, the company's economic situation is so bad that I will be forced to bite you all hard on the elbows.") You can even give them a brief outline of your presentation so that they know which major points you will be covering.

Rule 18: Pronounce Clearly

You are excited. You want everyone to be as thrilled about your discovery of The East Pole as you were. Butwhenyougetsoexcitedthatyoustarttotalklikethis, no one will understand. Slow down, and put a little bit of silence between each word. A little space is fine, and can make you look intellectually contemplative. Too   much space   just   starts   to   aggravate   people   as they   wait   for   you   to   get   finished already!

Being too quiet is also a problem. There's no need to shout, but just bring the sound up from your throat instead of just shaping it with your mouth. Don't be afraid to open your mouth wide!

And it doesn't have to all be at one speed or volume. If you want them to be excited about something, show your excitement by getting a bit faster and louder. If you want them to think carefully on a point, slow it down, even pause before and after it. A good pause is an attention-getter. Just don't overuse it.

Rule 19: Dress Cleanly

You don't necessarily have to dress up. If you are talking to a comfortably dressed group, you can dress just as comfortably. But even if you are in jeans and a t-shirt, they should look clean and fresh, not worn to shreds. Looking sharp shows that you pay attention to details, and people will value what you have to say.

Rule 20: Don't Talk Down

I can't explain this one to you. Just trust me on this one. For reasons you cannot understand, you shouldn't talk down to your audience.

Didn't that sound obnoxious? You bet!

Don't assume that your audience is stupid or that they'd be unable to understand something even if you took the time to explain it fully. Sure, you know more about what you are telling them than they do (if you don't, why are you doing the talking?), but there's a reason why you want them to know what you are telling them, so they obviously are useful people. They don't already know what you are telling them, but that just means they have things to learn, as we all do.

Rule 21: Don't Take Too Long

The people you are talking to probably have other things to do. Keep an eye on the time. If you are falling behind and see a slide that really doesn't need explanation, then don't. Move right ahead to the next one.

Don't leave one slide up for too long. If for some reason you have a lot to say before moving to the next slide, turn the projector off so that the focus will be on you, not the same old unchanging slide. (But maybe you would have been better off breaking the information from that slide into several separate slides?)

Rule 22: Don't Worry About It!

It's only talking, and you've been talking most of your life. You're not going to be perfect, and no one expects perfection from you. Heck, if you sound *too* perfect, people might think you're trying to put something over on them. If something goes wrong, just, say "Whoops," correct yourself, and move on. If they don't understand something, they'll ask you. There's no need to worry about everything.

And the weird thing is that if you don't worry, you'll do better. Confidence is very convincing, so smile and relax.

The Least You Need to Know

➤ Rehearse and prepare notes, but don't use a script.

➤ Talk to someone, but not always the same someone.

➤ Look at each new slide, but don't talk to the slide and don't just read what's on the slide.

➤ Stop for questions.

➤ Keep it simple.

➤ Use examples and use humor.

➤ Check your equipment and the room before the presentation.

➤ Introduce yourself to your audience, and tell them where the presentation is going.

➤ Pronounce clearly.

➤ Don't talk down to your audience.

➤ Don't take too long.

Buttons and Menus and Mice, Oh My!: Working Wonders with Windows

By the End of This Appendix, You'll Be Able to...

➤ Control the computer using the mouse

➤ Start and handle programs using Windows 95, Windows 98, or Windows NT

➤ Use buttons and menus to give commands

➤ Complain about your computer using the right words

This appendix is about *Windows*, the program that handles how you control all the other programs. A number of different versions of Windows are around, but you're probably using Windows 95, Windows 98, or Windows NT. These all work pretty much the same.

Maybe this is the first time you've used your computer, or maybe it's not. If you have used a computer before, you probably know most of the stuff in this appendix, but read it over anyway to become comfortable with the terminology used in this book. (For example, did you know that we are no longer calling the W key "the W key?" Instead, we're calling it the *Harold Stassen Memorial Digital Wuh-Sound Input Device*.)

A Mouse in the Hand

Attached to your computer is probably a white lump with two or three buttons on it. You use this device to control the computer. The Geeks in Charge of Naming Computer Things (GICONCT) decided that because you would be spending so much time with your hand on it, they should name it after something you would never put your hand on. It's called a *mouse*. You use the mouse by putting your hand on it and sliding it across a flat surface (usually a *mouse pad* made for just such usage).

Try sliding your mouse around. When you slide it, you should see something move on your computer screen. When you slide the mouse side to side, it also moves side to side. When you slide the mouse forward, it moves up the screen, and when you move the mouse back, it moves down the screen. This thing is called a *pointer*, and it's under your command. It will follow you to the edge of the Earth—or at least the edge of the screen.

Missing a Mouse?

If your computer doesn't have a mouse, it probably has a *trackball* (push your hand across the top of the ball, and the pointer is pushed in the same direction) or a *pad* (drag your finger across this flat rectangle, and the pointer is dragged similarly).

The Point of the Pointer

The pointer is used to point to different things on the screen. When you want to give the computer a command about a certain part of what's being displayed, you use the pointer to tell the computer which part.

The pointer takes on different shapes at different times. Usually, it's an arrow, which makes a very clear pointer. When you're pointing to an area of text, the pointer might turn into something that looks like a thin, tall capital *I*. This is called an *I-bar*, and it's handy because you can put the thin vertical bar of the I between two letters, letting you point to a specific place in the text.

Sometimes the pointer turns into a picture of an hourglass. This means that the computer is busy doing something, and you have to wait until it's done. If you get sick and tired of seeing the hourglass, it's either time to get a faster computer or time to go do something else, like whittling. (If you can whittle yourself a new computer, you can do both at once!)

Clicking's a Snap!

It's not enough to point to something to give a command. After all, the pointer is always pointing to something. You have to have a way of letting the computer know that it's time to act on what you're pointing at, and that's what the mouse buttons are for.

The mouse has at least two buttons. The left one is the one that you'll use most of the time. When we talk about *clicking* something, we mean that you *point* to it with the pointer and then press the left mouse button. Don't hold it down, just push down and then let up on it quickly. To *double-click* something, you point at it and, instead of clicking once, you click twice.

Right-clicking is just like *clicking*, only you use the right mouse button rather than the left one. You won't do this nearly as often.

If your mouse has three buttons, you probably won't be using the middle one, at least not in the beginning. That third button is there mostly for advanced users, who can set it up to do special things with certain programs.

Check This Out

Lefties Are All Right!

If you have a mouse that's set up for left-handed use, you will use the right button for normal clicking and the left button when we tell you to right-click.

Clicking a Button

On your screen is a rectangle with a little colorful Windows symbol in it and the word **Start**. It's probably in the lower-left corner of the screen. (If you don't see it, try pointing to the very bottom of the screen; a gray bar should appear with **Start** at the left end.) This is a *button*, a rectangular area on screen that, when you click it, issues a command to the computer. At this point, the **Start** button is probably the only button on your screen, but soon you'll have more buttons on your screen than there are on a dry cleaner's floor!

Notice how the button looks like it's pushed out from the gray bar that it's on. Try clicking the button, and you'll see two things. One is that the button looks pushed in. This means the button is currently *active*, that it is having an effect. The other is that a list of items appear above the button (see the following figure). This list, called the *Start menu*, shows a number of commands that you can give to the computer. Pushing the Start button told the computer to show you the commands. Click the button again, and the list disappears and the button appears pushed out again.

Pressing the Start button made the Start menu pop up.

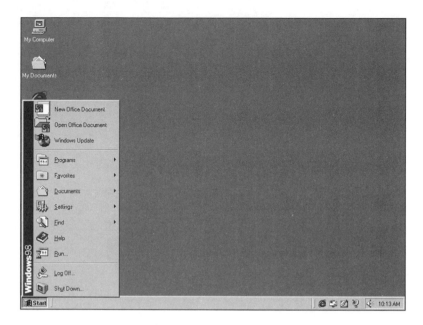

Try *right-clicking* the big open background area of the screen display (this is called the *desktop*). A short list of commands that you can choose pops up. This is called a *shortcut menu*. By right-clicking many things in Windows, you get a menu of commands that apply to what you clicked. Right-click the desktop, and you get a shortcut menu of commands that can change the desktop. Right-click a strawberry, and you get a strawberry shortcut menu, which isn't half as good as a strawberry shortcake menu!

Dragging Ain't No Drag!

Sometimes, you have to move something from one part of the screen to another. This is called *dragging*, and it's quite easy. To take a swing at it, let's try dragging one of the *icons* around your desktop. (The icons are the little pictures with words underneath. Each one stands for a different program, file, or device on your computer.)

Find the icon with the picture of a computer on it (it probably says **My Computer** underneath it). Point to that icon. While pointing to it, push down the left mouse button and hold it down. With the button pressed down, slide the mouse around. A transparent copy of the image follows your pointer. It's the ghost of your computer!

Slide the pointer over to an area of the desktop where the ghost icon isn't overlapping any other icon. Let go of the mouse button, and one of two things happens:

➤ The icon disappears from where you dragged it and reappears where you moved it, or...

➤ The icons rearrange themselves in neat columns, with the icon appearing in a new spot.

If the second thing happened, it doesn't mean your dragging didn't work. Your copy of Windows is set up to keep the desktop tidy, and the moment it saw that something was out of the group, it neatened everything up. If your real desktop worked as well as your computer desktop, you'd always be able to find a pencil when you needed one!

In either case, you can put things back to the way they were by dragging the icon you moved back to where you took it from. If the rearranging icons covered up the place where the icon was before, drag it just a bit higher on the screen than the icon that took its place, again making certain the ghost icon doesn't overlap any other icon.

When You Need a Menu

You've already seen how the Start menu and the shortcut menu can appear when you need them, hiding away like squirrelly, umm, squirrels the rest of the time. Menus provide access to tons of commands without taking up a lot of screen space when you don't need them.

Start Up the Start Menu, You Upstart!

Click the **Start** button again. Take a look at the Start menu. Each line has a picture and a word or phrase explaining what that command does. Some of the lines also have an arrowhead at the right edge, pointing toward the right. The arrowhead indicates that ancient native peoples used these menus, probably while running Windows 1273.

Actually, the arrowhead means that that command brings up another menu. Slide your pointer up the menu. Notice how, as the pointer passes over each command, it changes color. This color change is called *highlighting*. Just like the way that blue water in your toilet shows you that Tidy Bowl is there for you, the colored bar shows you that that command is there for you. Click the line marked **Programs**.

Programs had an arrowhead on it, so that means that another menu will appear next to it. It may be just one column, but it may be several. Find the line marked **Windows Explorer** (it should be near the end of the last column), and click it. This starts a program that lets you sort through the files on your disks.

Why Don't You Drop Down and See Me Sometime?

A big rectangle appears onscreen, filled with all sorts of stuff in it. This is the Windows Explorer *window*, the area of the screen where the Windows Explorer program displays controls and information (see the following figure).

Your Windows Explorer window may look different depending on your Windows version and settings.

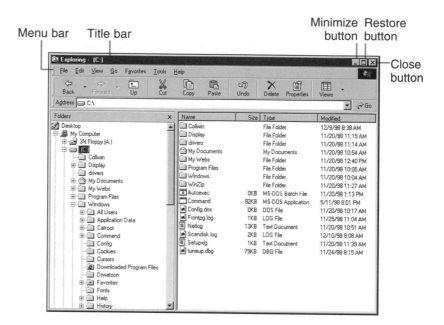

At the top of a window are two bars. The first, called the *title bar*, has a name for the window. On the Windows Explorer window, it says Exploring followed by the name of your hard disk.

Managing Menu Mishaps

If you accidentally bring down the wrong menu, don't worry. Just click the menu name again, and that menu disappears!

The second bar is called the *menu bar* (as opposed to, say, a *bar menu*, which would have a list of drinks and prices for those 10-year-old boiled eggs they keep in a jar). It has a series of words on it. Each word is the name of a menu. Try clicking the word **View**. A menu of commands appears below it—these are commands that have to do with the way that the program is displaying the list of what's on your disk. Try clicking the command **Refresh**. This tells the program to recheck what's on the hard disk and to display the information again; you should be able to see when the display is being redone.

Some programs try to keep their menus simple using a system called *personalized menus*. This means the program guesses which commands you're likely to use and shows only those commands when you click the menu. At the bottom of the menu will be a down-arrow. Click the down-arrow, and the rest of the commands become visible.

Keyboard Kwikies!

Sometimes you don't want to keep moving your hand back to the mouse and then back to the keyboard, you just want to keep typing. Reaching your foot for the mouse is too much exercise after a while! Luckily, there are ways to give menu commands without clicking the menu.

If you click the **Edit** menu, you will see some commands with things like **Ctrl+V** or **Ctrl+A** on the end of them. This tells you the shortcut for that command. For example, the **Ctrl+V** on the end of the Paste command means that you can do a Paste command at any time by holding down the key marked **Ctrl** and pressing the key marked **V**. Other keys you might see referred to include the **Shift** key and the **Alt** key. If a menu item is followed by **Shift+Alt+X**, for example, that means that you can issue that command by holding down the Shift key and the Alt key, simultaneously, and tapping the X key. Of course, if you're new at typing, you might need both hands and your nose to do this.

On the menu bar, one letter of each word is underlined (for example, the V in <u>V</u>iew is underlined.) This means that you can bring the menu up by holding down the **Alt** key and pressing the underlined letter's key (such as **Alt+V**). On the menu that appears, one letter in each command is underlined; just press the key for that letter (such as the R in <u>R</u>efresh) to issue that command. So, in full, to get the refresh command, press **Alt+V**, and then let go of the Alt key and press the **R** key. It may sound like a lot of work—but if you think that's a lot of work, you should talk to your grandpa, who will tell you that real work is carrying 16 tons of rocks a mile up hill every day, just to earn your lunch (a rock sandwich). (Of course, your grandfather actually sold shirts for a living, but that's no reason why you should have it easy!)

Gray Means No Way

Most of the menu commands are in easy-to-read lettering, probably black. If you see one that's almost the same color as the background (probably gray), it means that you can't use this command now. (These are commands that only work under certain conditions.)

Windows Don't Have to be a Pane!

If you're using several programs simultaneously, you can end up with a screen full of windows, overlapping and even completely hiding each other. This can make your desktop as messy as that "stuff" drawer in your kitchen, where you *know* there's an almost-working 9-volt battery, if only you could find it! Luckily, there are tools that let you move around windows, change their size, and even hide them for a while (very handy if you're playing Space Bunny Attack and hear your boss coming).

Wipe Away Your Window

At the right end of a window's title bar are three buttons. The first, which has a straight line in it, is the *Minimize* button. Click this, and the window disappears! Don't worry, it's not gone for good, so you can still help the Space Bunnies save the galaxy. If you look at the *taskbar* (the bar with the Start button on it), you'll see a button with the title of each window you are currently using. Click the button that has the title of the window you just minimized, and the window reappears, good as new, with each Space Bunny still intact.

Seize the Size!

The middle button will have one of two pictures of it. If it has two overlapping rectangles, this window is currently in *Full-Screen mode*, so that it automatically takes up all the screen space available. When a window is in Full-Screen mode, you can't move it or change its size. It is seemingly invincible, but for one fatal flaw, its Achilles' Heel (or, for those of us with more modern heroes, its Kryptonite). If you click this button (called the *restore* button), it goes from Full-Screen mode to *Resizable* mode, and then you can do what you want with it! You've torn down all of its defenses!

If the middle button has just a single box on it, the window is already in Resizable mode. Clicking this button (called the *maximize* button) will put the window into Full-Screen mode. This is good if you want to see as much as possible in the window. (More Space Bunnies!)

Become a Mover and a Shaker... and a Resizer!

For you to move a window, it has to be in Resizable mode. Point to the window's title bar and then drag it. Depending on how your computer is set up, you may be dragging the whole window or just an outline of it. Drag it up, drag it down, drag it, drag it all around! When you let go of the mouse button, the window will now be where you dragged it to!

If you want to change the size of a window, point at the lower-right corner of the window. The pointer will turn into a slanted arrow with arrowheads in both directions (like a "two-way" street sign would look, if there were any need for such things)! Try to drag the corner, and you'll find that you're moving the corner of an outline of the window. Move it so that the outline is the size that you want the window to be, and then release the mouse button. The window will now appear in the rectangle. With a little practice, you'll get so quick at dragging that you'll be ready for the drag races!

Wiping Out the Window

The button on the far right of the title bar, the one with an X in it, is the *Close* button. After you finish using a window, click this and the window disappears. This also tells the computer that you're done using the program that opened the window; so if you're running a program where you create a file (like a word processor), be sure you've saved the file before clicking this.

Let's Rap About Dialogue!

Sometimes, a program wants to ask you for information. To do that, it uses a *dialog box*, a type of window. Most dialog boxes don't have a menu bar and can't be resized, but they can be moved around. More importantly, you give the computer the information it wants with one. Or, if you don't want to buckle into the computer's demands, you can just ignore the dialog box. Of course, then the computer won't do what you want it to, but sometimes it's important to show who is boss!

A dialog box is a basically a form. Just like paper forms can have blanks to fill in, boxes to check off, items to circle, and so on, computer forms have a lot of different ways of getting information. After all, filling out a form on a computer should be just as much fun as filling out a paper one!

To see some of these in action, click the **Start** button, and select the **Find** command. When the second menu (sometimes called a *submenu*) appears, pick the **Files or Folders...** command. (The ... at the end of a command name lets you know that if you select that command, you'll get a dialog box (see the following figure). You can't complain that you weren't warned!)

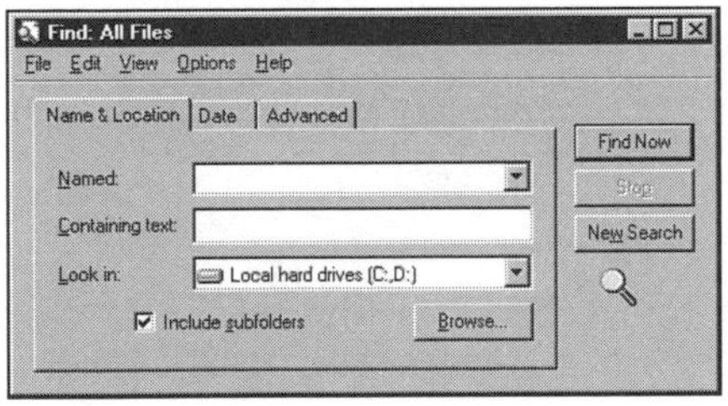

A dialog box.

Tab: It Isn't Just for Dieters Any More!

On the Find File dialog box, you can see a file folder shape with a form on it. At the top of it, in the tab where the name of the folder would go, are the words **Name & Location**. Next to it are two other tabs, just like if you got a set of good file folders with the staggered tabs. Click one of those other tabs, and another form appears. Clicking the three tabs, you can easily choose which form you want to work on!

A Text Field Is the Type for Type

Check the **Advanced** tab and the **Name & Location** tab. On one of them (depending on which version of Windows you're running), you'll find a white area marked **Containing Text**. This is a *text field*, one that you can type into. To put some words into that field, click in the field, and then type. You can use the cursor keys and the Backspace key to correct any typos you make. Or, you can leave your mistakes in, and just confuse the computer!

Drop Down and Give Me Twenty!

On the **Advanced** tab is a field labeled **Of type**, which has a button at the end with a down arrow. This is a *drop-down list*, good for choosing one item from a list of items. Click the button (the *drop-down button*, which is a better name for it than *Mildred*), and a list of items will appear under it. Click any item, and the list goes away, and that item appears in the field.

What the Scroll Is That?

At the right side of the *drop-down list*, you will see a vertical bar with a box inside it. This is a *scrollbar*, which sounds like a wizard's tavern. Actually, it's Windows's way of telling you that it has more to show you than it can fit in the area it has to work in. The bar area represents the whole list. If the box is at the top of the bar, it means you're seeing the start of the list; if it's at the bottom of the bar, you're looking at the bottom of the list.

To see more of the list, just drag the box down the bar. The lower you drag it, the farther down the list you will see. (If you see a sideways scrollbar at the bottom of a display, it means that what the computer is trying to show you is wider than the space it has. A sideways scrollbar works just like a regular one, if you're lying down!)

Check Out the Check Box!

Click the **Name & Location** tab. At the bottom of the form you'll see a little box marked **Include subfolders**. This is a *check box*. It either has a check mark in it, which means *yes*, or it's empty, which means *no*. To change a check box from checked to unchecked (or vice versa, or even the other way 'round), just click it!

Option Button, Option Button, Who's Got the Option Button?

Click the tab marked either **Date Modified** or just **Date**. At the left of the form, you'll see two columns of circles. These circles are called *option buttons*. These "buttons" are used to select one thing from a small list of choices. You use them to select one from a list of choices, and when you select one by clicking it, a dot appears in the circle. You can only have one button selected in each column at a time; when you click one, the dot disappears from the previous selection.

Try clicking the lowest option button. When you click it, the field next to that option turns white; but if you then select the button above that one, that field turns gray. That's because that field is only used if you use that option. When it turns gray, the computer is telling you that you don't have to fill it in. Think of the fields like fields of snow—a white field is good to be in, but stay away from the gray ones!

The Least You Need to Know

➤ Sliding the mouse across your desk moves a pointer on the screen.

➤ *Clicking* means to point the pointer at something and press once on the left mouse button.

➤ *Double-clicking* means to point at something and press the left button twice, quickly. *Right-clicking* means to point at something and press the right button once.

➤ A *menu* enables you to select from a list of commands by clicking the menu name to bring up the list and then clicking the command you want.

➤ A *dialog box* is a form that the computer displays, asking you for information.

Speak Like a Geek

People who design or use computers like to make up new words to describe the various pieces of the computer and the things these pieces do. Even worse, they like to take already existing words like *mouse* and *window* and give them new meanings.

Here's a cheat sheet for you. With it, you should be able to understand what they're talking about, and even spit it right back out at them!

Access   A database program made by Microsoft. Database programs let you organize lists of information and help you find information on those lists.

Action buttons   Special AutoShapes that look like buttons and automatically have hyperlinks attached to them.

alignment   Refers to where the text is positioned side-to-side within a text box.

animation   Moving something onto the slide during animation or making it appear gradually instead of all at once. A list may appear item by item, for example, rather than all at once.

AutoShape   A set of predrawn shapes that PowerPoint lets you add to your slide easily.

box   The rectangular area containing any object on a slide.

bullet   A pointer used to highlight items on a list. Bullets are usually dots, but they can be little arrows or any of a number of other designs.

button   The word *button* is used for two different things. There are the buttons on the mouse, which you push to tell the computer to take action on something onscreen. An onscreen button is usually a rectangular area that you click to perform some action.

CD-ROM   Short for *Compact Disc-Read Only Memory*, this is a shiny disk that looks like an audio CD, but has computer data on it. Your computer needs a CD-ROM drive to be able to read the information on a CD-ROM.

chart   Refers to a numerical graph, except when used as part of the term *organizational chart*.

check box   A small white square that you use to select an option. Click the square to put a check mark in it (which means you want the option); click again to take the check mark out.

click   Clicking something is when you point the pointer at it, and then press and release the left mouse button once. (If you're using a left-handed mouse, you use the right button.)

clip art   A piece of art meant for use in your documents.

Clip Gallery   An organized collection of clip art, sounds, and videos that you can use in your documents.

Clipboard   An area of memory used to store things that you have copied or cut from your document so that you can paste them somewhere else.

Close button   The button with an X at the right end of the menu or title bar. Clicking the menu bar's Close button closes the document while leaving the program open. Clicking the Close button on the title bar closes the document and the program.

copying   Storing a copy of whatever is currently selected into an area of memory called the *Clipboard*.

CPU   Short for *Central Processing Unit*, the CPU is the chip that does most of the computer's thinking. The 486 and the Pentium are two types of CPUs.

cropping   Trimming one or more sides of a picture.

cursor keys   Keys with arrows on them that are used to change where your typing will appear in a block of text.

cutting   Removing something from a document and storing it in an area of memory called the *Clipboard*.

database   A program that helps you create and organize lists of information and makes it easy to pull specific information out of that list.

datasheet   A grid where you enter information for a numeric chart.

deleting   Removing.

desktop   The open area that is underneath any open windows in Microsoft Windows. If there aren't any programs running, what you see is the desktop.

dialog box   A window that appears when the computer wants information from you. It can have a mixture of tabs, buttons, fields, check boxes, and radio buttons in it.

document   Any single picture, letter, report, spreadsheet, presentation, or other item that you have created and stored on the computer.

donut   The standard source of energy used to power programmers.

double-clicking   Pointing to something with the mouse pointer and pressing and releasing the left mouse button twice, rapidly. (If you're using a left-handed mouse, use the right button.)

downloading   Copying a file from another computer to yours, using a modem connection or a network.

dragging   Moving the mouse with the left button pressed down. To drag an object, point to it, press, and move. (Left-handed mice use the right button.)

drop-down button   A button with a downward-pointing triangle on it at the end of a field. Clicking this button makes a menu of possible values for the field appear.

drop-menu   The menu that appears when you click the drop-down button.

email   Short for *electronic mail*, this refers to letters or files sent over a computer network from one use to another.

Excel   A spreadsheet program made by Microsoft. Spreadsheet programs are used to do math and to create graphs.

field   A white rectangle where you can type information that the computer wants.

file   A group of information stored under a single name so that the computer can find it. A PowerPoint presentation can be a single file, or it can use several files, with the main file containing the information about what other files are used.

fill effects   Styles of filling a shape with a blend of colors or a picture.

film recorder   A device that lets your computer put images onto photographic film.

floppy disk   A flat square removable item used to hold computer information. For the computer to read the information, you have to stick it into a *floppy disk drive*. It's called a *disk* because there's a flat magnetic circle inside that actually holds the information.

folder   The information on the hard disk is organized into *folders*. Each folder has a name and can contain files and more folders.

font size   How big your letters appear.

fonts   Styles of type. For instance, Courier New and Arial are fonts that come with Windows.

footer   Material that appears at the bottom of every slide, except the title slide.

function keys   A row or column of keys marked F1, F2, and so on. These are used by many programs to perform special commands. Exactly which command is performed by each key changes from program to program.

GIF   The *Graphics Interchange Format* is a way of organizing information about a picture so that the computer can understand it and recreate the picture.

gigabyte   Sometimes abbreviated GB, this is a measurement of information size. A gigabyte is about a thousand megabytes.

graph   A chart that plots numeric values.

hard disk   A device built in to your computer that is used to store information permanently. Information on the hard drive doesn't go away when you turn off the machine; it has to be erased by a computer command.

header   Material that appears at the top of every slide, except the title slide.

Help system   A group of many short articles and instruction guides that are organized so that you can find the one you want.

HTML   Short for *Hypertext Markup Language,* this is the format used to store displays on the World Wide Web so that your Web browser can understand it.

hyperlink   The linking of an object to a slide, a program, or a Web address so that when you click the object (or when you pass the mouse over it), the slide, program, or Web page is opened up.

icon   A small picture that represents a file, program, or function.

ink-jet printer   A printer that prints out by squirting little dots of ink onto the paper.

Internet   A series of computers linked around the world that let you get information from one computer to another by passing it down the line.

Internet Explorer   A Web browser program created by Microsoft. Web browser programs let you view the displays on the World Wide Web.

intranet   A series of computers linked together within your company or organization. Intranets work like the Internet, only on a smaller scale.

JPEG   A format used for storing a picture on a computer. The name comes from the *Joint Photographic Experts Group* that developed the format.

keyboard   The part of the computer with the typewriter-like bunch of keys.

kiosk   A standalone computer designed to be easily accessed and easily used for getting information.

Kiosk mode   A slideshow display mode that doesn't allow the user any controls that aren't built in to the slide itself.

laser printer   A printer that prints by pressing toner onto the paper.

LCD   Short for *Liquid Crystal Display*, a display made up of little segments that can be clear or colored, depending on whether electricity is being applied.

LCD panel   A computer monitor that you can put on an overhead projector so that the image that would be on the computer screen is seen wherever the projector is aimed.

LCD projector   A device capable of projecting a computer screen image onto a movie screen.

loop   Repeat.

Meeting Minder   A PowerPoint feature you can use to take notes during the slideshow and add things to your scheduling program.

megabyte   Sometimes abbreviated MB, this is a measurement of information size. A megabyte can store about a thousand pages of text, a dozen full-screen pictures, or seven seconds of high-quality stereo sound.

megahertz   The computer has a central rhythm, a beat that it uses to drive everything it does. The speed of this is measured in *megahertz* (abbreviated MHz), which stands for millions of beats per second. Today's fast computers dance to a rhythm of 450 million beats per second, or 450 megahertz.

menu   A list of commands that you can select from. You can see the menu by clicking the right name on the menu bar.

Menu bar   The second bar at the top of a window. The menu bar has a list of menus on it. Click any menu name to see the menu.

Microsoft   The biggest PC software company. They make PowerPoint, Windows, Office, and many other products.

modem   A computer device that lets your computer share information with other computers using the phone lines.

mouse   A device that helps you control the computer. Slide the mouse across the mouse pad, and a pointer on the screen moves in the same direction. The buttons on a mouse enable you to tell the computer to take action on what you are pointing to.

mouse over   Passing the mouse pointer over a displayed item without clicking the mouse button.

narration Speech that you record on the computer to play along with your slides.

network Computers that are connected to each other so that they can exchange information.

Normal view A PowerPoint view of your slideshow where you can see a slide, the Speaker Notes for that slide, and the outline of your presentation.

Notes Page view A PowerPoint view of your slideshow where you can see one slide at a time and the Speaker Notes from that slide.

object The word *object* is used for two different things in PowerPoint. It can refer to anything that you put on a slide (a line, a picture, a sound, and so on) or specifically to anything that PowerPoint needs to run a separate program to deal with (such as a chart or graph).

Office A set of programs sold as a group by Microsoft. Office includes the Word word processor, Excel spreadsheet, PowerPoint presentation creator, and Outlook scheduling program. Some versions of Office include additional programs.

Office Assistant An animated character that appears in a window and offers help information.

online Refers to anything done over a network or over a modem connection.

Option buttons Another name for *radio buttons*.

organization chart A diagram that shows who works for whom in your company.

Outline view A PowerPoint view of your slideshow where you can see all the text from your slides and make changes to it.

overhead A transparent sheet with an image on it. You display overheads by putting them on an *overhead projector*, which shines light through it and magnifies it onto a screen.

overhead projector A device that shines light through an overhead so that the image appears on a movie screen or a wall.

packing Storing everything you need for your presentation into a single file.

pasting   Taking whatever's in the area of memory called the *Clipboard* and putting it into your document.

PC   Short for *personal computer*, this refers to any small computer meant to be used by one person at a time or any computer designed primarily to run MS-DOS or Windows.

pointer   A small picture on the screen that moves when you move the mouse. The picture is usually an arrow, but sometimes it can be a small bar or a finger.

PowerPoint   A program designed to help you make presentations.

presentation   An information show created with PowerPoint. Presentations can include slides, notes, and narration.

processor   Another term for *CPU*, the chip in the computer that does most of its thinking.

pushed in   Refers to a button that looks like it's below the level of the toolbar. A button that's pushed in means that button's feature is now in effect.

radio buttons   A set of small circles next to a list of options. Select the option you want by clicking the radio button next to it. Only one radio button in a group can be selected at a time; when you select another button, the selected one becomes unselected.

RAM   Short for *Random Access Memory*, this is a bunch of computer chips where the computer stores information that it is currently using. Information in RAM goes away when you turn the computer off.

Redo   A command that counteracts the effect of a just-issued undo command.

resizing   Changing the size of a picture or box. Resizing stretches or squishes the item to fit the new size.

right-click   Right-clicking something is when you point the pointer at it and then press and release the right mouse button. (If you're using a left-handed mouse, you use the left button.)

saving   Copying the document you're working with (including all new changes) to a disk.

scanner   A device that takes a picture of a hard copy page and sends that picture to your computer.

scrollbar   A scrollbar is what you use to select which part of a document you want to see, when that document is too big to show in the space provided. There's a box on a bar. The box shows the relative position of what you're seeing in the document. Drag the box to see another part, or use the up and down buttons at either end of the scrollbar to move up or down in the document. (Sideways scrollbars have left and right buttons.)

selecting   Indicating the item onscreen that you want your commands to affect. You select something by clicking it or by dragging a box around it.

service bureau   An outside company that will put your computer created images onto slides, overheads, posters, and other tough-to-create forms.

shortcut menu   A menu that appears when you right-click something. Shortcut menus usually have commands that deal specifically with the thing that you clicked.

slide   One screen of information in PowerPoint or a single transparent picture used with a slide projector.

Slide Master   A special slide that isn't shown itself, but everything you put on the Slide Master appears on all your slides besides the title slide.

slide projector   A device used to project transparent pictures onto a screen.

Slide Sorter view   A PowerPoint view of your slideshow where you see a number of slides at a time. This is good for rearranging your show or doing things that effect a number of slides.

Slide view   A PowerPoint view of your slideshow, where you see one slide at a time and can change all of the contents and graphics.

sound card   A computer board inside your computer that connects your computer to speakers, giving it the capability to put out sound and music.

Speaker mode   A slideshow display mode that allows the most control over moving through the show or performing other functions.

Speaker Notes   A PowerPoint feature that allows you to create notes for each slide and to see them onscreen as you give your presentation.

Spelling Checker   A PowerPoint feature that checks every word on your slide as you enter it and underlines it with a wavy red line if it thinks it is misspelled.

spreadsheet   A program that does math, using information laid out in a grid.

Start button   A button on the left edge of the taskbar that you click when you want to start a program.

Style Checker   A PowerPoint feature that checks the format of your text and underlines it with a wavy green line if it thinks it looks bad.

tab   This has two meanings. There's the Tab key on the keyboard, which is used to move your typing spot to a fixed position. There are also the tabs in a dialog box, which are named buttons that you use to select which set of settings you want to work with; click a tab, and the settings having to do with the name on the tab appear.

Taskbar   A bar usually found at the bottom of the screen that includes the Start button as well as buttons for all the programs you are currently running.

template   A file containing a design for the look of your presentation. You can choose a template before starting to build your presentation, or apply the template to an already-written presentation.

text   Typed information, such as paragraphs, numbers, and so on.

timings   Stored estimated times for the showing of each slide, used either to automate the slideshow or used by the Slide Timer to keep you informed of whether you're running behind time.

title   A special piece of text at the top of the slide that identifies the slide. PowerPoint considers the title text to be the name of the slide.

Title bar   The bar at the top of the window. This usually has the name of the program being used followed by the document name.

Title Master   A special slide that isn't shown itself, but everything you put on the Slide Master appears on the title slide.

title slide   Usually the first slide in your slideshow, this has the title of your presentation.

toolbar   A row of buttons and drop-down lists that have related functions. For example, PowerPoint uses several toolbars, including a toolbar of Web-related controls.

trackball   A device used instead of a mouse. Roll the ball in any direction, and the pointer on the screen moves in that direction.

transition   The visual method of replacing one slide on the computer screen with the next.

transparency   Another word for *overhead*.

transparent color   A color selected on a picture that will be treated as clear instead. If you put a picture with a transparent color on your slide, you can see through the parts with transparent color to whatever is under the picture.

Undo   A feature that takes back your last command.

uploading   Copying a file from your computer to another computer, using a modem or a network.

URL   Short for *Uniform Resource Locator*, it's another name for a Web address—the string of letters, slashes, and punctuation that tells the computer where to find a given display on the Web.

video   In computer terms, *video* refers to a changing picture stored as a series of still images, which are shown one after another. Video files can include the sound that goes with the picture.

Web browser   A program that lets your computer show you the displays on the World Wide Web, as well as any other displays stored in HTML format.

window   A moveable, resizable rectangular area of a computer display that has a title bar and menu bar at the top.

Window mode   A slideshow display mode that shows the show in a window rather than full screen.

Windows   A computer operating system made by Microsoft that's designed around using the mouse and the window displays. Windows 98 is the version of Windows released in 1998.

wizard A program feature that takes you through all the steps needed to do something, taking care of all the steps it can for you.

Word A word processor made by Microsoft. Word processing programs are used for creating and changing letters, reports, and other text.

WordArt A logo design tool built in to PowerPoint and some other Microsoft products. The term can also refer to a logo designed with that tool.

word processor A program that you can use to create letters, reports, and other text documents, as well as letting you change and correct things before you print them out.

World Wide Web A system that you can use to see information displays stored on various computers connected to the Internet. To see these displays, you need a connection to the Internet, and you need a Web browser.

Index

Other Related Titles

The Complete Idiot's Guide to Microsoft Word 2000
Dan Bobola
ISBN: 0-7897-1860-X
$16.99 US

The Complete Idiot's Guide to Microsoft FrontPage 2000
Elisabeth Parker
ISBN: 0-7897-1806-5
$16.99 US

The Complete Idiot's Guide to Microsoft Outlook 2000
Bob Temple
ISBN: 0-7897-1981-9
$16.99 US

The Complete Idiot's Guide to Windows 98
Paul McFedries
ISBN: 0-7897-1493-0
$14.99 US

Easy Windows 98
Shelly O'Hara
ISBN: 0-7897-1484-1
$19.99 US

The Complete Idiot's Guide to Microsoft Office 2000
Joe Kraynak
ISBN: 0-7897-1848-0
$16.99 US

The Complete Idiot's Guide to Microsoft Access 2000
Joe Habraken
ISBN: 0-7897-1900-2
$16.99 US

The Complete Idiot's Guide to Microsoft Excel 2000
Sherry Kinkoph
ISBN: 0-7897-1868-5
$16.99 US

Get **FREE** books and more...when you register this book online for our Personal Bookshelf Program

http://register.quecorp.com/

 Register online and you can sign up for our *FREE Personal Bookshelf Program*—immediate and unlimited access to the electronic version of more than 200 complete computer books! That means you'll have 100,000 pages of valuable information onscreen, at your fingertips!

 Plus, you can access product support, including complimentary downloads, technical support files, book-focused links, companion Web sites, author sites, and more!

 And, don't miss out on the opportunity to sign up for a *FREE subscription to a weekly email newsletter* to help you stay current with news, announcements, sample book chapters, and special events, including sweepstakes, contests, and various product giveaways.

 We value your comments! Best of all, the entire registration process takes only a few minutes to complete, so go online and get the greatest value going—absolutely FREE!

Don't Miss Out On This Great Opportunity!

QUE®is a brand of Macmillan Computer Publishing USA. For more information, visit *www.mcp.com*